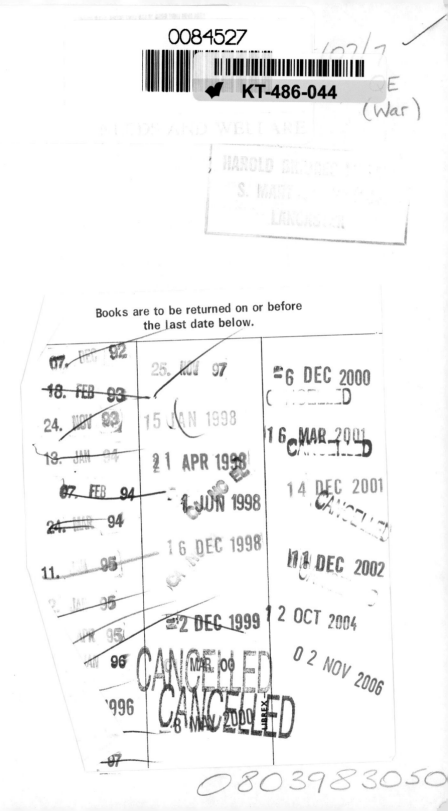

NEEDS AND WELFARE

edited by

Alan Ware and Robert E. Goodin

SAGE Modern Politics Series Volume 26
Sponsored by the European Consortium for
Political Research/ECPR

SAGE Publications

London ● Newbury Park ● New Delhi

First published 1990

SAGE Publications Ltd
6 Bonhill Street
London EC2A 4PU

SAGE Publications Inc
2455 Teller Road
Newbury Park, California 91320

SAGE Publications India Pvt Ltd
32, M-Block Market
Greater Kailash – I
New Delhi 110 048

British Library Cataloguing in Publication Data

Needs and welfare. – (Sage modern politics series;
    v. 26)
    1. Welfare services. Political aspects
    I. Ware, Alan   II. Goodin, Robert E.
    361

    ISBN 0–8039–8304–2
    ISBN 0–8039–8305–0 pbk

Library of Congress catalog card number 90–61730

Typeset by Mayhew Typesetting, Bristol, England
Printed in Great Britain by Dotesios Printers Ltd,
Trowbridge, Wiltshire

Contents

Preface

The chapters in this book are revised versions of papers originally written for the Joint Sessions of the European Consortium for Political Research in Paris in April 1989. The workshop on 'Needs, Contributions and Welfare' was convened by Alan Ware and had been sponsored by the ECPR's Standing Group on Political Theory. The Standing Group was first organized in 1973 as a Planning Session at the ECPR's Joint Sessions in Mannheim. The arrangements were formalized in 1987 when the ECPR Secretariat invited a Standing Group to be organized, with Elias Berg, Robert E. Goodin and Andrew Reeve acting as its first co-conveners.

The workshop in Paris involved twenty participants and, for reasons of space, it was simply not possible to include all the papers presented there in this book. The workshop benefited enormously from the thematic coherence of the papers, and the fruitful, friendly and constructive interchanges between the participants. This was very important in the evolution of this volume, and the editors wish to thank all the participants for their contribution to the development of ideas discussed in the book. For their comments and help we would also like to thank Heiner Ganßmann, Michael Laver, Philippe Van Parijs and Andrew Reeve.

Alan Ware
Robert E. Goodin

1

Introduction

Alan Ware and Robert E. Goodin

The idea of need is politically controversial. Debates on the subject intensified in the 1980s as some western governments reduced programmes which had enabled many of their citizens' needs to be met. This collection of essays is about the idea of need and how needs can be, and are, met in western societies. The essays are concerned with a wide range of topics about needs and welfare provision – both in theory and in practice.

In this brief introduction we attempt to set within a broader context the arguments examined in the later essays. Our starting point is the issues which unite and divide those political scientists, theorists and journalists who write about needs.

The concept of needs

In the first place, there is widespread acceptance that needs are different from wants.[1] A person may need something she may not want (as with food in the case of an anorexic) and want something she does not need, as with the umpteenth car purchased by a billionaire. Unlike wants, needs are not wholly subjective. Except under special circumstances, we usually assume that the person himself is the best judge of whether he wants something or not. With needs, however, other people may be just as well placed, or in a much better position, to decide a specific person has a need for certain resources.

It is also widely accepted that to say 'x is needed' is to refer to an instrument – I need something *for some purpose*. All humans need fresh water to keep themselves alive, but in examples such as this one we often do not require the person who is asserting that there is a need to specify what that purpose is – it is all too obvious. Moreover, there are cases where virtually everyone can agree that a particular person is in need – as with a person without water in a desert.

Beyond these points, however, a widespread consensus about needs is lacking. Indeed, there are a number of key issues on which there is considerable disagreement.

While there is agreement that needs can be determined objectively, there is disagreement about whether they constitute an 'absolute' standard against which anyone said to be in need can be tested. Those who argue that needs are in some sense 'relative' may be making one of three very different kinds of argument.

There is one argument that even an 'absolutist' would accept. While everyone needs resources to provide food, water, shelter and so on, just *which* resources are required will depend on the physical circumstances facing a person. The needs of an Eskimo are not the same as those of an Amazonian Indian. But an 'absolutist' would maintain that *only* physical, and not social, circumstances modify the package of resources required to meet a person's needs. The second and third arguments about 'relativism', however, are concerned with social dimensions of needs.

Many conservative writers argue in favour of an absolute notion of need and then deny the importance of need as a political concept in western democracies, on the ground that virtually everyone in those societies has the resources required for physical survival. Opposed to them, many non-conservatives argue that it is not the capacity for physical survival alone that is relevant in determining who is in need, but also the availability of resources to enable people to act as agents in the particular society in which they live. This, for example, is the approach of Weale (1983: 35) who argues that: '. . . minimum needs are not simply satisfied by providing the physical necessities of life, for example, adequate food, clothing and shelter, but require also for their satisfaction a level of provision for persons that is suitable for social agents, interacting with others in a specific society.'

This approach sees needs as 'relative' in the sense that what is needed is determined by the modus operandi of the particular society in which a person lives. To be in need is to be unable to act as a full agent in that society. Consequently, one line of criticism open to 'absolutists' is to take Margaret Thatcher's approach and to deny that a society is anything more than an aggregation of individuals.

However, there is a third argument that needs are relative, and this forms the subject of Robert E. Goodin's chapter in this book. Goodin identifies a 'strong' sense of relative needs: within a specific society some needs are relative in that what a person needs depends on what goods and resources other people already have. In a society in which physical strength largely determines the distribution of resources, people may have a need not just for enough food for survival but for food containing sufficient calories to enable them to obtain the strength with which to compete with their fellow citizens. While meeting other kinds of needs can be accomplished by the provision of resources to those in need, with 'strong' relative needs providing resources cannot eliminate need – it merely increases the stakes in a competitive process. Meeting these needs requires a very different approach, and it is one in which the role of the state would be central.

The role of the state in meeting needs

Virtually no one denies that the state must play some role in meeting needs. However, for many writers of the New Right who trace their intellectual origins back to nineteenth-century liberalism, the state's role is confined merely to providing aid to those people whose needs cannot be met by an informal network (mainly families), the market, or by voluntary provision. The state serves as the last resort for those who 'fall through the net' of other agencies. On this view families provide much care for those who cannot provide for themselves, a competitive market will enable a great many resources to be distributed widely, and donations (of money and labour) will sustain an extensive voluntary sector. This is not, of course, how western states have actually operated for most of the twentieth century, since in its first 70 or 80 years there was a vast increase in the role of the state in meeting people's needs. But for some writers it is vital that the welfare states that were established be largely dismantled and that a return be attempted to a supposed nineteenth-century golden age of public–private relations.

Whatever the attractions of such a model, there are a number of objections to using it as the basis for supplying needs. As Norman Johnson points out in chapter 8, there are already severe pressures on the informal, market and voluntary sectors in maintaining their present level of welfare services, let alone increasing their supply to take over the activities of the state. Then, as Alan Ware argues in chapter 10, the expansion of market relations on the lines advocated by the New Right may actually be incompatible with a voluntaristic response to social needs – or, at least, with a response grounded in altruism.

Moreover, a model of late nineteenth-century states in which voluntary welfare organizations are conceived as largely independent of the state is highly misleading. It is not even an accurate portrayal of the United States where, despite the much-proclaimed voluntaristic tradition, there is a long history of cooperation between, and interpenetration of, the state and voluntary sectors (Salamon, 1987; Ware, 1989). In those countries where the state has always had wider boundaries of legitimate operation this New Right model does not accord at all with the development of services to meet social needs. In chapter 9 Stein Kuhnle and Per Selle show that in one such country, Norway, there has always been a close integration of the two sectors. There was never a golden age of independent welfare provision which was somehow ended with the rise of the welfare state.

Those who argue for a more extensive state role than does the New Right may base their case on a number of grounds. At the beginning of chapter 5 Brian Barry argues that many justifications in Anglophone countries for state welfare provision are really extensions of justifications for a 'poor law'. The poor law constituted a strictly limited redistribution of resources from those with property to those in poverty. Modern welfarists who espouse this sort of view support far more extensive state benefits than did earlier proponents of a poor law; but the point of such benefits is still to redistribute from those who are not in need to those who are.

Of course, this individualistic sort of justification for state welfare provision is only one strand of the arguments used in support of state intervention, even in the English-speaking world. In chapter 4 Michael Freeden's analysis of the welfare thought of British writers at the turn of the century reveals a communitarian strand of argument. Prominent Liberal writers, such as Hobhouse and Hobson, were not concerned with the redistribution of resources to the poor but with the community realizing opportunities and capacities.

A more 'social' justification still for welfare provision is that associated with the idea of social citizenship. Those who propound this kind of argument believe that citizenship entitles a person to a set of rights – and this includes economic and welfare rights, such as rights to health services, a certain level of education and so on. That citizens have welfare rights entails a corresponding duty on the part of the state to supply resources and services to every citizen commensurate with those rights being respected.[2]

Quite clearly, the claim that each citizen has a right to have his or her needs met – a 'right to welfare' – is disputed by many on the political right. But even among those who defend extensive welfare provision, there is disagreement about these rights. Obviously, those who assert that there are such rights are not concerned about whether in a particular country a *legal* right to welfare exists – that can be easily resolved – but whether there is a natural or human right to welfare. One difficulty with this assertion is that if a citizen of Britain or West Germany has such a right then, surely, the same must be true of a citizen of Uganda or Bangladesh. Yet it is equally apparent that the latter lack the economic resources necessary to perform their alleged duties to their citizens. It seems that, if this is a human right, it is one that could not be redeemed by everyone. This apparent objection to the claim that there are rights to welfare forms the subject of Peter Jones's essay (chapter 3).

Models of social provision

We have already alluded to an important distinction in welfare provision which we must now consider further. Both individual action and public policies may be designed to help those already in need or they may seek to prevent people falling into need in the future. At the individual level in nineteenth-century Britain, for instance, we find people making donations to charities (to assist those already in need) and also insuring, through contributions to a friendly society, against certain risks that might place their own family in need. At the level of the state we also find, from the early stages of public welfare provision, a difference between policies created to alleviate actual needs and those based on the insurance principle. We can thus discern two distinct models of welfare provision: a *residualist (or needs-based) model* and an *insurance (or contributions-based) model*. In the early-to-mid-twentieth century a third model emerged which combined features of the other two, but which was nonetheless quite distinct; this is the *social citizenship (or rights-based) model*.[3] In practice, the differences between the three models are often blurred with particular welfare programmes containing elements of more than one model. Nevertheless, for purposes of analysis it is useful to distinguish between the models, and the differences between them are best illuminated by considering three questions: who is covered? what is the level of coverage? and what, if any, is the (re)distributive impact?

1 Residualist (or needs-based) model

Who is covered?
This model seeks to provide universal coverage, in the sense that everyone (defined either as a citizen or a permanent resident) is entitled to assistance if they are in need. Need is defined in a minimalist way, in that it relates to basic resources required for survival. Only those who actually fall below the minimum receive any assistance, but coverage extends to anyone who happens to do so. In so far as the need is for financial assistance, some form of test has to be applied to discover whether a person is in need or

not, and this usually involves them having to divulge all the assets available to them ('means testing'). While coverage is universal, the state may still do little to ensure that those in need are aware of the programmes and it may also do little to remove feelings of being stigmatized among those accepting 'handouts'.

Level of coverage

Coverage is strictly limited; it involves bringing people up to some minimal standard so that they have enough to survive. In principle, however, there is no ceiling on what could be spent – expenditures are simply determined by how far those in need fall below that standard. This (potentially) unlimited state commitment contrasts with that of the insurance model, in which benefits are linked to the previous contributions (if any) of beneficiaries.

(Re)distributive impact

At any given time the residualist model redistributes resources from those not in need to those in need. Of course, as with the operation of the British poor laws, the minimal standard may be set so low that redistribution overall is very limited. Moreover, the object of redistribution is to prevent people from being in need *now*; it is not to compensate them for having been in need in the past, nor to ensure that they are not in need in the future. Yet these qualifications do not alter the basic point: to ground public policy on the basis of the maxim 'to each according to his needs' is to implement an egalitarian policy. As Vlastos (1962: 40) notes, when commenting on this maxim: 'Since needs are often unequal, this looks like a precept of unequal distribution. But this is wrong. It is in fact *the most perfect form of equal distribution*' (original emphasis).

2   Insurance (or contributions-based) model

If the British poor law remains one of the principal exemplars of the residualist model, it is Germany which provides a good exemplar of the insurance model in operation. Imperial Germany, which is usually regarded as the precursor of the modern welfare state, was the first country to introduce an extensive system of state-directed insurance. German social insurance was, and has remained, linked to employment and state bureaucracies were formed to administer the system.

Who is covered?

This model does not provide coverage to everyone, but only to those who have made required contributions in the past. These contributions do not necessarily have to be made by the individuals themselves, but could be made on their behalf by, for example, their employers, spouses or parents. This depends on the conditions of the particular scheme.

Level of coverage
Payments and services are related in the insurance model to the contributions that have been made. Coverage is not related to need. Consequently, payments may be made to those who are not in need, while those who are may have no entitlements whatsoever.

(Re)distributive impact
Social insurance is not designed to redistribute resources from one income group in society to another. (Or, rather, in its pure form it does not redistribute between people; as we have mentioned before, in practice many programmes of welfare provision are amalgams of the different models outlined here.) Instead, social insurance redistributes across time within the life cycle of single individuals or their families. The purpose of social insurance is nonetheless to help prevent insured individuals from being in need at times of their lives when they are most at risk. Social insurance thus represents an extension of the kind of insurance provided earlier by friendly societies.

3 Social citizenship (or rights-based) model

In the early-to-mid-twentieth century a number of countries went beyond these two models and created systems of social welfare that were based largely on the idea of social citizenship. The most extensive development of this model was to be found in Scandinavia. Although in some sense it can be seen as a fusing of different elements of the first two models, it constitutes an entirely separate model.

Who is covered?
Anyone who is a member of a community is covered and is entitled to receive payments and services. Membership may be defined in terms of a person's legal citizenship but more usually on the basis of permanent residence. Like the residualist model, provision is universal; but, unlike it, there is never any means testing. A person has a right to welfare derived from membership of the community. This does not mean that in such a system some programmes do not test to see if someone is in need – for

instance, only those who need hospital treatment gain admission to a hospital bed.

Level of coverage

People receive payments and services to enable them to be full participants in their society; whatever is required to facilitate full participation is provided. Provision is based on a notion of needs that is socially relative and not absolutist in character.

(Re)distributive impact

In principle, this model should redistribute resources from those who have more than enough to those without enough. In practice, considerable doubts about this process occurring in any welfare state have been expressed. For example, some commentators on the British welfare state (such as Le Grand, 1982) have argued that its overall impact is non-egalitarian and that it benefits the middle class rather than the working class. The middle class have the skills and other advantages allowing them to make better use of universal benefits. Moreover, utilizing fairly standard rational-choice assumptions about the behaviour of voters and politicians, it can be shown that a welfare state would be likely to experience a transfer of resources in favour of the middle class (Stigler, 1970).

While, for purposes of analysis, it is useful to emphasize the distinctive features of each of the models, in reality the distinctions become blurred. There are a number of political pressures on a state which uses either the residualist or the insurance models primarily to adopt elements of the other or of the social citizenship model.

A weakness of the residualist model is that, unless the needy constitute a very large proportion of the electorate, they may be vulnerable to the mobilization of electoral opposition against them. Consequently, those who wish to protect the needy may try to move programmes in the direction of an insurance model. Because contributors have bought their entitlements, it is more difficult to eliminate or reduce such programmes in times of retrenchment, and beneficiaries are less subject to the exercise of discretion by state officials (Goodin, 1988: ch. 7).

Again, there are also pressures for the residualist model to move in the direction of a social citizenship model. Services and programmes that are 'only for the poor' tend to be inadequate, partly because of the lack of political 'clout' by the poor. Allowing everyone to benefit from services, even if the middle classes get more than their fair share, is a necessary condition for everyone receiving adequate levels of provision, and is a coherent political strategy for those defending the interests of the poor (Goodin and Le Grand, 1987: ch. 10).

Furthermore, political pressure to extend coverage of contributory programmes to non-contributors may result in the insurance model becoming more like a social citizenship model. The needy are then provided for by diluting the contributory basis of the insurance principle; and it is even more likely to be diluted by the breaking of the link between the level of payments made and the level of benefits received (Titmuss, 1963: 173–87).

But if there are pressures for a blurring of the boundaries between different models, some forces for change seem to be stronger than others. In chapter 6 Joakim Palme shows that, in the case of pensions, the move to a citizenship model came in countries which had earlier had means-tested residualist systems, while countries that came to have insurance-type systems tended to stick with them.[4] But, as was the case in Britain, not all needs-based pension schemes were superseded by citizenship-type schemes.

Differences in the organizing principle of welfare provision help to explain the responses in different countries to the alleged 'crisis' in the welfare state, which was prominent in political debate in the early 1980s. Welfare programmes were much more vulnerable in those countries where the citizenship principle and the insurance principle were weakest. But there was also a directly political element in this response to the supposed inability of western states to meet their welfare obligations in an era of high inflation and low economic growth. In those European countries with proportional representation and coalition governments it was more difficult to translate any electoral swings to the right into direct assaults on the welfare state. In Britain, however, the situation was very different. The Conservative party came into government in 1979 with a working majority but having obtained the votes of less than 44 per cent of the electorate; division within the opposition allowed it to retain absolute power with even smaller shares of the vote in two subsequent elections. In chapter 7 Richard Parry relates the Conservative government's attempt to transform welfare provision in Britain to a political strategy – a strategy based on underlying changes in the British electorate.

From a British perspective, even one informed also by the experience in Reagan's America, it is all too easy to see the 1980s as an era in which the role of the state in welfare provision generally came to be questioned seriously. But such a conclusion stems from adopting too parochial a viewpoint. As De Swaan (1988: 229) has noted: 'The coalition to maintain the basic arrangements of the welfare state still holds in most countries. Even determined conservative regimes, such as Thatcher's or Reagan's, have not undone the basic tenets of collectivization and transfer-capital accumulation.' The New Right may have placed issues on the agenda of welfare politics that had been absent in the consensual mid-century years, but the western state is likely to remain what it became during the course of the twentieth century – the main institution responding to need in western society.

Notes

1. For an explanation of why needs cannot be reduced to wants, see Braybrooke (1987), Doyal and Gough (1984), Frankfurt (1984) and Wiggins (1985); cf. Goodin (1988: ch. 2).

2. On the justification for state welfare provision provided by a notion of social citizenship, see King and Waldron (1988); cf. Goodin (1988: ch. 2).

3. This typology of models of welfare provision parallels that of Titmuss (1974).

4. Of course, the insurance-type schemes which remain are themselves not really genuine *insurance*; they have been modified so that they no longer conform with the actuarial bases of true insurance.

References

Braybrooke, David (1987) *Meeting Needs*. Princeton, NJ: Princeton University Press.

De Swaan, Abram (1988) *In Care of the State*. Cambridge: Polity Press.

Doyal, Len and Gough, Ian (1984) 'A theory of human needs', *Critical Social Policy*, 4(1): 6–38.

Frankfurt, Harry (1984) 'Necessity and desire', *Philosophy and Phenomenological Research*, 45(1): 1–13.

Goodin, Robert E. (1988) *Reason for Welfare*. Princeton, NJ: Princeton University Press.

Goodin, Robert E. and Le Grand, Julian (1987) *Not Only the Poor*. London: George Allen & Unwin.

King, Desmond S. and Waldron, Jeremy (1988) 'Citizenship, social citizenship and the defence of welfare provision', *British Journal of Political Science*, 18(4): 415–53.

Le Grand, Julian (1982) *The Strategy of Equality*. London: George Allen & Unwin.

Salamon, Lester M. (1987) 'Partners in public service: The scope and theory of government-nonprofit relations', pp. 99–117 in Walter W. Powell (ed.), *The Nonprofit Sector*. New Haven and London: Yale University Press.

Stigler, George J. (1970) 'Director's law of public income redistribution', *Journal of Law and Economics*, 13(1): 1–10.

Titmuss, Richard (1963) *Essays on the Welfare State*. London: George Allen & Unwin.

Titmuss, Richard (1974) *Social Policy*. London: George Allen & Unwin.
Vlastos, Gregory (1962) 'Justice and equality', pp. 31–72 in Richard B. Brandt (ed.), *Social Justice*. Englewood Cliffs, NJ: Prentice-Hall.
Ware, Alan (1989) *Between Profit and State*. Cambridge: Polity Press.
Weale, Albert (1983) *Political Theory and Social Policy*. London: Macmillan.
Wiggins, David (1985) 'Claims of need', pp. 149–203 in Ted Honderich (ed.), *Morality and Objectivity*. London: Routledge & Kegan Paul.

2

Relative Needs

Robert E. Goodin

Misery consists, not in the lack of things, but in the needs which they impose. . . . 'Great needs', said Favorin, 'spring from great wealth; and often the best way of getting what we want is to get rid of what we have'. (Rousseau, 1762: 45)

What is or is not a need may be contentious. Whether the need has or has not been met, in any particular set of circumstances, may be likewise. But what follows in public policy terms from recognizing something as an unmet need is utterly uncontentious. It is, according to the conventional wisdom, indisputably better for people to be provided with more of what they need, up to the point that they need no more of it.

This principle of maximizing the supply of needed resources may, of course, be subject to a ceteris paribus clause – especially if you think that needs-based claims should not enjoy completely absolute priority over every other moral claim imaginable. Still, there seems little hesitation in saying that that is broadly the right way to respond to the claims of needs. What follows from the proposition that there is a need for more housing? That we should build more of it, obviously. What follows from the proposition that there is a need for more education? That we should supply more of it, surely. What could be more straightforward?

It is the theme of this chapter that, perhaps surprisingly, maximizing the supply of needed resources is not always the right response to unmet need. At least for certain important classes of needed resources – and perhaps for most classes of needed resources, at least in part or across certain portions of their ranges – the best way of meeting unmet needs may entail decreasing rather than increasing supply. More specifically, the best way of satisfying unmet needs may not be to cause those who are relatively more needy to have more of the needed resource, but rather to cause others to have less of it.

This chapter starts from two commonplaces about needs, their priority and their relativity. It proceeds to develop a paradox, arising principally out of the latter attribute but deriving much of its sting from the first. The counter-intuitive conclusion indicated above is then teased out of that paradox, and its implications for public policy in various areas are explored.

Two commonplaces

It is often said that, in any conflict between satisfying people's desires and meeting people's needs, the latter is to take priority. Intrapersonally, that proposition constitutes the core of the case for paternalism: it tells us to serve a person's needs, whether he or she wants them satisfied or not. Interpersonally, that proposition guides the allocation of social resources, giving priority to the satisfaction of one person's needs over another's 'mere desires'.

Whether it is needs as such that deserve such high priority treatment, or whether it is merely something that correlates with needs, is an open question. But that correlation – if that is all that it is – is typically thought to be strong enough for claims of needs to exert a strong moral pull on us. Exactly how strong a pull is another open question. But the priority to be accorded to needs over wants is typically said to be very strong, and is often said to be virtually (if rarely literally) absolute.

Those are contentious issues, which I have addressed at length elsewhere.[1] For present purposes, they need not be finally resolved. It is enough here merely to observe that needs enjoy at least a strong de facto priority over mere wants. That is the first commonplace with which I shall here be conjuring.

The second commonplace is that needs can be relative as well as absolute. There are, in fact, a great many different ways in which – and a great many things to which – they might be relative. In this chapter, I shall be focusing on one of them in particular. However, I must first mention briefly at least some of the others, if only to set them to one side.

Most fundamentally, perhaps, we can see needs as always being relative to the goals for which the resource in question is needed. Needs are inherently instrumental, in this respect. Certain important consequences, political as well as philosophical, follow from that fact.[2] That, however, is not the relativization of needs that will here principally concern me, though I shall make passing use of this point later.

Beyond that, there are various other respects in which needs are relative to the society in which you find yourself. Needs are, in many diverse ways, relative to time, place and social circumstance. One has no need for a fur coat in Havana or a bikini in Antarctica. The ancients had no need for fissionable materials, nor do subsistence farmers have any need for mainframe computers. A community of atheists has no need for sacramental wine, nor a community of teetotallers for a cellar master. The English working class has no need for hunting lodges, nor has the English landed gentry any need for tickets to the local football match.[3]

Those society-wide relativizations of need might matter crucially to one or another of the various applications of the term in social discourse. Historical debates over whether the standard of living has risen or fallen since the Industrial Revolution, or World Bank debates over what exactly the 'basic needs' strategy would require for any given country, clearly must take such relativizations of the notion of need very much to heart.

Here, however, I shall be focusing instead on a deeper sense in which needs might be relative. My point is not just that needs are essentially conventional, or in some other way relative to time, place and social circumstance.[4] That is true, too. But that is not the end of the matter. What in particular you need does not just depend on the society in which you are living.

My focus here will instead be on the way in which, within a single society, what one person needs may also be relative. My needs may be relative, not only to the society in which I live, but also to what others in my society already have. One person's needs-fulfilment may be a function (positively, or more typically negatively) of other people's needs-fulfilment in the same society. What resources one person needs in order to satisfy the goal of meeting certain needs may be relative to the resources available to others in the same society for meeting their similar goals.[5]

The former style of social relativization of needs is a model of 'relativism'. It relativizes needs to societies: what you need depends on the society (its objective circumstances and its extant values) in which you find yourself. The latter and deeper style of social relativization of needs is genuinely a model of 'relativities'. It relativizes your needs to the needs-satisfactions of other members of your society: your needs-satisfaction, on that latter model, depends not just on the society in which you are living but also on how well you, compared to everyone else in that society, are doing towards meeting the standard that that society sets as the benchmark of needs-satisfaction. Henceforth when talking of 'relative needs' I shall mean the term in that latter, stronger sense.

There are clearly certain needs that are, by that standard, not relative at all. They are completely fixed by nature and wholly independent of social context. The minimum caloric intake required to sustain a human body of given size and weight at a given level of physical exertion in a given climate might be one such example.[6] At the very least, we can say with confidence that how much sustenance you need to exert a certain amount of force on the natural world is independent of the caloric intake of others around you.

Other needs, though, are more dependent on social context. The clearest examples, perhaps, are those arising in connection with Peter Townsend's (1954, 1962, 1979) discussion of 'relative poverty'. Whether you need access to a television set to participate in social conversations in your society depends on what proportion of the population around you has access to one, and on how much social conversation is dominated by last night's programmes in consequence.[7] How many calories you need might even depend on what society expects you to do by way of expending calories, which in turn depends on how many calories others around you have available to expend: if they are all playing tennis, you need to have the strength to join in the game if you are not to be excluded from that aspect of social life altogether.

In all such practical illustrations of the social relativity of needs, it is almost inevitably unclear which sense of relativity – strong or weak – is at work. Sharp though the distinction may be in logic, it is inevitably blurred in practice, because the strong sense actually implies the weak one. If what you need is relative to what others around you have, for individuals one-by-one, then it follows that what you need will also be relative to some society-specific aggregate (mean consumption, or some such).

Townsend's examples are as ambiguous, between these two senses of social relativity of needs, as are others. Sometimes the point of the example seems to be just that needs are conventional, and relative to time and place and cultural location in that sense.[8] But at least sometimes the examples seem capable of bearing an alternative interpretation. At least sometimes the point seems to be that your needs depend not only on what local convention requires of you but also on how well everyone else in your society satisfies those requirements. Your needs-fulfilment is dependent on, and relative to, theirs. What you truly need depends on what they already have. The more needed resources they have, the more of them you need.

The paradox

If needs are relative, in the strong sense that how much you need does indeed depend on how much others have, then there are in principle two quite distinct ways of meeting needs. One is to increase the supply of needed resources to the relatively more needy; the other is to reduce the supply of needed resources to the relatively less needy. Or, of course, we might pursue the mixed strategy of doing both at the same time.

Now, there is nothing paradoxical about the first option. It is not in the least odd to suggest that we reduce aggregate neediness in the population by giving more to the relatively more needy. There is nothing paradoxical in the suggestion that aggregate neediness could be reduced by distributing any extra resources disproportionately in favour of the relatively more needy, for example. Nor is there anything paradoxical in suggesting that we pursue that goal by redistributing needed resources away from the relatively less needy and towards the relatively more needy. Such strategies, insofar as they are designed to give the relatively more needy people relatively more needed resources, are intuitively wholly accessible and perfectly appealing.

Notice, however, that the second option – equally eligible, on the logic of meeting relative needs – does not stop with anything nearly so unexceptionable as that. It is concerned primarily that we should take needed resources *away* from the relatively less needy people in the population. What we then do with those resources is, under that second strategy, strictly speaking of no concern. To be sure, we would make more of an impact on the reduction of relative needs if we were to conjoin the second strategy with the first, both taking from the relatively rich and giving to the relatively poor. But in the unalloyed version of the second strategy, that is not strictly necessary: the desired effect could be achieved perfectly well simply by taking resources from the relatively less needy, and then throwing them into the sea. That would be a perfectly good, albeit perhaps non-ideal, way of reducing the relative disparity between the two groups – and in so doing, reducing the relatively more needy group's unmet (relative) needs.

The logic of that inference is impeccable. Yet there is something undeniably paradoxical about meeting needs by wantonly destroying needed resources. There is something unquestionably odd about recommending impoverishment as a strategy for needs-satisfaction.

Of course, the general structure of the problem is familiar from other contexts. But the standard ways we have for solving such problems in those other contexts are generally unavailable to us here. It is often said, for example, in discussions of equality that if all we care about is equality per se then levelling down is as good as levelling up. Throwing the treasures of the rich into the sea is a perfectly good way of producing equality, too. If enough of the rich's treasures are tossed away, all would be equal – albeit equally poor.

The standard response, in the case of equality, is that equality is *not* all we care about, nor does equality even enjoy any particularly strong priority over everything else that we also care about. Thus, for example, we care about minimizing poverty or maximizing the average standard of living as well as about minimizing inequality. And it is those other, competing, compelling goals that make 'levelling down' an unacceptable strategy of equality.

The same response, however, works less well in the context of arguments about relative needs. Needs claims have quite high (if not quite absolute) priority over all other claims. The stronger we think that that priority is, the more relaxed we should be about sacrificing other goals to them, through a socially wasteful process of levelling down to maximize relative needs-satisfactions. Of course, which strategy we should ultimately prefer depends on what alternative mechanisms are available for satisfying relative needs, and on how effective they happen to be. But it is perfectly possible that the goal may be of sufficiently high priority, and the alternative means of pursuing it sufficiently unpromising, that the strategy of wantonly destroying the resources of the rich, Pol Pot style, might turn out to be the socially preferred strategy.

Here, then, the paradox resists the standard solvents. It is not just that some lower priority social goal (efficiency, or whatever) is suffering unnecessarily when we throw some needed resources of the relatively less needy into the sea, and that our intuitive attachment to that lower ranked goal makes us uneasy about that practice. We feel, intuitively, that the goal of meeting needs *itself* somehow suffers in the process of throwing needed resources into the sea. Surely, we say to ourselves, making everyone in society go as short of food as the hungriest member is no way to meet people's needs.

Characterizing really relative needs

The upshot, I think, is just that people like Townsend have overplayed their hand in pretending that all social needs are relative, in any strong sense. Some are, some are not. And the air of paradox already identified pretty well dissolves once we remind ourselves of that fact.

What is wrong with the strategy of throwing food into the sea, in order to meet people's needs, is that their need for food is – to a very large extent, anyway – absolute, and not at all relative to how much others in their society are eating. Even if it is impossible for everyone to eat as much as they need, it is better – not just better for individuals themselves, but even better in terms of (absolute) needs-satisfaction across the society as a whole

– for more people to eat adequately than for fewer to do so.

The question, then, becomes how to separate out needs that are indeed socially relative, in the strong sense. Some, such as Sen (1983), might attempt to do this by distinguishing between needed resources that are of end-use value, on the one hand, and ones that are of merely instrumental value, on the other hand. The point about food – the reason that you are better off with more food than with less, however much or little food others around you might have – is that food is of end-use value to you. You derive benefits from food through the very act of your eating it; you are not depending on any further chain of social consequences, in which food consumption plays some crucial role, in order to get the good in view from the morsel in your mouth.

Thus it would seem that your need for some resource can only be socially relative, in the strong sense, if the resource is of merely instrumental value to you. That is a necessary, not sufficient, condition, of course. Not all goods of merely instrumental value are necessarily relative, in the strong sense. But it is, apparently, true that only goods that are of instrumental value are capable of being socially relative in the strong sense.

This partitioning of the problem takes us less far than we might have hoped, however. The trouble is that – as announced earlier – needed resources are always of merely instrumental value.[9] In saying that something is needed, you must always be able to go on to say *for what* it is needed. The answer might well be 'for just about anything else you care to do'. Resources of which this can truly be said are the ones we feel most comfortable describing as 'needs', in the colloquial sense.[10] But their instrumental nature is in no way undercut by the universality of the instrument.

This observation poses an obviously difficult predicament for the standard analysis of relative needs as pertaining only to resources of merely instrumental value. If all needed resources are instrumental, in some sense, then the distinction between absolute and relative needs cannot be analysed in terms of a (non-existent) distinction between needed resources that are of end-use value and ones that are of merely instrumental value. All are instrumental.

Everything will therefore have to depend on the second feature – which was always going to have to be a necessary part of the definition of relative needs, anyway – of competitive utilization. All needed resources are instrumental. But some instruments' usefulness to you is independent of others' stock and use of similar instruments, while some instruments' usefulness is not so independent. Food is an example of the former: it is instrumental in keeping you alive, but your meal's usefulness to you in that regard is independent of anyone else's stock or use of the food in their larder. Money is an example of the latter: it is instrumental, too, but how useful it is to you in pursuing your ends depends on how much others have and use of it in bidding against you for scarce resources that you both desire but cannot both simultaneously enjoy.[11]

Now, the paradox identified above dissolves in the context of needed resources that are instrumental and competitive in their utilization. If your stock and use of resources actually impinges upon others' enjoyment of theirs, then it is easy enough to see how restrictions on your stock and use of resources might enhance overall social enjoyment: what you lose through such restrictions may be more than compensated by what others gain through them. Where instrumental, competitive-utilization resources are concerned, throwing the resources of the rich into the sea may well be a good way to reduce relative social needs overall.

It is worth emphasizing, however, that for the paradox to dissolve in this way the competitiveness must be genuinely objective. It must, somehow, be inherent in the very nature of the goods themselves that one person's utilization of them as instruments towards his or her ends is inherently competitive with another person's utilization of them in similar fashion. Stories that trace the competitiveness to some purely subjective attribute will simply not suffice.

For an example of the latter, inadequate, variation on this theme, consider the familiar story about 'relative deprivation'. People's felt deprivation is relative to their aspirations and expectations, which are relative in turn to their reference group and average accomplishments within it.[12] A similarly subjective story about relative needs would be that what people think they need is relative to what they expect to be able to do, which is relative in turn to what others around them are doing.

As a story about subjective satisfactions – of either wants or needs – that account is impeccable. Yet surely there is still something paradoxical about any inference that we should therefore destroy needed resources, just to reduce people's subjective anxieties about their relative deprivations. Perhaps the air of paradox persists simply because we do not take subjectivities of this sort altogether seriously: we think that people *are* (objectively) better off with more needed resources, even if others have still more of them, however sensitive the people themselves may be to meaningless relativities. Secondarily, perhaps, we may be particularly tempted to take that hard line on merely subjective deprivation because we suppose that people always have it within their own power to ease any objectively groundless sense of deprivation that they may feel just by revising their aspirations or their choice of who to take as their reference group. Purely subjective problems admit of purely subjective solutions.[13]

If the relativities matter not just subjectively but objectively, though, then it is a different story. Instrumental resources that are competitive in their utilization in that way are a wholly legitimate matter of concern, because the more of them that others have the less good mine will objectively do me. Since it is not thinking that made it so in the first place, thinking otherwise will not cease to make it so: it is not within my power to make objective relativities cease to matter, in the way that it is with subjective relativities. With objectively competitive resources, I inevitably am and I must inevitably remain objectively worse off, the relatively more others have of them. From that fact it follows that we may all be made objectively better off – less needy, in ways that objectively matter – by removing resources from the relatively well-endowed, even if those resources are then merely thrown into the sea.

Policy implications

The argument so far has been designed to establish that, while (*pace* Townsend) not all needs are relative, at least some needs are genuinely relative in the strong sense in which how much you need depends on how much others around you have. Let us call these, generically, needs for 'status goods'. The balance of this chapter is devoted to identifying certain specific needs of this sort, and tracing out their policy consequences.

It must be emphasized at the outset, however, that very few goods (hence needs) fall squarely into one category or the other. Most needed resources are valued partly for what they can do for you, independently of others' utilization of similar resources, and partly for what they can do for you in competition with others. In virtually all the discussions that follow, therefore, I shall persistently be saying 'in so far as' the resources are needed as status goods, certain policy consequences follow. There is no presumption that that is the only role that they play, or the only need that they serve. In so far as they do indeed carry some other value, and serve some other end, then the appropriate social policies vis-à-vis those needed resources are to that extent potentially quite different.

With that caveat in place, let me simply catalogue what I take to be some of the main headings of social needs, tracing in what ways the needed resources are status goods and what policy prescriptions follow from that fact.

Housing

Consider, first, housing needs. It is indisputably true that, to some extent, people's needs for shelter are absolute, and not at all relative to the housing standards enjoyed by others around them. Of course, what sort of housing you need in the desert is very different from that which you need in the mountains, and what sort you need in damp climates is very different from that which you need in dry ones. But that is just a matter of social relativity in the weaker sense: invariate standards of health and hygiene just generate different implications in different climatic conditions.

There is, then, a 'basic need' for housing that is absolute, and not at all socially relative in the strong sense. It is a sad truth, of clear importance for public policy, that not everyone's basic housing needs are presently being met. Even (perhaps especially) in wealthy societies, some people still sleep rough, and many still live in insanitary environments. Far from all of them do so in any way that could be remotely described as 'through their own choosing'. The first task for public policy on housing must, unquestionably, be to respond to absolute need of this sort.

Beyond that, however, there is a demand (that is often described as a 'need') for housing that is indeed socially relative, in the strong sense. Accommodation is often scorned as 'substandard', not on the grounds that it is absolutely unsatisfactory (unhealthy, unhygienic, etc), but merely on the grounds that it falls short of the 'standard' typical of that society. Thus, for example, Marx and Engels write:

> A house may be large or small: so long as the surrounding houses are equally small, it satisfies all social demands for a dwelling. But let a palace arise beside the little house, and it shrinks from a little house to a hut. . . . However high [the poor man's] house may shoot up in the course of civilization, if the neighbouring palace grows to an equal or even greater extent, the occupant of the relatively small house will feel more and more uncomfortable, dissatisfied and cramped within its four walls.[14]

In so far as housing is indeed a status good of that sort, various policy consequences follow. The first is that relative needs satisfaction will be maximized by a regime that enforces broad equality in housing standards. Over the minimum standard set by people's absolute basic needs for housing, equally small houses are just as good as equally large ones. Within the range here under discussion, it is the equality of everyone's accommodation rather than its absolute size that matters.[15]

The second policy consequence is that, on various other grounds, it is probably socially preferable that housing should be equally modest for all rather than equally grand for all, again once we are over the minimum standard set by absolute basic needs for housing. Contrast, for example, the terraced three-bedroomed houses of an English town with the suburban sprawl of three-bedroomed houses set on a quarter of an acre in Sydney's western suburbs. The joys of living 'in the country' are wholly lost when you have to share it with so many near neighbours; the distances involved make walking to neighbourhood shops infeasible and driving, with the attendant traffic congestion at rush hours, mandatory.[16] Thus, in so far as relativities really are all that matter to people in this range of housing choice, everyone would be better off (have their 'relative needs' for housing better met) with smaller houses on smaller building plots.

In practical policy terms, this presumably means that relative housing needs would be better met through programmes of building restriction rather than by programmes of building. Land use controls ought be used – in the name of meeting relative needs, even – to prevent a socially counterproductive turn in the competition for ever-grander houses on ever-larger plots in previously unspoilt locations. Negatively, governments ought to refrain from providing infrastructural subsidies (through road building, sewer extensions, etc.) to developers. Positively, governments ought to take steps to protect the 'green belts' around urban centres.

None of those policy measures is in the least novel, of course. The novelty lies merely in justifying those measures in the self-same needs-based terms that are usually employed to justify the house building that I would hope to stop. Depending on the exact nature of the needs, maximizing the supply of dwellings may be counterproductive of satisfaction of housing needs. If the needs in view are socially relative in the strong sense (so the housing is required merely as a status good) then smaller but more equally sized houses will meet that need better than larger and more variably sized ones.

Food and clothing
The same that has been said of shelter can be said, mutatis mutandis, of the other two members of the classic trio, food and clothing. Both unquestionably, to some extent address needs that are utterly absolute. Again, how much and what kinds of food you need to eat, and how much and what kinds of clothes you

need to wear, depend on vagaries of local climate and so on. But that is social relativism of a relatively superficial sort. At root, one's basic need for certain quantities of food and clothing is surely as absolute as one's need for shelter from the ravages of the environment.

Again, however, people are generally said to have 'needs' for food and clothing that go well beyond those absolute necessities. What sort of food you need to eat, and what sort of clothing to wear, is to some extent relative to what others around you are eating and wearing. In part, perhaps, that is because of the contribution food and clothing make to one's capacity to utilize one's human capital effectively in the labour market: a well-fed and well-clothed worker can work more efficiently than a less well (albeit perfectly adequately, by absolute standards) fed and clothed worker.[17] In larger part, no doubt, the social relativity of needs for food and clothing derives from the role of those commodities as symbols and signals in every culture.[18] Who would trust an ill-clad person who prefers cabbage to caviare with a position of responsibility in our culture?

The upshot, here again, is that food and clothing beyond the absolute basic necessities is largely a 'status good', your need for which is a function of how many other people around you already have it.[19] In so far as that is true, it once again follows that how much of these fancy goods matters less, socially, than how they are distributed. The satisfaction of relative needs, across the whole society, is more a matter of equalizing stocks than of maximizing them.

Social symbolisms are sufficiently flexible, and policy instruments sufficiently blunt, that it is probably hopeless ever to expect to impose even rough equality on consumption of food and clothing. Sumptuary laws have, historically, met with little success since Richard the Lionheart tried to prohibit the extravagant wearing of fur by the Crusaders under his command.[20] Still, there is one measure that might even nowadays be worth considering.

Highest status typically attaches to imported goods. (That is partly due to their relative scarcity, no doubt; but it is at least partly due to their being exotic, whether or not particularly scarce.) If we want to maximize satisfaction of everyone's relative needs for status goods of food and clothing across the whole society, one way to do it would therefore be to discourage importation of fancy goods, to which high status will quite probably be attached.

The standard way of doing that is to impose a swingeing import tax, of course, on the ground that the more expensive a product is the less of it will be consumed. But that is exactly the wrong way to discourage status goods competition, of course. The higher the price, the more a mark of status the good's consumption is. Thus, instead of taxing French champagne heavily, Australians keen to avoid status competition should ban it altogether. No one will suffer, in absolute terms, from being forced to drink the domestic product instead. There are, of course, the standard 'trade war' rejoinders to this proposal to be considered. My point here is just that, if people's relative needs are what is at issue, that is the best way to meet them.

Education

Education falls into the same broad pattern. To a certain extent, more education makes you absolutely better off: you are better able to manipulate nature around you; you enjoy life more, and so on. To some extent, however, one's need for education is socially relative. That is clearly true in the weaker sense, in which how much information you need to have depends on whether you are living in a primitive culture or a technologically sophisticated one. It is also true in the stronger sense, in which how much education you need depends on how much others around you have.

The most interesting way in which education serves as a 'status good' has to do with 'credential inflation' in the labour market. Suppose that the amount of information and intellectual sophistication required to perform perfectly satisfactorily the job of an entry-level clerk in the civil service is equivalent to three A-levels, or a high school diploma in the US. Suppose, however, that employers will always prefer to hire more qualified rather than less qualified candidates for any given job, for any of a variety of reasons.[21] Then each person, hoping for a better job, has an overwhelming incentive to acquire qualifications well beyond those that are strictly needed to do the job for which he or she will apply. It is a 'prisoner's dilemma' situation among prospective employees, wherein each would be better off if they all refrained, but wherein no one has any incentive so to refrain from acquiring credentials superfluous to the task.[22]

In so far as education is needed only to confer relative advantage in labour market competition (and I hasten to add here, as before, that this is only part of the story), the policy implications are clear, at least for a country with a centralized educational system. We need merely decide how many jobs there are (and are likely to be) requiring what levels of educational attainment; then we ought to restrict entry to those educational schemes to numbers roughly proportionate to the projected need for people with those skills, after allowing for natural wastage. In countries leaving such matters to the market, and where people are allowed to buy as much education as they can afford, restricting credential inflation will obviously be harder: but perhaps a first step would be to grade each job, according to the skills strictly required for its performance, and to prohibit employers from discriminating against applicants on the grounds that they do not have educational qualifications in excess of what is deemed necessary.[23]

The general aim, with education as with other status goods, would be to equalize rather than maximize across society. The rationale, here as with other status goods, is not to promote equality for its own sake but rather as a way of maximizing relative needs-satisfaction across the whole of society. The fewer superfluous credentials each has, the fewer all others will need.

Legal aid

On the face of it, 'justice' is an absolute virtue. It is better to have more of it than less, for each and every person. Any injustice done to you is a wrong, which is not mitigated by any similar wrongs that might have been done to others around you. From the obvious truth of that proposition, we might (wrongly) infer another: it is always better for people to have more legal services than fewer; more specifically, it is always better for people to have legal representation than not to have it.

Legal representation is commonly described as a social need, and legal aid schemes to provide such representation to those who cannot afford it are generally justified on those grounds. In so far as it is a matter of providing attorneys for those accused of crimes, such legal aid schemes undoubtedly contribute to 'justice' in absolute terms: where the state will prosecute, it is wrong for the accused to stand undefended. Similarly, perhaps, in so far as it is a matter of defending against a civil action: where the plaintiff will be represented by counsel, it is a matter of absolute natural justice that the defendant should be likewise.

In other respects, however, legal services are a relative rather than an absolute need. How much legal assistance you need depends on how much others on the other side of the courtroom have to bring to bear. To a large extent, you need lawyers to defend you against lawyers. If no one had lawyers, no one would need lawyers, in civil actions at least. In that sense, legal representation is a 'status good', in the technical sense that how much you need depends on how much others around you have.

In so far as legal aid is indeed a status good of that sort, various more-or-less radical policy prescriptions follow. The rather grander way of putting the point would be to say that we should try to follow the abortive Indian attempt to return (for purposes of civil cases, at least) to less structured forms of pleadings, familiar in England from the early history of Chancery.[24] The less grand way of putting the point would be simply to say that we should try to expand upon the model of the 'small claims courts' already in operation in various Anglo-American jurisdictions. The point, in each case, would be that legal representation would then be less necessary, and also less advantageous.

In this case as the others, the general idea is to equalize rather than maximize the supply of legal services across the society. If lawyers are needed only to defend us against other lawyers, then we would be equally (or indeed better) off with fewer rather than more. The less legal aid each has, the less all others will need.

Conclusion

These brief remarks on a random assortment of policy issues are meant merely to be illustrative. The selection is not systematic; the discussions are not remotely comprehensive on any of the proposals; given how unrealistic, politically, most of the proposals actually are there is little point in fleshing them out further. Still, some more general points of deeper interest emerge from those more particular policy proposals.

There are two components of needs-satisfaction. On the one hand, we have needs that are absolute: the satisfaction that any one person derives from needed resources of this sort is independent of others' utilization of similar resources. On the other hand, we have needs that are relative: there, the satisfaction that any one person derives from needed resources does depend on how many similar resources others have and use. These two components of needs-satisfaction are analytically separable even if in policy terms they are often empirically intertwined.

In so far as our aim is to maximize satisfaction of absolute needs, the policy prescription is just the familiar one. There, we should indeed maximize people's supplies of needed resources, up to the point that they need no more of them according to standards of absolute need.

In so far as our aim is the satisfaction of relative needs, however, the policy prescriptions are really quite different. There, policy should be guided by two principles. The first is equalization rather than maximization of resources that are needed in this relative way. Maximization of relative needs-satisfaction across the whole society is (given the way 'relative needs' in the strong sense have here been defined) equivalent to the minimization of differentials between people's holdings across the whole society. It is the equality of holdings across society, rather than the absolute levels of those holdings, that matters for this purpose: unlike absolute needs-satisfaction, everyone's being equally poor in these respects is just as good as everyone's being equally rich, so far as relative needs-satisfaction is concerned.

Though those two outcomes are equally good in terms of relative needs-satisfaction, there are other grounds for choosing between them. In so far as a resource is needed only to procure competitive advantage over others with similar resources, and in so far as competition of that sort is socially counterproductive (eating up resources that could, alternatively, have been put to more productive uses), it is socially preferable that relative needs be satisfied by providing everyone with equally few resources of this sort rather than equally many. Minimizing everyone's equal supply of relatively needed resources then, is, the second principle that should guide policy in this area.

These two principles, taken together, have further implications for the preferred mode of provision of these relatively needed resources. Roughly speaking, the options are to provide them through market mechanisms that have been suitably adjusted or to provide them in kind via direct social provision.[25] Equalization of resources could, in principle, be accomplished through either route. (In practice, of course, there may be far more political resistance to the dramatic equalization of income and assets that would be required to accomplish this via the market mechanism than there would be to the direct provision of non-fungible needed goods in certain more limited categories.) The second goal, however, cannot credibly be pursued through market mechanisms.

It is in the very nature of the competitive market process that each will try to 'up the ante' in the status goods sweepstakes, and that each must at least match the other's bid to stay in the competition. This spiralling of the status good competition is socially counterproductive but utterly inevitable, adjust initial market assets as you may. Furthermore, the ordinary market technique for discouraging certain social pursuits will not work with status goods: whereas the higher the price of most goods the fewer of them are consumed, with status goods the higher their price the more a mark of higher status (and hence the more valuable a token in social competition) they are. Thus, equalizing relatively needed resources at minimal levels is impossible through market mechanisms.

There are many things that can be said in favour of a policy of meeting social needs through direct social provision of the needed commodities.[26] Here, I have added yet one more. Where the needs are relative, in the strong sense, the great advantage of the state over the market as provider of those resources is that the state can (at least in principle) say 'no' in a way that the market simply cannot. With relatively needed resources – ones needed only to procure competitive advantage, in a competition that is itself socially counterproductive – uniform provision, at lower levels, will achieve all the good without doing any of the harm that would be done by market-style maximization of those resources. The real advantage of direct state provision for those sorts of needs is that the state can, in a way the market cannot, actually restrict supply of those sorts of resources.[27]

Whether there will actually be the political will for the state to say 'no' in this way is, perhaps, an open question. There should be. If the competition in status goods is genuinely counterproductive – if everyone really would be better off if everyone (themselves included) were prevented from pursuing them – then there should be a substantial majority, approaching unanimity, in favour of banning the counterproductive competition. But that assumes that everyone is realistic in assessing this as a competition that no one can win. Psychometric studies militate against any such easy assumptions. It is a common phenomenon for people to think that they are better than average, or in the top half of the distribution, on any range of favoured attributes you care to mention. And if that tendency is so strong as to encourage large numbers of people to think that, against all the odds, they are likely to be among the very few winners of this status-goods competition, then the natural, rational majority for banning such competitions might start to slip away.

Of course, needed resources are never wholly of one sort or wholly of the other – neither wholly absolute nor wholly relative. So these conclusions must be phrased with care. What my argument implies is that, apropos of any needed resource that has a 'status good' relativistic component (and most seem to have such a component, at least across part of their ranges), there is something to be said for uniformly minimal supply achieved through direct state provision; and there is something, conversely, to be said against markets which, adjust them as we may, will always tend to maximize supply of those resources. That there is 'something to be said' for such a policy does not imply that that is a conclusive consideration. Countervailing considerations must always be borne in mind before final policy recommendations can be given. Still, that is an important, if partial, finding.

It is important, if for no other reason, because it flies so squarely in the face of conventional wisdom. Ordinarily we think that maximization of needed resources is socially desirable – as indeed it is, where absolute needs are concerned. Writers employing a relative standard of needs help themselves willy-nilly to that standard presumption. They tend to assume, without argument, that the right response to relative deprivation is to try to bring everyone up to the standards enjoyed by the median member of that society. Where the needs at issue are genuinely relative, though, that is not necessarily – and, if I am right, is necessarily not – the right response. Minimization rather than maximization of those resources might be socially optimal. There, less really may be more, and there we may well want to rely on the state to enforce those minimalist strictures upon ourselves.

Notes

I gratefully acknowledge the comments and criticisms of participants at the Paris ECPR workshop from which this collection emerges, particularly Heiner Ganßmann, Philippe Van Parijs and Keith Dowding, and Alan Ware's detailed written comments.
1. In Goodin (1988: ch. 2). On the principle of precedence of needs over wants more generally, see Braybrooke (1968, 1987) and Frankfurt (1984).

2. Barry (1965: 47–9); Braybrooke (1987: ch. 2); Wiggins (1985: 154–5). One consequence is this: if needs are always instrumental in this way, then meeting needs cannot have absolute priority over everything else, including achieving the ends for which the needed resources were required in the first place (Goodin, 1988: 29–32).

3. The latter example is Townsend's (1954: 133–4), more or less – ironically enough, in light of Piachaud's (1981) powerful critique of his later book (Townsend, 1979) on precisely this point.

4. This is presumably the force of Adam Smith's comment, quoted approvingly by Townsend (1962: 219) and used as the basis for his subsequent work on 'relative poverty' (Townsend, 1979), that: 'By necessaries I understand, not only the commodities which are indispensably necessary for the support of life, but whatever the custom of the country renders it indecent for creditable people, even of the lowest order, to be without'.

5. In perhaps one of the earliest appreciations of this class of needs, Sir James Steuart (1767: bk. 2, ch. 21) calls these 'political necessities' required for the pursuit of 'rank in society', and distinguishes them from 'physical necessities' required for physical survival.

6. Townsend (1962: 216–18) offers nutritionalist grounds for resisting any such simple standard. Dasgupta and Ray (1986/1987; see more generally Streeten et al., 1981) offer the more profound observation that dietary deficiencies handicap the malnourished in labour market competition; in that sense, your need for food really would be relative to others' consumption.

7. A similar 'critical mass' analysis has been given to account for the failure of satellite television to take off in Britain so far: there is no point buying a dish if you are unlikely to run into anyone with whom you can gossip about last night's satellite television programmes.

8. Townsend's (1979) claim that you are relatively poor if you cannot afford to eat roast beef on Sunday, in a society where everyone else does, is clearly one such example.

9. This might be connected to the standard complaint against means-ends reasoning: there is never any true 'end' in the chain; any end is always, at the same time, merely a means to some higher-order end, which is always merely a means in turn to some yet higher-order end, and so on (see Braybrooke and Lindblom, 1963).

10. That is clear from the discussions of, e.g. Doyal and Gough (1984: 14), Daniels (1985: chs 1 and 2) and Goodin (1988: 35 and 36–40).

11. Among the models on which this discussion is based are: Shubik's (1971) 'games of status'; Hirsch's (1976) 'positional goods'; and Sen's (1977, 1981, 1985a, 1985b) 'exchange entitlements' as means of securing 'basic capabilities'. It follows from what I say here that relative needs will be a problem only in circumstances of scarcity: if everyone could have all that they wanted of everything, then there would be no reason for resource disparities to translate into consumption disparities; everyone could, and would, be equally satiated (Ellis and Heath, 1983). Still, scarcity in that sense will presumably always be with us.

12. This draws on the model developed by Hyman (1942), Runciman (1966), Campbell (1972) and Duncan (1975: 273).

13. That is the emphasis of Frankfurt (1984: 9–13), for example.

14. This passage from Marx and Engels (1958: Vol. 1, 93–4) is reproduced from Streeten et al. (1981: 19). As phrased, it sounds as if subjectively relative deprivation rather than any objective forces are at work behind this sense of impoverishment. But there may be objective forces at work, too: after all, the more space your neighbour's house occupies, the less open land there is nearby and the further you have to walk to get past the neighbour's house when going to local shops.

15. I take it as a mathematical truth that a policy of equalization will minimize relative need, measured on virtually any index of dispersion. Of course, some individuals may care about relative needs more than do others; and if we are trying to minimize some subjective measure ('relative frustration' or some such) we may therefore be tempted to let those to whom the relativities matter more have relatively more than those to whom the relativities matter less. For reasons given at the end of the third section of this chapter, I take it that our concern is with objective rather than subjective facts about relativities, though.

16. This point, made in a general way by Hirsch (1976: 32–41), is richly illustrated with examples from the American case by Jackson (1985).

17. For an elegant formalization, see Dasgupta and Ray (1986/1987).

18. That is the theme of Douglas and Isherwood (1978). In a way, their argument makes the relativity of the need subjective rather than objective. But the subjectivism comes at the level of the collectivity whose code is constituted by symbols, and it is therefore beyond the power of any individual to alter. It is therefore immune to the objections raised at the end of the third section.

19. Some might, of course, profess a purely aesthetic preference for a fancy frock, denying that there is any social-status component in their preference for it. But as Brian Barry interjected, when this point was offered in the Paris workshop

at which this argument was originally discussed, 'However aesthetically excellent the frock, I cannot help thinking that a lady would be pretty pissed off seeing several others walking down the street wearing an identical one'.

20. Schoeck (1969: 261). According to the official ideology, at least, the requirement that British schoolchildren wear set uniforms is designed to avoid status competition based on clothes; but I take it that that model would be harder to impose on the rest of society.

21. This might be for some 'good' reason: better qualified candidates might perform marginally better, or marginally more reliably, or might be better long-term career investments for the employer. More often, the practice seems to be employed, not because higher qualifications are thought to make candidates more promising in any sense at all, but just as a tie-breaker among candidates who are by all reasonable criteria equally promising.

22. Elster (1976) elaborates on the brief remarks of Hirsch (1976: 41–51).

23. Politically, perhaps it is unlikely that a society that is sufficiently laissez faire to leave education to the market would be tempted by this interventionist a measure. But educational attainment tends to correlate with race and sex, and those groups that have been discriminated against in the past are credential-poor in consequence in the present; so this measure might be justified as a mild form of reverse discrimination of the least objectionable sort. On that basis, it might fly politically even in the US.

24. Goodin (1982: ch. 4). On the Indian case, see Galanter (1974).

25. The 'adjustments' to markets here in view are distributional adjustments – redistributing resources, but then letting market forces operate in the ordinary way. There is, perhaps, a third alternative to the two here canvassed, viz. a socially regulated market. I am inclined to regard this as not a distinct alternative but rather as just a combination of the other two; and the extent to which the regulated market option can meet the problems here exposed in market strategies is directly proportional to the extent to which 'command' elements in the hybrid overshadow genuinely 'market' components. There may, of course, be good reasons for 'direct state provision' to operate through private contractors. But the market forces at work in tendering for the contract from government are very unlike the market forces at work in supplying direct to the public, in this regard.

26. It is a more direct – and hence, presumptively, more efficient – way of getting the needed resources into the hands of those who need them, rather than relying on roundabout adjusted-market mechanisms. 'Specific egalitarianism' is politically far more popular than is global egalitarianism: we, collectively, seem to care far more about grossly unequal distributions of food, shelter and so on than we care about grossly unequal distributions of income and wealth more generally (Tobin, 1970). In-kind transfers of specific commodities are more efficient ways of satisfying demand, where the community is characterized by greater variation in people's income than in their tastes for those commodities (Browning, 1975; Weitzman, 1977). And so on.

27. We might ordinarily regret the uniformity of state provision as suppressing valued goals of individuality and diversity. But in so far as the market caters to people's tastes for status goods of the sort required to meet socially relative needs, it cannot be credibly said to be catering to idiosyncrasies of individual tastes at all. A desire for a status good is not an autonomous expression of the individual's own personality; rather, the good imparts social status (and is desirable, and desired for that reason) only by virtue of a social convention that all involved internalize.

32 Needs and welfare

References

Barry, Brian (1965) *Political Argument*. London: Routledge & Kegan Paul.

Braybrooke, David (1968) 'Let needs diminish that preferences may prosper', *American Philosophical Quarterly Monographs*, 1: 86–107.

Braybrooke, David (1987) *Meeting Needs*. Princeton, NJ: Princeton University Press.

Braybrooke, David and Lindblom, C.E. (1963) *A Strategy of Decision*. New York: Free Press.

Browning, E.K. (1975) 'The externality argument for in-kind transfers: Some critical remarks', *Kyklos*, 28: 526–44.

Campbell, Angus (1972) 'Aspiration, satisfaction and fulfilment', pp. 441–66. in A. Campbell and Philip E. Converse (eds), *The Human Meaning of Social Change*. New York: Russell Sage Foundation.

Daniels, Norman (1985) *Just Health Care*. Cambridge: Cambridge University Press.

Dasgupta, Partha and Ray, Debraj (1986/1987) 'Inequality as a determinant of malnutrition and unemployment', *Economic Journal*, 96: 1011–34; 97: 177–88.

Douglas, Mary and Isherwood, Brian (1978) *The World of Goods*. Harmondsworth: Penguin.

Doyal, Len and Gough, Ian (1984) 'A theory of human needs', *Critical Social Policy*, 4(1): 6–38.

Duncan, Otis Dudley (1975) 'Does money buy satisfaction?', *Social Indicators Research*, 2: 267–74.

Ellis, Adrian and Heath, Anthony (1983) 'Positional competition, or an offer you can't refuse?', pp. 1–22 in A. Ellis and Krishan Kumar (eds), *Dilemmas of Liberal Democracies*. London: Tavistock.

Elster, Jon (1976) 'Boudon, education and the theory of games', *Social Science Information*, 15: 733–40.

Frankfurt, Harry G. (1984) 'Necessity and desire', *Philosophy and Phenomenological Research*, 14: 1–13.

Galanter, Marc (1974) 'Why the "haves" come out ahead: Speculations on the limits of legal change', *Law & Society Review*, 9: 95–160.

Goodin, Robert E. (1982) *Political Theory and Public Policy*. Chicago: University of Chicago Press.

Goodin, Robert E. (1988) *Reasons for Welfare*. Princeton, NJ: Princeton University Press.

Hirsch, Fred (1976) *Social Limits to Growth*. London: Routledge & Kegan Paul.

Hyman, H.H. (1942) 'The psychology of status', *Archives of Psychology*, no. 259.

Jackson, Kenneth (1985) *The Crabgrass Frontier*. New York: Oxford University Press.

Marx, Karl and Engels, Friedrich (1958) *Selected Works*. Moscow: Foreign Languages Publishing House.

Piachaud, David (1981) 'Peter Townsend and the Holy Grail', *New Society*, 54(982): 419–21.

Rousseau, Jean-Jacques (1762) *Emile*, trans. Barbara Foxley. London: Dent, 1911.

Runciman, W.G. (1966) *Relative Deprivation and Social Justice*. London: Routledge & Kegan Paul.

Schoeck, Helmut (1969) *Envy*, trans. Der Neid. New York: Harcourt, Brace & World.

Sen, Amartya (1977) 'Starvation and exchange entitlements: A general approach and its application to the Great Bengal Famine', *Cambridge Journal of Economics*, 1: 33–59.

Sen, Amartya (1981) *Poverty and Famines*. Oxford: Clarendon Press.

Sen, Amartya (1983) 'Poor, relatively speaking', *Oxford Economic Papers*, 35: 153–69.

Sen, Amartya (1985a) *Commodities and Capabilities*. Amsterdam: North-Holland.

Sen, Amartya (1985b) 'Well-being, agency and freedom', *Journal of Philosophy*, 82: 169–221.

Shubik, Martin (1971) 'Games of status', *Behavioral Science*, 16: 117–29.

Steuart, James (1767) *An Inquiry into the Principles of Political Economy*, ed. A.S. Skinner. Edinburgh: Oliver and Boyd, 1966.

Streeten, Paul et al. (1981) *First Things First: Meeting Basic Human Needs in the Developing Countries*. New York: Oxford University Press for the World Bank.

Tobin, James (1970) 'On limiting the domain of inequality', *Journal of Law & Economics*, 13: 363–78.

Townsend, Peter (1954) 'Measuring poverty', *British Journal of Sociology*, 5: 130–37.

Townsend, Peter (1962) 'The meaning of poverty', *British Journal of Sociology*, 13: 210–27.

Townsend, Peter (1979) *Poverty in the United Kingdom*. Harmondsworth: Penguin.

Weitzman, M.L. (1977) 'Is the price system or rationing more effective in getting a commodity to those who need it most?', *Bell (now Rand) Journal of Economics*, 8: 517–24.

Wiggins, David (1985) 'Claims of need', pp. 142–202 in Ted Honderich (ed.), *Morality and Objectivity*. London: Routledge & Kegan Paul.

3

Universal Principles and Particular Claims: From Welfare Rights to Welfare States

Peter Jones

Of all the attempts to defend the welfare state by appealing to welfare rights, perhaps the most ambitious is the attempt to claim welfare rights as human rights. That claim is incorporated in the United Nations Declaration of Human Rights, the latter half of which asserts a number of rights, commonly described as socio-economic, whose content coincides substantially with what are typically thought of as welfare rights.[1] Perhaps more imposing than documents such as this, which merely 'declare' what rights people have, are the writings of a growing number of philosophers who *argue* the case for recognizing welfare rights as human rights.

Some of these argue that welfare goods minister to the most basic of human needs, that if human beings have a right to anything they have the right that those most basic needs should be met, and that consequently merely being human is enough to make one the possessor of welfare rights (cf. Bay, 1968; Scheffler, 1976; Peffer, 1978; Mallman, 1980; Vlastos, 1984; Sadurski, 1986; Baker, 1987: 14–22). Others have attempted to ground welfare rights in the very concept of morality itself by arguing that the goods secured to people by welfare measures are themselves pre-requisites for authentically moral conduct; to recognize human beings as moral agents is therefore implicitly to acknowledge their possession of welfare rights (Gewirth, 1978, 1982, 1984; Plant et al., 1980: 37–96; Plant, 1988; cf. Doyal and Gough, 1984).

Not only do these philosophers defend the idea of human welfare rights. Typically they also offer rights-*based* defences of welfare states.That is, in justifying welfare states, they take rights, rather than duties or goals, as their fundamental moral category; and, in so far as welfare states are conceived as requiring the performance of duties and the pursuit of goals, those duties and goals are grounded in these logically more basic rights.[2]

My concern in this chapter is to examine whether this way of conceiving welfare rights can be squared with welfare states as we know them. The arguments I have cited defend welfare rights in universalist terms and in terms which, prima facie at least, would lead one to suppose that all human beings possess welfare rights, that they all possess the *same* welfare rights, and that there is therefore something wrong, or something very much in need of moral explanation, if the world is one in which people do not, as a matter of fact, enjoy the same welfare rights.

Yet the arguments I have cited are also deployed in defence of welfare *states*. Indeed, most commonly, it is simply taken for granted that each person's welfare rights are held only in relation to the state of which he or she is a member. But, since different states have different levels of resources at their disposal, this presumption results in the citizens of different states being endowed with very different welfare rights. How can that be? How can people with identical entitlements deriving from identical moral foundations end up with such varying claims upon the world's resources? I begin by clearing away four preliminary considerations.

A first response might be that these universalist justifications are intended to justify only so much of current welfare provision as could reasonably be made available by all states. Anything beyond that lowest common denominator should be conceived as exceeding what people are owed as a matter of right or, at least, as exceeding what they are owed as a matter of *universal* right. This response clearly will not do – at least not for those who employ the universalist arguments I have cited. Most of those theorists seek to defend welfare states as they have developed in the west and, in some cases, to argue that they imply a right to more and better welfare goods and services than those that are currently provided by these developed states.

A second possible response is of a more practical kind. An international redistribution of resources to meet people's welfare rights might be rejected because it would do more harm than good. It might, for example, simply drive up domestic prices or undermine the productive base of the recipient society. This is a matter on which I am not qualified to judge, although I find it inconceivable that every sort of international transfer, no matter how carefully and sensitively handled, must be harmful to the recipients. But, even if I am incorrect, it would still be important to settle whether rich populations have no obligations in respect of the welfare rights of poor populations, or whether, in principle, they do have such obligations but, in practice, they ought not to discharge them because any such attempt would only make things worse.

Thirdly, objections to socioeconomic human rights are some-times countered by showing that some traditional civil and political rights run into identical difficulties. If life gets difficult for socioeconomic rights because of scarce or unequal resources, so does it for more traditional rights such as the right to a fair trial or the right to personal security which also make a call upon resources (Plant, 1988; Sadurski, 1986; Donnelly, 1985: 90–96; Shue, 1980). I do not wish to deny that the latter sort of rights are usually asserted by those who reject socioeconomic rights, or that those rights make demands on resources. But all that shows is that the problems associated with socioeconomic rights are not unique to those rights; it contributes nothing to their solution.

Fourthly, variations from one society to another in the sorts of welfare goods and services that each makes available to its members are, in some measure, capable of quite innocent explanation. Human beings living under different climatic conditions require different forms of shelter and housing. Different diseases prevail in different parts of the world and make different medical priorities and precautions appropriate. Those who take a universalist approach to welfare matters have no problems with this. The same principles can require different measures in different circumstances.[3] Nor need we confine acceptable variations to those having their origin in different natural conditions. Cultural variations might also have to be accommodated. None of this need embarrass the universalist but, equally, none of this takes us very far in accounting for variations in welfare provision in the current world. Most of that variation is not simply a matter of some receiving something different from others, but rather of some receiving more and better than others.

A division of moral labour

Universal welfare rights, we may suppose, must ultimately imply universal welfare responsibilities. But it is simply not practicable to suggest that all of those individuals who should be net contributors should, as individuals, make transfers to all of those individuals who should be net recipients – let alone that they should, as individuals, make provision for specific welfare goods and services. There clearly has to be some means of coordinating and collectivizing individuals' efforts. The most obvious mechanism this suggests is a network of international institutions that can act as intermediaries between individuals and the performance of their duties to one another (cf. Shue, 1988). But we might, as an alternative, follow the suggestion of Robert Goodin (1988b) and conceive the existing world of states as a sort of division of moral labour for the same purpose. Universal rights give rise to universal (or 'general') duties. But those general duties might be more conveniently and effectively performed if humanity were divided up into groups with each group being assigned responsibility for honouring the rights of its own members. Thus, the world of states might be conceived as one in which the general duties of mankind have been transformed into a number of special duties so that they could be discharged more effectively. While at the level of ultimate principle the duties that we owe to our compatriots are neither more nor less than those that we owe to foreigners, at a subordinate level there is reason to accept that individuals owe special duties to their fellow-citizens.

Does this then provide us with a satisfactory explanation of how universal rights of welfare can be transformed into a set of particular claims against particular states? It might. But the content of those particular claims would then be very different from those that characterize the contemporary world. As Goodin himself observes (1988b: 685), if the special responsibilities of states for their citizens are conceived as no more than administratively convenient devices for discharging general duties, it matters that those administrative arrangements really do discharge the relevant general duties as adequately as possible. If resources are distributed so unequally among societies that some states are unable to discharge the responsibilities they have been assigned, then a reallocation of resources among states is called for to put that right. Thus, while this 'assigned responsibility model' may be plausible in itself, it does little or nothing to reconcile the universality of welfare rights with welfare states as they currently exist.[4]

Four interpretations of communities and citizens

Before examining other ways in which the uniform rights of humans might be squared with the diverse rights of citizens, I want to distinguish four different ways of understanding people's membership of political communities. These differences are often overlooked but I think their distinction helps to clarify just what it is that we are being asked to accept about citizenship. I link citizenship to community not because the two concepts are necessarily closely related – they need not be – but because they seem to be closely associated in the minds of those who write about citizenship.

The first way of understanding citizenship takes an ideal of community as its ultimate inspiration. It is that which provides the thrust for what citizenship should be and what it should entail.

Rights to welfare may be seen as instrumental to the attainment of that ideal or, more likely, they may be seen as essential constituents of it.

This position is in some measure 'universalist', in that it holds up a single common ideal for all humanity although, of course, humanity has to divide into separate groups in order to attain it. But, since each community should be able to develop its own particular identity and form of life, that universalism may turn out to be pretty minimal. In Dworkin's classification (1977: 171–2), it clearly belongs to the family of goal-based rather than rights-based theories even though many of those who have espoused it – most notably T.H. Marshall (1950, 1981) – have wanted to make recognition of rights an essential part of it. In fact, the more closely a community approaches the ideal of mutual care and concern, the more the assertive language of rights may become inappropriate and unnecessary (cf. Jones, 1980: 136–42).

Contrasted with this are theories which view citizens as united by common principles of right rather than by the pursuit of a shared conception of the good: theories which are pre-eminently deontological rather than teleological. In these theories citizenship is a more limited notion. In some sense citizens still form a single community, for they live in a bounded society and are subject to a common set of rules and institutions. But the status of citizenship is essentially one of enjoying certain basic and equal rights rather than one of sharing a 'common life' in any stronger sense.

Individuals are conceived as being free to shape their own lives as they choose within these shared rules of citizenship. Some or all of them may, of course, opt for more communitarian ideals and they are free to do so, but these must be their own individually chosen goals and their pursuit must continue to respect the limits imposed by principles of right. Nor, on this view, is citizenship seen as arising from any 'natural' tie between those who form a single political community. Rather citizens are citizens merely by virtue of their being bound together by common institutions and rules. Theories of this sort – of which those of Rawls (1971) and Dworkin (1977, 1985) are pre-eminent examples – are more obviously universalist than communitarian theories in that they strongly emphasize fundamental principles which must be recognized and respected in all societies and which therefore imply a single uniform conception of citizenship for all societies.

Implicit in both of the views that I have so far described is the belief that human beings should seek to shape the world according to certain ideas of the right or the good rather than merely accept the world as they find it. I want now to describe two views which are more guided by what there is rather than what there might be.

A third view, which I shall describe as 'radical particularism', takes as simply given that people are members of particular societies. That is just a fact of life. It is also a moral fact of life. The rights and obligations that the members of a society have in relation to one another they have only as members of a particular society at a particular time. Citizens as citizens are already enmeshed in particular sets of normative relations which must be taken as moral 'givens' and it is not open to us to abstract individuals from those given contexts and consider, in separation from them, how they ought to relate to one another. Thus this view makes no supposition that the principles or ideals which govern one society should also govern others, nor that there is a single set of rights which should be enjoyed by citizens of all states. On some understandings of Burke, this is the sort of position to which he is committed. Those who stress nationhood rather than mere statehood might also be led to this position.

Sharing some affinity with this position, but distinct from it, is a view I shall describe as 'moderate particularism'. This view shares with the previous one an acceptance that people just are members of particular societies and that, as a matter of moral fact, they have special ties to those societies. Like the third position, and unlike the second, it conceives a political community not as a body of individuals united only *by* a set of common rules, but as a united community *with* a set of common rules. To all intents and purposes citizens are 'naturally' bound to the communities to which they belong and it is therefore unacceptable to examine their rights and duties as though we were examining what constituted just relations between contingently related individuals.

However, unlike radical particularism, moderate particularism is willing to generalize about the status of citizenship. Just as each child is uniquely related to its parents but we may still talk in general terms about the moral relation of parent and child, so each citizen is uniquely related to his or her community but we may still talk in general terms about the rights and responsibilities of citizenship.[5]

Citizenship and universal rights

Which of these four conceptions of citizenship is compatible with a doctrine of universal rights of citizenship, including universal welfare rights? Clearly radical particularism is not. That particularism might argue for the maintenance of a welfare state, for example, by appealing to the established traditions and expectations of a community (cf. King and Waldron, 1988: 431–6). It might also advocate the creation or extension of a welfare state by arguing that change in that direction is 'intimated' by the society's current arrangements. But an assertion of universal welfare rights would be contrary to the very nature of radical particularism (cf. Walzer, 1983: xiv–xv, 6–10, 64–94). Communitarianism also looks unpromising. It might recommend a common strategy for the attainment of its ideal and recognition of rights might form a part of that strategy. But the assertion of universal fundamental rights is not the driving force behind the ideal and it is ill-suited to an insistence that all people everywhere possess uniform entitlements.[6]

What of the other two positions? Of these, the more obviously friendly to the assertion of universal rights is the second. However, strictly, there is no reason why moderate particularism should not also accommodate an idea of universal rights of citizenship – if by that we mean only that there are certain rights which every political community must accord to its members. Obviously this depends on how moderate this form of particularism remains but, in principle, the idea that each citizen is naturally rather than contingently tied to his or her political community can coexist with the ascription of a uniform set of rights to citizens, even though each citizen will hold those rights only in relation to his or her community.

Can we use either of these approaches to citizenship to reconcile the uniformity of human rights with the diversity of particular claims acknowledged in the contemporary world? Can either make room for the belief that, when human rights are translated into citizens' rights, the same entitlements give birth to claims which somehow become different in substance even though they remain identical in foundation? Again there are a number of possibilities to consider.

Shoring up civil and political rights
One explanation of why equal rights should constitute claims to unequal resources goes like this. There is a high degree of unanimity that, if people have rights as citizens at all, those rights include civil rights to fundamental freedoms such as freedom of expression and freedom of association and political rights such as the right to participate in some way in the political processes of one's society. But if those civil and political rights are to be of genuinely equal value, they must be underwritten by a guaranteed

minimum of material well-being for, without that, the rights of citizens may be formally equal but will be effectively unequal.[7]

Now, if that is why welfare rights matter, we can easily see why equal welfare rights will need to be unequally resourced in societies of unequal wealth. The level of material well-being, education, etc, that a person will need in order to operate on terms equal with others in civil and political matters will depend on the general standard of living of the society in question. For example, welfare goods and services will have to be more generously resourced in America than in Kenya if they are to be of equal instrumental value to Americans and Kenyans. Thus we have a reason why people's equal entitlements should lead to unequal provision.

As a justification for welfare rights, I find this unpersuasive – both because it claims too little and because it claims too much. It claims too little because, if we were really serious about ironing out the inequalities in political influence or 'effective' freedoms produced by material inequalities, we would have to go far beyond the measures normally associated with welfare states. It claims too much because I cannot believe that this is why welfare goods and services really matter to people, or why they should matter. If I live in slum housing, or am in chronic pain, or cannot provide an adequate diet for my children, or live constantly on the edge of hypothermia, probably the last thing on my mind is that these conditions impede my freedom to publish or my right to run for Parliament. Or, to put it less tendentiously, for most people welfare goods matter for the immediate impact they have on the quality of their lives and not because of their instrumental importance for their civil and political rights. Probably nobody but political philosophers would have thought otherwise.

That is not to say that civil and political rights do not matter. Nor is it to deny that political and civil rights may be important to people in attempting to improve their lot in life (but notice that that puts the order of importance the other way round). Nor, again, is it to claim that welfare rights are entirely without significance for civil and political rights. Some, such as education, are obviously important. It is simply to say that, for the most part, worries about civil and political rights are more convincing as subsidiary than as primary reasons for being concerned about welfare rights.

Socially relative human rights
However, the relativizing of rights to the specific circumstances of each society might be argued for in a broader and altogether more

persuasive way. It is often, and rightly, observed that the nature of individuals' needs cannot be divorced from the character of the society in which they live (Weale, 1983: 35–8, 76–9). People conduct their lives in significantly different social contexts and what they need in order to achieve a given level of well-being cannot be divorced from the particular context in which they live. Thus, 'minimum needs are not simply satisfied by providing the physical necessities of life, for example adequate food, clothing and shelter, but require also for their satisfaction a level of provision for persons that is suitable for social agents, interacting with others in a specific society' (Weale, 1983: 35).

Recognition that needs are 'socially relative' in this way is potentially of much greater significance than the prosaic point that we noted earlier: that the needs of individuals might differ according to the natural or cultural environment in which they find themselves. For, if needs are 'socially relative', there is much greater scope for allowing that some people simply need *more* than others – that the same needs can demand a different quantitative as well as a different qualitative response. Thus it might be argued that, if an individual is to function as a member of a society like the USA or West Germany, she needs a higher minimum income than she would require if she were a citizen of Kenya or the Philippines. Likewise people living in the developed west might be said to need an education that is not merely different from that required by members of the less developed world; they also need education that is more extensive and recognizably 'better'.

It is important to be clear about the sense in which these 'socially relative' needs are said to be 'relative'. It is sometimes suggested that need is a socially relative concept, in that each society simply defines 'need' for itself (e.g. Benn and Peters, 1959: 144–6). There are no common human needs and no absolute human needs. There are only different societies, each with their own ideas of what is an acceptable minimum standard of living. On the whole, the higher the average standard of living of a society, the higher it will pitch its notion of the acceptable minimum.

Now if this is what is meant by 'relative need', it clearly discredits any notion of universal need and therefore any notion of universal rights based on it. Need becomes a concept whose content is entirely relative to the society in which it occurs. But need can be 'relative' in a quite different sense. Americans might be said to need more than Kenyans not because they have a more extravagant conception of need but because the welfare recipient in America has to have more than the welfare recipient in Kenya if each is to function in the same way and at the same level in their respective societies.

So it is not that we are impelled to use different and contradictory conceptions of need for Americans and Kenyans. It is simply that minimum incomes (among other things) have to be set at different absolute levels if they are to achieve effectively equal levels of welfare in the two societies. Understood in this way, the notion of 'relative need' is compatible with the idea of human beings possessing fundamentally (if not immediately) identical needs and therefore with their possessing fundamentally identical welfare rights. It is simply that unequal amounts of resources have to be disbursed in order to secure equivalent levels of social well-being.

I do not intend to dispute that needs are often relative in this second sense; they clearly are. But is that *so* true that it can go all the way in accounting for the disparities in welfare provision in the contemporary world? I think not. In the first place, it seems a more compelling consideration for some welfare matters than for others. Social security measures certainly have to be adjusted to the society for which they provide. But it is not at all obvious why the 'relative' health care needs of people in poorer societies should be reckoned any less demanding, or more easily satisfied by a lower standard of medical treatment, than those of people in affluent societies. If health care is reckoned an important 'status good' (cf. Goodin, in this volume) then, of course, we re-enter the logic of relativity, but it would seem perverse to hold that the good of health care was wholly, or even primarily, of that sort. Secondly, if all of these differences were no more than adjustments to secure equal outcomes in different societies, we would have to conclude that welfare recipients in affluent societies were (absolutely) no better off than those in poor societies and that, given a choice, people would be wholly indifferent between the two. That too seems unsustainable.

Human rights and the duties of citizens
What I suspect is the most common (though often unarticulated) supposition about the relation between universal rights and the rights of citizens goes something like this. Yes, all human beings matter as human beings, all have certain basic needs and all have rights in virtue of having those needs. But the responsibility for meeting those needs is not similarly universal. Each political community has the duty to see that the human rights of its citizens are fulfilled, but its duties remain within its own borders – at least

as far as full welfare rights are concerned. It may be that in special emergencies such as famines or earthquakes a people's duties extend beyond its own borders and those in desperate need might properly claim a right to the help of foreign populations. But, in the ordinary course of life, each community is obliged to concern itself only with the universal rights of its own citizens.

Now, formulated in this way, this position could amount to no more than a reassertion of the idea that, for purely practical reasons, humanity must accept a division of moral labour. However, we have already seen that, while this 'assigned responsibility' model might have to tolerate some discrepancies in the treatment meted out to different communities, it can hardly sanction the vast differences in material circumstances that characterize the contemporary world. Nor do those who hold to the position I am describing here typically think of their special responsibilities to their fellow citizens as matters of mere administrative convenience. Nor, again, do they necessarily find anything untoward in the citizens of some communities having claims to goods and services which greatly exceed what is possible, let alone achieved, in other communities. So on what else might this common supposition be founded?

One possibility goes back to the sort of view of political societies found in the writings of John Rawls. Rawls regards political communities as 'schemes of co-operation' in which people combine their labours and arrange their lives for their mutual advantage. Now common principles of justice apply to all such schemes of cooperation. These principles require, among other things, that certain rights be established and respected in all communities – rights to basic liberties such as freedom of conscience and freedom of expression. (I will ignore the one major exception that Rawls allows.) To that extent therefore Rawls's universal principles yield universal rights. In addition, some have argued that welfare rights can be derived from Rawls's principles, particularly from his 'difference principle', even though that may involve some modification of his own arguments (King and Waldron, 1988: 439–42; Weale, 1978; 1983: 80–99; Michelman, 1975; Gutmann, 1980: 119–44).

But even if Rawls's theory can be interpreted in that way, those rights would turn out to be very different for different societies. For Rawls's principles are concerned only to ensure a just distribution of income and wealth *within* each scheme of social cooperation. Since some schemes will have more resources to dispose of than others, the goods and services that will be claimable as a matter of right in some societies will exceed, and quite properly exceed, those claimable as rights in others.

What appears to legitimate these differences are two related notions. First, the duties that are owed here are duties to fellow cooperators, not duties to human beings as such. Secondly, the wealth that is generated by the scheme of cooperation belongs to the cooperating community itself which is why that community provides the boundaries within which that wealth is to be justly distributed.

If this is the sequence of thought that leads to the acceptance of different welfare rights for different bodies of citizens, virtually nothing remains of the idea of universal welfare rights. For what has disappeared from view here is not merely any sense of duties beyond borders or of rights of equal substance, but also any notion of *universal* entitlements.

Certainly, on this view, welfare rights stem from principles of justice which are equally valid for all societies. But particular citizens' rights to welfare goods derive from their being participants in particular schemes of cooperation and not from their being human beings with characteristically human needs. Their welfare rights are grounded not in a title which they share with the rest of humanity but only in their claim, as citizens of a particular society, to receive their just share of the resources of that society.[8]

Can moderate particularism do better? Here the claim would be that individuals' basic needs as human beings should be attended to by the political community to which they belong. In contrast to the 'assigned responsibility' model, this is not regarded as a mere administrative convenience. Nor is it understood as the product of some quasi-contractual arrangement. Rather it signifies the belief that merely 'belonging' to a particular political community is something of fundamental moral significance in and of itself. This, I suspect, gets closer to the thinking of those who simply take for granted that, where human rights require more than mere forbearance, it (naturally) falls to states to provide for the human rights of their citizens.

This way of coupling together 'universal rights' with 'special duties' is not necessarily unsatisfactory – although there is reason to question whether we should describe the situation in that way. If the duties are 'special' because they are owed only to a particular community, are not the rights also 'special' because they are held only against a particular community? And if the rights are 'universal' because citizens of all societies have the same rights, are not the duties also 'universal' because citizens of all societies have the same duties? However, I take it that the justification for describing the rights as 'universal' but the duties as 'special' lies in the fact that the moral situation contemplated here is ultimately rights-*based*. That is, people come forward as human beings with rights but are then responded to by citizens with duties.

However, I remain uncomfortable with this way of disposing of the issue, and not merely because of an asymmetry between the relevant rights and duties. For the most part, the issue of socioeconomic human rights has been discussed in terms of rights and duties, as though what was principally at stake was how universal rights could be matched to the duties of particular societies. But should welfare rights be seen principally as rights *against others*, as though their primary point were to demand the performance of duties by others? Are they not, in larger measure, rights *to* or *over resources*? It is true, of course, that some welfare goods take the form of services, as in the cases of health care and education. But, fundamentally, moral welfare rights are not rights against doctors to be given medical treatment or rights against teachers to receive education. They are rights held in relation to a society (more or less broadly defined) which require that society apportion resources so that everyone has access to a basic minimum of goods such as health care and education.

The guiding motto is 'bread for all before jam for some'. Granted that, the crucial question becomes not so much, 'who has the duties that correspond to the rights?' but rather, 'in relation to what set of resources are the rights held?' Now, moderate particularism typically includes a view not only of who is morally tied to whom but also of what resources belong to which community. It embodies a view of what might be called national or community property rights.

Even the UN Declaration speaks of the right to social security being held 'in accordance with the organization and resources of each State' (article 22). The conjunction of universal rights and particular claims offered by moderate particularism is therefore not so much a matter of who has the duty to respond to whose welfare rights as one of which pool of resources should be drawn upon to meet each claimant's welfare rights. Each citizen's welfare rights are a claim only on his own society's resources and that claim can be met only to the extent that his own society's resources permit.

Once again, therefore, we end up with allegedly universal welfare rights that are radically unequal in content. Indeed, this interpretation of welfare rights is, ultimately, not very different from the Rawlsian view. All that remains 'universal' here is a notion that certain distributive principles are equally valid for all societies; but the specific rights that those principles yield will be closely dependent on the total sum of resources at each society's disposal. Everyone may end up having rights to *some* food, housing, medicine and education. But that is hardly remarkable. The crucial question in relation to welfare rights is 'how much?' To be told that one has a right to some housing or some education is about as enlightening as being told that one has a right to some freedom of expression.

Moreover, consider how we would feel if we were told that there was a universal right of free expression because all human beings were free to say something, even though (as a matter of what was morally right and not merely as a matter of fact) some were entitled to say things that others were not. To say that one person is entitled to say what another is not is to deny that they possess the same rights of free expression, and it is hard to see why a different logic should apply to welfare rights.

It has been suggested that socioeconomic rights which are beyond the means of pre-affluent societies might still be ascribed to the members of those societies but as 'conditional' rights (Meyers, 1981). All human beings can then be said to possess an identical set of socioeconomic rights, subject only to the condition that the economic circumstances of their respective societies permit those rights to be fulfilled.

But is that to say any more than that people possess the same rights under the same conditions and different rights under different conditions – and that, since the relevant conditions are currently different, all humans do not possess the same rights? Notice, too, that the relevant conditions here are not wholly empirical. They implicitly refer to who owns what. The assumption is that, although rich societies might have a surplus large enough to make good the shortfall in poor societies, there is no obligation on one to transfer resources to the other. In other words, national property rights 'trump' socioeconomic human rights. That too may lead one to doubt whether these allegedly universal human rights really warrant that description.[9]

Democracy and collective self-determination

The identification of political boundaries with the boundaries of communal property rights, then, has radical implications for the idea of human welfare rights. Indeed, one of the most striking features of the sort of welfare state theory that we have just been examining is the way in which it combines a demand for redistribution within communities with a hostility to any similar redistribution between communities. It is as though the political

philosophy of Robert Nozick (1974) were found perfectly unacceptable when applied to individuals, but perfectly acceptable
when applied to states. I have already explained how Rawlsian
and particularist thinking produce these conclusions. However, a
further transposition of Nozickian ideas from individuals to
collective entities might also help to explain this combination of
commitments.

Assertions of human rights usually exist alongside, or indeed
incorporate, assertions of the rights associated with democratic
government and collective self-determination. That in turn raises
questions about how far those outside the democratic or self-
determining unit should be held responsible for matters that are
determined within it and which are therefore beyond the control
of outsiders. Should nation A be held responsible for dealing with
the consequences of decisions taken by nation B? In the case of
individuals, we would ordinarily hold that, if they want the
freedom to make decisions on their own behalf, they must also
accept responsibility for coping with the consequences of those
decisions. It would seem intolerable and inequitable if individual
A had persistently to save individual B from the consequences of
his or her own actions, if at the same time A could exercise no
control over how B acted. That would be to make one person the
slave of another's freedom (Jones, 1985). In the same way it
might be said that, if political communities wish to be autonomous, they must bear the full responsibilities that go with that
autonomy.

Welfare goods and services do not simply spring out of the
ground. They have to be produced and provided. If a people
claims the sole right of control over the sorts of policy matters
relevant to the provision of welfare goods and services, then it
cannot expect others to make good the failings of those policies.
Responsibility without power is no more acceptable than power
without responsibility. Consequently, if we accept the usual
canons of democracy and self-determination, we must accept that
the welfare rights to which human beings can lay claim cannot but
be constrained by the political circumstances in which they exist
as citizens.

Again, I think this must count for something. When human
rights come up against collective rights of self-determination, one
or the other must be compromised. Most usually, devotees of
human rights would argue that it is collective self-determination
that should give way. Part of the practical point of asserting
human rights is to set limits to what governments can do to
subjects, or what majorities can do to minorities. However, where

satisfaction of those rights requires the production and provision of positive goods and services, it would be quite unrealistic to suppose that what a society should do could be determined merely by reference to general principles (cf. Plant, 1985b: 20). Inevitably, the relevant decisions will have to be made in a context of competing claims on resources, conflicting values, imperfect information and judgements about the likely consequences of various policy options. That, then, is one reason why what a person can properly claim, by way of welfare rights, cannot be wholly divorced from the contingencies of the state of which he or she is a citizen.

However, there are a number of qualifying points to be made to this argument. First, some limit must be set to the discretion afforded to political processes if the idea of a human right to welfare is to retain any meaning. Secondly, we do not always adhere to the harsh logic of requiring people to suffer the full consequences of their actions. Smokers and gluttons still receive hospital treatment. There is even more reason to relax this logic in the case of societies, for the idea that a government's every decision embodies the will of its every citizen is plainly a fiction. Ignoring a population's plight might therefore mean ignoring victims rather than culprits. Thirdly, and most importantly, how much of the disparity between societies' resources can be traced to different uses of their collective rights of self-determination? I cannot answer that precisely (and perhaps nobody can) but, whatever the answer, it would still seem bound to leave a very large portion of the inequalities between societies unexplained.

Conclusion

What then are we to conclude? There are clearly some sound reasons for accepting that, if we ground welfare rights in people's rights as human beings, we can still accept some differences in the welfare rights possessed by the members of different societies.

Some of this may be explained simply by the different natural and cultural contexts in which people find themselves. Rather more may be explained by differences in what people need if they are to function in equivalent ways as members of the societies in which they live. Some variation too may have to be accepted as the price of acknowledging collective rights of self-determination. But after all of this has been taken into account, there still remains a gap between the inequalities that basic human needs and human rights would seem to allow and the inequalities between states in the welfare goods and services that they can, and do, make available to their members.

Thus we are faced with a simple choice. Either we take human rights to welfare goods seriously, in which case we must accept an international redistribution of resources on the scale that that implies. Or, if we set our face against such international redistribution because we believe that political boundaries do have moral significance, we should give up any pretence of believing in human rights to welfare. If we opt for the latter, we can still cling both to the idea of welfare rights and to the idea of moral welfare rights but, whatever it is that grounds those welfare rights, it cannot be mere humanity.

Notes

1. Some believe that the inclusion of socioeconomic rights in the UN Declaration was a mistake arising from a muddle (Cranston, 1967; Melden, 1977; 179–80). Others, however, argue that there is nothing logically improper about their inclusion in the Declaration (Raphael, 1967; Watson, 1977; Donnelly, 1985: 90–96).

2. On the idea of a rights-based morality, see Dworkin (1977: 171–2) and Mackie (1984).

3. It is arguable that some of the welfare rights included in the UN Declaration are not unadulterated human rights but are, at best, human rights already adapted to a specific set of circumstances – those of western industrialized societies (Milne, 1986: 2–3).

4. The same would seem to be true of Alan Gewirth's attempt (1988) to derive a justification of ethical particularism from universalist premises, even though he takes a route different from Goodin's.

5. In reality, those who subscribe to these two sorts of particularism are unlikely to divide into two sharply separate camps. The general and the particular may be mixed in different proportions. Thus Walzer, although he describes his own position as 'radically particularist' (1983: xiv), is still willing to generalize in some measure about the proper constitution of political communities, though to an extent that falls well short of what I have described as moderate particularism. The ethical significance that Miller (1988) is willing to give to nationality also seems to occupy a position somewhere in between radical and moderate particularism.

6. For an excellent statement of this communitarian approach to social policy, see Harris (1987) who draws on the ideas of 'citizenship theorists' such as Marshall, Robson and Titmuss but who develops these into a far more rigorous and coherent theory. Harris gives an important place to citizenship rights but, significantly, bases these not upon human rights but upon an 'irreducible' ideal of community and community membership. For a sceptical appraisal of communitarian justifications of the welfare state, see Goodin (1988a: 70–118).

7. For examples of arguments that link welfare rights to civil and political rights – though not always as simply as I have suggested here – see King and Waldron (1988: 425–31), Daniels (1975), Gutmann (1980: 122–9, 190–202), Plant (1985a).

8. However, some writers have attempted to rework Rawls's ideas to produce a theory of international, rather than intra-national, distributive justice; see Beitz (1979) and Richards (1982). For criticisms of these reinterpretations, see Barry (1982: 232–4), and Miller (1980: 144–6).

9. In a similar vein, Sadurski (1986: 63–4) has suggested dealing with this issue by distinguishing between having a right and having the capacity to use that right. I may have the right to publish a newspaper even though I lack the financial means to make use of that right. Similarly, people in poor societies might be said to possess welfare rights but simply to lack the means necessary for making use of those rights. That also seems fraudulent. I may intelligibly be said to have the right to go to press (in that others are duty-bound not to prevent my going to press) even though I will never be in a position financially to launch a newspaper. But, if I cannot claim a right to receive medical treatment because it is not possible to make that treatment available to me, surely I do not merely lack the capacity to exercise that right; I cannot be said to have a (claim) right to that medical treatment. Welfare rights *are* fundamentally rights to resources and consequently there is not the same scope for distinguishing between possessing those rights and possessing the means to make them effective as there is in the case of 'action' rights.

References

Baker, John (1987) *Arguing for Equality*. London: Verso.

Barry, Brian (1982) 'Humanity and justice in global perspective', pp. 219–52 in J. Roland Pennock and John W. Chapman (eds), *Ethics, Economics and the Law (Nomos XXIV)*. New York: New York University Press.

Bay, Christian (1968) 'Needs, wants and political legitimacy', *Canadian Journal of Political Science* 1(3): 241–60.

Beitz, Charles (1979) *Political Theory and International Relations*. Princeton, NJ: Princeton University Press.

Benn, S.I. and Peters, R.S. (1959) *Social Principles and the Democratic State*. London: George Allen & Unwin.

Cranston, Maurice (1967) 'Human rights, real and supposed', and 'Human rights: a reply to Professor Raphael', pp. 43–53, 95–100 in D.D. Raphael (ed.), *Political Theory and the Rights of Man*. London: Macmillan.

Daniels, Norman (1975) 'Equal liberty and unequal worth of liberty', pp. 253–81 in Norman Daniels (ed.), *Reading Rawls*. Oxford: Basil Blackwell.

Donnelly, Jack (1985) *The Concept of Human Rights*. London: Croom Helm.

Doyal, L. and Gough, I. (1984) 'A theory of human needs', *Critical Social Policy* 4(1): 6–38.

Dworkin, Ronald (1977) *Taking Rights Seriously*. London: Duckworth.

Dworkin, Ronald (1985) *A Matter of Principle*. Oxford: Oxford University Press.

Gewirth, Alan (1978) *Reason and Morality*. Chicago: University of Chicago Press.

Gewirth, Alan (1982) *Human Rights: Essays on Justifications and Applications*. Chicago: University of Chicago Press.

Gewirth, Alan (1984) 'The epistemology of human rights', *Social Philosophy and Policy*, 1(2): 1–24.

Gewirth, Alan (1988) 'Ethical universalism and particularism', *Journal of Philosophy*, 85(6): 283–302.

Goodin, Robert E. (1988a) *Reasons for Welfare: The Political Theory of the Welfare State*. Princeton, NJ: Princeton University Press.

Goodin, Robert E. (1988b) 'What is so special about our fellow countrymen?', *Ethics*, 98(4): 663–86.

Gutmann, Amy (1980) *Liberal Equality*. Cambridge: Cambridge University Press.

Harris, David (1987) *Justifying State Welfare: The New Right versus the Old Left*. Oxford: Basil Blackwell.

Jones, Peter (1980) 'Rights, welfare and stigma', pp. 123–44 in Noel Timms (ed.), *Social Welfare: Why and How?* London: Routledge & Kegan Paul.

Jones, Peter (1985) 'Toleration, harm and moral effect', pp. 136–57 in John Horton and Susan Mendus (eds), *Aspects of Toleration*. London: Methuen.

King, Desmond and Waldron, Jeremy (1988) 'Citizenship, social citizenship and the defence of welfare provision', *British Journal of Political Science*, 18(4): 415–43.

Mackie, J.L. (1984) 'Can there be a rights-based moral theory?', pp. 168–81 in Jeremy Waldron (ed.), *Theories of Rights*. Oxford: Oxford University Press.

Mallman, Carlos A. (1980) 'Society, needs and rights: a systemic approach', pp. 37–54 in K. Lederer (ed.), *Human Needs*. Cambridge, Mass.: Oelgeschlager, Gunn and Hain.

Marshall, T.H. (1950) *Citizenship and Social Class*. Cambridge: Cambridge University Press.

Marshall, T.H. (1981) *The Right of Welfare and Other Essays*. London: Heinemann.

Melden, A.I. (1977) *Rights and Persons*. Oxford: Basil Blackwell.

Meyers, Diana T. (1981) 'Human rights in pre-affluent societies', *Philosophical Quarterly* 31(123): 139–44.

Michelman, Frank (1975) 'Constitutional welfare rights and *A Theory of Justice*', pp. 319–47 in Norman Daniels (ed.), *Reading Rawls*. Oxford: Basil Blackwell.

Miller, David (1980) 'Social justice and the principle of need', pp. 173–99 in Michael Freeman and David Robertson (eds), *The Frontiers of Political Theory*. Brighton: Harvester.

Miller, David (1988) 'The ethical significance of nationality', *Ethics*, 98(4): 647–62.

Milne, A.J.M. (1986) *Human Rights and Human Diversity*. Basingstoke: Macmillan.

Nozick, Robert (1974) *Anarchy, State and Utopia*. Oxford: Basil Blackwell.

Peffer, Rodney (1978) 'A defense of rights to well-being', *Philosophy and Public Affairs*, 2(3): 65–87.

Plant, Raymond (1985a) 'Welfare and the value of liberty', *Government and Opposition*, 20(3): 297–314.

Plant, Raymond (1985b) 'The very idea of a welfare state', pp. 3–30 in Philip Bean, John Ferris and David Whynes (eds), *In Defence of Welfare*. London: Tavistock.

Plant, Raymond (1988) 'Needs, agency, and welfare rights', pp. 55–74 in J. Donald Moon (ed.), *Responsibility, Rights and Welfare*. Boulder: Westview.

Plant, Raymond, Lesser, Harry and Taylor-Gooby, Peter (1980) *Political Philosophy and Social Welfare*. London: Routledge & Kegan Paul.

Raphael, D.D. (1967) 'Human rights, old and new', and 'The rights of man and the rights of the citizen', pp. 54–67, 101–18 in D.D. Raphael (ed.), *Political Theory and the Rights of Man*. London: Macmillan.

Rawls, John (1971) *A Theory of Justice*. Oxford: Oxford University Press.

Richards, David A.J. (1982) 'International distributive justice', pp. 275–99 in J. Roland Pennock and John W. Chapman (eds), *Ethics, Economics and the Law (Nomos XXIV)*. New York: New York University Press.

Sadurski, Wojciech (1986) 'Economic rights and basic needs', pp. 49–66 in Charles

Sampford and D.J. Galligan (eds), *Law, Rights and the Welfare State*. London: Croom Helm.

Shue, Henry (1980) *Basic Rights: Subsistence, Affluence, and US Foreign Policy*. Princeton, NJ: Princeton University Press.

Shue, Henry (1988) 'Mediating duties', *Ethics*, 98(4): 687–704.

Vlastos, Gregory (1984) 'Justice and Equality', pp. 41–76 in Jeremy Waldron (ed.), *Theories of Rights*. Oxford: Oxford University Press.

Walzer, Michael (1983) *Spheres of Justice*. Oxford: Martin Robertson.

Watson, David (1977) 'Welfare rights and human rights', *Journal of Social Policy*, 6(1): 31–46.

Weale, Albert (1978) *Equality and Social Policy*. London: Routledge & Kegan Paul.

Weale, Albert (1983) *Political Theory and Social Policy*. London: Macmillan.

4

Rights, Needs and Community: The Emergence of British Welfare Thought

Michael Freeden

Differences of definition and of ideology divide proponents of negative (forbearance) rights and positive (welfare) rights. The former category, I would submit, is not a fertile one for the promoters of welfare principles. Even the latter category has developed in an unanticipated way, under the influence of philosophical models and perspectives that played no part in the origins of welfare state theory. Indeed, some of those approaches may have impoverished our comprehension of welfare principles and diminished our expectations of the welfare state.

The early development of the British welfare state was accompanied by innovative theoretical assumptions, some of which are now partially lost or abandoned, and whose retrieval can significantly deepen our understanding of the core of welfare state thinking. In particular, three areas stand out for attention: the wide range of arguments employed to ground welfare rights; a sophisticated and augmented version of needs-based rights; and a shift away from the older individualistic understanding of a right towards a communitarian interpretation of its origins and functions.

It has become a commonplace among supporters as well as critics of the welfare state to observe that its ideology is anchored to a needs-based notion of rights (Plant et al., 1980: ch. 2). The early development of that rights–needs relationship was however much more complex; moreover, competing or parallel notions of rights combined with it to constitute packages of welfare rights arguments. Progressive social and political thought in turn-of-the-century Britain, both of the liberal and the moderate socialist varieties, experimented ideologically with a plethora of welfare rights principles. Thus, the view that state assistance and regulation were in part merited responses to individual contributions to the community was extended to form a wider view of membership, though one that fell short of the socialist versions of automatic and full citizenship that human affiliation to groups bestowed. Membership may refer generally to a recognition of belonging to a group that entails some forms of equal treatment. The concept of citizenship that emanated from late nineteenth-century social thought referred to a more active, egalitarian notion expressed in participation, in status, as well as in wide sharing of available social goods. Concurrently, changing conceptions of human nature and of social structure had a major impact on welfare thinking. Those processes were not smooth ones, nor were they completed during the period examined here, from the 1890s to the 1920s. In close connection with political events, however, an important theoretical reformulation of rights and welfare – based increasingly on individual and social needs while retaining generalized ideas about individual contributions – was made available for ideologists, social philosophers and politicians to draw on.

Towards a redefinition of rights

At the end of the nineteenth century, the concept of rights was associated with three main approaches. Benthamite utilitarians, in pursuit of the greatest happiness of individuals, denied the existence of any but civil rights. Conservatives played variations on the Burkean theme of concrete, particular, historical rights. Finally, the natural rights heritage, while still retaining a residual liberal pedigree, was increasingly employed by a rising middle class defending newly won privileges. Progressive social reformers who wished to use the language of rights were hence in a quandary: the political connotations of rights language were far too restrictive for their purposes. Their response was twofold: many skirted around the concept of rights, preferring to talk about obligations, duties and responsibilities, while implying – unintentionally or unconsciously – that those terms nevertheless entailed rights. Others re-examined the natural rights doctrine itself. For despite its obvious shortcomings, it still provided the only starting point for those who wanted to promote the ethical and essentialist case for the egalitarian and universal protection of fundamental human attributes. It is hence understandable to find theorists reassessing natural rights discourse, if only as a new vehicle through which to convey their concerns about the intolerable human costs of the Industrial Revolution.

An important bridge between the old world and the new was forged by a book, much quoted at the time by liberals and socialists alike: *Natural Rights*, by the progressive Idealist D.G. Ritchie. It performed the essential function of suggesting a new agenda to social reformers. Ritchie rejected the old canon of natural rights because of a particular meaning it attached to 'nature'. It postulated an individual separated from society, abstract, ahistorical and unchanging. In effect, this generalized specific ends convenient to the existing members of a particular society. As a result, the idea of natural rights underwent a deradicalization that divested it of its original intentions, supporting instead 'what is now the established economic and social order' (Ritchie, 1894: 19). The principled thinking behind natural rights theory, however, was vital on two counts: first, the notion of fundamental ethical norms, protecting what was of value in humanity, was a necessary basis for a properly conducted society; secondly, a more subtle and broader redefinition of human nature could salvage the intent of natural rights doctrine while jettisoning its individualistic and extra-social connotations. This Ritchie accomplished through an original mixture of ethical and utilitarian argument, which from that time on was to constitute the heart of most modern welfare thought. His mixture is also of interest in the context of contemporary debates because it did not follow the prevalent path of counterposing rights-based theory to utilitarianism, a path that proffers an individualistic caricature of the latter as an Aunt Sally to be knocked down (see for example Frey, 1985).

On the one hand, Ritchie (1894: 87) argued:

> if there are certain mutual claims which cannot be ignored without detriment to the well-being and, in the last resort, to the very being of a community, these claims may in an intelligible sense be called fundamental or natural rights. They represent a minimum of security and advantage which a community must guarantee to its members at the risk of going to pieces, if it does not with some degree of efficiency maintain them.

This passage identifies the welfare of a community as the test of a successfully claimed right, yet that welfare was concurrently related to the benefit of its members. That inseparability – the individual *in and of* community, but an individual that was not subsumed in community – must be seen as a keynote theme of future welfare discourse.

On the other hand, Ritchie helped to extend notions of human nature in two directions. He urged that 'if we say that in the end of the state should be included the development of a people's natural gifts, the very word "development" would suggest growth and progress'. He therefore singled out as a fundamental defect of Benthamite utilitarianism 'the assumption of the identity of human nature in spite of differences of time and place and stage of growth' (Ritchie, 1894: 98). Evolution supplied Ritchie with an empirical developmental model of human nature superimposed upon its intellectual forebears – namely, the more abstract and wishful developmentalism of Idealist theory or of the enlightenment conception of man. The second direction was to expand and conflate happiness and health in a wide sense, opening up a more multi-faceted view of human nature than previous rights-theorists had allowed for. Ritchie's new utilitarian creed relied heavily on health metaphors, strengthening a significant trend in the welfare debate, and linking it emphatically with the concept of need: 'Happy citizens – and that in the long run means healthy citizens, healthy in mind, body and estate – will prove the most useful citizens' (Ritchie, 1894: 99).

The importance of Ritchie's redrafting of the rights agenda can be appreciated only against prevalent modes of thinking. Many social reformers, including progressive ideologists, still found it difficult to detach the concept of rights either from individualist claims or from demands for political status; nor could they readily associate what we would now call 'welfare rights' with the growing awareness of human needs. Locating socially important needs at the basis of fundamental rights was thus an arduous process ranging across paternalist, commercial, contractarian and social-benefit justifications. Only two concrete areas of social reform – old-age pensions and unemployment – utilized the language of rights, though even there rights were frequently justified on grounds unrelated to needs.

Old-age pensions: Rights and the social interest

Old-age pensions were arguably the least controversial field of reform, some scheme or other having been advocated from all major positions on the political spectrum. The 1908 Act was accompanied by a public debate replete with the language of obligation and duty towards the elderly, thus emphasizing their legitimate claims. The argument most frequently heard was voiced by the Labour MP Will Crooks (*Hansard*, 4th series, vol. 192, 193ff [9.7.1908]): 'They are the veterans of industry, people of almost endless toil, who have fought for and won the industrial and commercial supremacy of Great Britain . . . We claim these pensions as a right.' For many advocates, pensions were a recognition of service rendered, a social reward for the performance of past social duties. Asquith (*Hansard*, 4th series, vol. 153, 1337 [14.3.1906]), then Chancellor of the Exchequer and responsible for the bill, argued that 'a man should be entitled as a right to claim an old-age pension subject to his satisfying a large number of conditions . . . as to character, conditions as to residence, and . . . conditions as to means'. Those rights were consequently not presented as protecting prerequisites for wholesome human functioning, but as entitlements purchased primarily through socially meritorious past behaviour.

J.M. Robertson (1912: 46), Liberal politician, writer and rationalist, took this argument one stage further. He described rights as 'deducible from the simple law of reciprocity, the principle of doing as you would be done by'. This suggested that past performance was not the only claim an individual had against the state; rather, a right could embody the morality of treating like cases alike. Practically, though, the related question of the state enforcement of such a morality (rejected as self-defeating by T.H. Green) was connected to a social utility argument, granted that all 'working, wealth-creating, service-rendering units' were enfranchised (Robertson, 1912: 48). Robertson evidently linked the notion of rights with that of *active* citizenship in a society, rather than with membership alone. As for old-age pensions specifically, he denied that the principles of 'natural right' (as the moral demand for reciprocity) and of public utility were mutually exclusive. Though Robertson was neither a communitarian nor a supporter of wholesale state regulation – indeed, he felt that reciprocity should stop short of 'the danger of an uncalculating altruism' – he regarded the welfare of the state, the welfare of individuals and a universal rule of mutuality as entirely compatible (Robertson, 1912: 63). The non-contributory nature of old-age pensions removed them from the sphere of market relationships, from the requirement to purchase a *private* right (i.e. a privilege). But Lloyd George (*Hansard*, 4th series, vol. 190, 565 [15.6.1908]), when himself Chancellor of the Exchequer, was inclined to present them as contributory in a broader sense: '. . . when a scheme is financed out of public funds it is as much a contributory scheme as a scheme which is financed directly by means of contributions . . . a workman who has contributed health and strength, vigour and skill, to the creation of the wealth by which taxation is borne has made his contribution already . . .'.

The establishment of universal, state-financed old-age pensions was hence the first important step towards the consolidation of a new welfare theory. First, it conclusively transferred an area of individual well-being from the private to the public sphere, thus proceeding with the evolution away from agreements among individuals, through private group arrangements such as friendly societies, and towards community assumption of responsibility for dispensing social justice (Freeden, 1978). Secondly, the extension of 'contract' from a precise to an imprecise contrivance severed the quantifiable exchange relationships that the laissez-faire age had assumed to exist among individuals, replacing them with a qualitative, 'extended-credit' perspective. The embryonic conception of a community as an aspect of the human *condition* rather than as a private-interest, calculable and voluntarily created market relationship dictated that transformation.

Nevertheless, this was only a first step. Most progressives were loath to decouple the argument for pension rights from the *quasi*-conditional notion of reward, and to attach it instead to an identification of the essential prerequisites for being human. Indeed, it was an opponent of the pensions scheme, the individualist Harold Cox (*Hansard*, 4th series, vol. 190, 596ff [15.6.1908]) who was quick to grasp the essence of the matter. Why, he asked the House of Commons, should one

> start by saying that people over the age of seventy were entitled to a pension any more than by saying, for instance, that all people afflicted with blindness should receive a pension? . . . if old age pensions were paid as a right, the man might claim to be treated as other individuals in regard to the right to buy a glass of beer.

Plainly, one underlying problem concerned the notion of limitless and insatiable needs, as well as the immense difficulty of differentiating between needs and wants. The other problem involved the reluctance of advocates of state intervention to follow through the logic of their position. Few contemporary thinkers would have echoed L.T. Hobhouse's relevant observation: 'Essentially they [the formulators of the Old Age Pensions Bill] contemplate an extension of individual or private rights as against the community, which is the same thing, viewed from the other end, as an extension of the responsibility of the State towards its individual members' (Hobhouse, 1908). This idea of rights was not merely a logical inversion of duties, but in Hobhouse's hands it had two further implications: the recognition of *communitarian* duties, and an appreciation of *unconditional* spheres of the duty–rights nexus.

Unemployment: the thin end of the communitarian wedge

Unemployment was the other area in which rights discourse was occasionally used, nowhere more so than in connection with the 'Right to Work' bills, unsuccessfully proposed a number of times by the Labour party before 1914. The right to work was the only major pre-war welfare demand specifically couched in terms of rights, albeit only by a minority of progressives. Precisely for that reason it presents a particularly illuminating insight into the question of rights and needs. Some of the intellectual groundwork for those proposals had already been constructed. In 1890 John Rae, the writer on English socialism, had published a number of enlightening and radical pieces on rights partly foreshadowing Ritchie's ideas, but also developing different ideas of his own. He presented the right to labour as a 'just claim of the unfortunate'. He grounded such rights on an individualistic basis – 'the principle of preventing degradation and facilitating self-recovery . . . the right to an undegraded humanity', but he signalled an important advance when admitting that the principle had no obvious boundaries: 'Schools, museums, libraries, parks, open spaces, footpaths, baths, are certainly means of intellectual and physical life, which keep the manhood of a community in normal vigour; but, it will be asked, if the State once begins to supply such things, where is it to stop?' The answer could only be provided 'by measuring the length of our necessities with the length of our purse' (Rae, 1890b: 881–2).

Hence a right, although practically restricted by financial contingencies, was predicated on 'need' in a broad sense. It was an inclusive protective capsule for all important human faculties. Starting out from natural rights perspectives, Rae (1890a: 438) insisted that, ultimately, the state had to secure 'those essentials of all rational and humane living which are really every man's right, because without them he would be something less than man, his manhood would be wanting, maimed, mutilated, deformed, incapable of fulfilling the ends of its being'. This statement, at the time one of the clearest concerning human rights and in marked contrast to the vagaries of most progressives, distanced itself from the restricted view of human nature implicit in natural rights theory; in a further passage Rae also moved away from the static conception of human nature entailed in that doctrine: 'the opinion of the time may vary as to what is essential for a whole and wholesome manhood' (Rae, 1890b: 883). Rae regarded the above rights as general claims 'of the unfortunate on society at large', but he also entertained 'special claims of certain weaker classes of society against certain stronger'. In these instances the state acted as guarantor and regulator of presumedly private relationships – fair prices, rents and wages. Again, the argument was crucially related to need: 'protection against extortion to the very necessitous man, who must accept any terms or starve . . . an authoritative prescription of fair interest is only a necessary requirement of justice and humanity' (Rae, 1890b: 884).

The Liberal government of the day had, through the able speeches of its spokesman, Winston Churchill (*Hansard*, 5th series, vol. 5, 499ff [19.5.1909]), championed labour exchanges because they put an end to 'treating a job as if it were a favour . . . as a thing which places a man under an obligation when he has got it'. But the inability to make the leap from obligation to right was again in evidence. When Churchill published some of his speeches under the title *The People's Rights*, his attitude towards rights was no less vague. There was no problem with regard to identifying democratic rights as against a diehard House of Lords. The section on the people's welfare, significantly, avoided rights language altogether (Churchill, 1911). The right to work was dismissed by the Liberal government, not only because it threatened to place intolerable burdens on the economy and on state machinery, but because it was seen to create a bond between individual and society too intense for most to tolerate.

For those very reasons, the proponents of the right to work had to pursue multiple strategies. The minimalist position presented it as a reformulation of the right to life, as part of the social obligation to protect citizens from destitution. Even Labour party members abided by an individualist justification, namely, the right to earn daily bread and to exercise labour power (G. Lansbury, *Hansard*, 5th series, vol. 21, 639–40 [10.2.1911]). On these grounds, the right to work was portrayed as wholly within the natural rights tradition, simply extending life (and perhaps the Lockean notion of property as mixing one's labour with material objects). A second strategy was 'to recognise the obligation to keep a man alive, and that it is more sensible to keep him alive and make of him a useful citizen, with the right to work' (W.P. Beale, *Hansard*, 5th series, vol. 4, 676 [30.4.1909]). Here considerations of social utility were uppermost: work signified participation in communal life and this right was unwittingly transformed into a quasi-duty, highly desirable for the community even if not precisely claimable by it. A third vantage-point was the suggestion that 'the Right to Work is only the obverse of the Duty incumbent on society to organise its work'. On that understanding it reflected the problems of industrial societies and the difficulties they faced because of 'vendible values' (J.H. Harley in Freeden, 1989: 230). Social regulation and rationalization necessitated the recognition of new claims that pertained not so much to changing ideas about human nature as to structural mutations of societies.

For the Christian Socialist H.S. Holland, however, the claim for work had wider implications. It 'comes out of the very heart of human nature'. It was part of a nexus of rights seen as:

> endowments to which [the individual's] place in the Community entitle him . . . He has a right, as a member of the Community, to demand the Community's consideration: to make requirements upon its resources. These rights are not demands he can make in his own name over against the counter interests of another body, called Society: they are, rather, rights which the Society creates for its own welfare, acting through its own members, identifying his own good with theirs.

That socialist perspective, while entitling individuals to call upon society for the provision of their needs, demanded a price: 'the full disposal of the worker, and the full control of his work'. For individual and communal claims were correlative, and 'the needs and necessities of the public welfare' governed the rights of the individual (Holland, 1909: 65–7). This ethical expression of human sociability and of organic social structure fused society and individual into an entity surpassing what most progressive theorists were prepared to countenance, and certainly surpassing any approach embodied in the working ideology of the welfare state.

The 'rights' of children

The question of the treatment of children offers a particularly interesting insight into a period of transition in social thought and practice. In the wake of the alarming discoveries of Booth, Rowntree and the recruitment officers during the Boer War, the debate about the nation's health led reformers to turn their attention to the welfare of the young. In the words of the social reformer Reginald Bray (1901: 122):

> A child has three needs: he is, first, an animal and needs to be a healthy animal; he is, secondly, a thinking animal and needs to think correctly; he is, lastly, a feeling animal and needs to feel aright. As a thinking, feeling animal he possesses character, which is a product of the physical, mental, and moral state of development.

Two points deserve immediate comment. First, children's needs were on this account indistinguishable from adult ones; secondly, Bray indicated the multi-faceted and interdependent nature of human needs, and hence of welfare strategies: 'the child must be regarded as a complex organism, so cunningly knit together that any change in one part reacts on the rest'. The negative-libertarian Asquith, however, was careful not to couch the protection of children in terms of rights, though he was proudly prepared to demonstrate 'what it has cost the State to recognise its duty to the children of the community' (*Hansard*, 4th series, vol. 172, 1175ff [18.4.1907]).

To this very day, children's rights frequently have to make way before alternative proprietary rights that parents claim over children. It is hardly surprising that Edwardian children were not treated as independent agents capable of directing valid claims towards other human beings. Much of the debate was meant to ensure that parents act as responsible trustees of their children's well-being, without invoking the corresponding rights that children might be thought to claim. As a contemporary observer wrote: 'We have been accustomed for so many generations to regard children as their parents' property that a statement of children's rights sounds unfamiliar and extravagant to the most progressive among us' (*Ethical World*, 1898: 771). Even the socialist Ramsay MacDonald, while conceding the replacement of parental primacy with a recognition of the claim of the child against the community, referred to children's 'rights' in inverted commas, preferring to debate the rights of parents to secure their children's education or the absence of the right of parents to impose their dogmas on children (Freeden, 1989: 37).

Promoters of child welfare recognized that parents had duties to their children. As those duties could not always be discharged under conditions of deprivation, it was agreed that the state might have to assume a secondary duty. Again, the language of the debate was significant. Rather than employing rights-language, a social-utilitarian argument was invoked, alluding that it was in the best interests of the state that children should be fed by education authorities, yet compulsion was thought fit to ensure that *individual* parents foot the bill for this social necessity (W.T. Wilson, *Hansard*, 4th series, vol. 152, 1390ff [2.3.1906]). Only if that proved impossible was there a case for public provision of one good meal a day for children. That debate on the feeding of schoolchildren also contains another common theme: 'From a business point of view the money would be well invested, because not only would the children be better equipped for fighting the battle of life, but it would be found that the expenditure on prisons, workhouses, and asylums was considerably reduced, and therefore the money invested would be returned with interest.' Such statements reaffirm the complexity of the arguments that supported welfare-state thinking, and reflect the political truth that the battle for social reform had to be won by persuading the well-off middle class to support it.

The community as claimant

We are now in a position to evaluate these early theoretical contributions which, although differing in their vision from contemporary welfare perspectives, underpinned initial welfare state assumptions. The advance towards a full conception of social rights was a tortuous one. Hastings Rashdall (1896: 323, 331), philosopher and cleric, and indebted to T.H. Green and Oxford Idealism, qualified the rights to well-being that the individual could claim against the state in two senses. First, 'there is no right that may not, under some circumstances, have to give way to the general interest'. Secondly, excepting the right to equal consideration, 'there is no right in the individual which does not spring from the demands of social well-being'. Rashdall was making a case for prima facie rather than absolute rights, and he grounded the vast majority of rights on what was conducive to the general good. Approaches such as these differ from typical current analyses supporting a communitarian welfare state (Harris, 1987), which resist the attempt to moot a definable public or common good, and eschew the awareness that welfare rights may not only be predicated on the interest of the community but claimed directly by the community itself, if necessary even *against* its members.

To appreciate the force of this argument one can turn to the two theorists who did more than any others at the time to redefine the parameters of welfare rights, J.A. Hobson and L.T. Hobhouse. During the 1890s Hobson elaborated a plea for defending side by side the 'just rights of individual and social property'. As he put it, 'the greatest single source of error in dealing with the Social Question is the failure to understand the claim of society to property based on the ground that society is a worker and a consumer'. Because society participated actively in the making of property values, it had 'a natural claim upon property'. This was a 'view of the rights and needs of society' essential to supporting 'the full healthy progressive life of the community' (Hobson, 1901: 150, 141, 148–9). Hobson was far from proposing the replacement of individual rights and needs by social ones; the latter simply extended and complemented the principles on which individual rights were based. His concerns remained with the realization of the equal opportunities for individual self-development. But to that individual standpoint 'must be joined a just appreciation of the social, viz., the insistence that these claims or rights of self-development be adjusted to the sovereignty of social welfare' (Hobson, 1909: xii). This sovereignty was based on a distinct feature: 'Just as property was necessary to the individual in order to realize personal rational ends, so did the moral life of the community require property as the sphere of social self-realization' (Hobson, 1900: 104).

Hobhouse was much indebted to the inventive originality of his friend, Hobson. He too allocated rights to communities, though more cautiously than the latter. In his famous book, *Liberalism* (1911: 149), Hobhouse asserted in connection with the enforcement of standards of public welfare, that 'the conscience of the community has its rights just as much as the conscience of the individual'. Two years later (Hobhouse, 1913: 31) he converged upon Hobson's position and maintained that 'if private property is of value . . . to the fulfilment of personality, common property is equally of value for the expression and development of social life'. With the aid of that common property, individual claims for social justice could be optimally catered for; in particular, that 'of securing to each man, as part of his civic birthright, a place in the industrial system and a lien upon the common product that he may call his own'. Hobhouse reserved the fullest treatment of the subject for his post-war work, where he emphatically stated that rights were not 'conditions precedent to social welfare, but elements in social welfare and deriving their authority therefrom'. However, while reiterating the Idealist claim that the individual had no moral rights which conflicted with the common good, Hobhouse acknowledged individual rights against a community that might misjudge that good (Hobhouse, 1922: 37, 40; Freeden, 1986: 249–51).

For both Hobson and Hobhouse social welfare was attainable through standards of communal well-being which established social needs. These could be directly realized by adopting a democratic and organic perspective. The identification of a social unit with claims parallel to those of the individual had significant consequences for welfare rights theory. It reduced the potentially antagonistic connotations of a right as something held against a state or society; it aspired to prescribe uniform, non-controversial criteria of human welfare; and it regarded any investment in the well-being of individuals as a matter of social utility, independent of personal merit or interest.

The maximization of need

An advance of no less consequence was effected by these liberal welfare theorists on the question of need. In a pathbreaking article (Hobson, 1893), Hobson effected a highly innovative rephrasing of natural rights. He not only rejected, as did Ritchie, their socially detached connotation, but associated them with a conception of human nature both more dynamic and more concrete than that employed by conventional natural-rights theorists (see Freeden, 1990a). Because Hobson understood the essence of human nature as involving activity, work and life as a wholesome process of consumption and expression, his primary conclusion was: 'that which is required to maintain the productive energy of workers is their natural property'. A physiological feature of human nature became a major identifier of human needs and determinant of social arrangements. Immediately, though, Hobson added a psychological given of human nature which necessitated further social arrangements. The 'natural' expenditure of physical energy was not instinctive or biologically determined. Mind had to instruct body to expend energy. This too was natural, but in the holistic sense of an organic linkage between body and mind. As he saw it, 'the human will is part of human nature, and the "property" required as a sufficient motive to act upon this will is as "natural" as that required to furnish the physical energy used up in production' (Hobson, 1893: 135). That right of property was 'natural' in the sense that, unless it was conceded, human nature would refuse the effort that was asked of it (Hobson, 1901: 105). The door was left open for moderate capitalist arrangements to stimulate motivation.

The importance of this formulation for welfare state theory as it developed in parallel to political practice cannot be overestimated. Modern welfare rights theory is unduly preoccupied with philosophical perspectives that assess wholesome humanity according to standards of successfully exercised agency or autonomy (Gewirth, 1982: 11–20). Welfare rights are uneasily fitted into this edifice by assigning them instrumental significance as essential prerequisites for such autonomy or, alternatively, structuring human welfare so that it ascribes priority to rational action over other facets of well-being (see Freeden, 1990b). This did not characterize British welfare thinking in its foundational stages. While rational choice was recognized as crucial to a full personality, other personality features were treated as independently valuable. The result was a more inclusive conception of human needs, incorporated into a far more extensive and complex pattern of rights. Physical, psychological and emotional needs could exist in conjunction with mental and moral ones; social needs could be singled out from individual ones. All these were organically linked and potentially harmonious.

Hobson's account of the needs–rights nexus merits further

examination. If we regard him as the most compelling and creative of the British welfare theorists, which I am inclined to do, what can we learn about the principles and options available through him (and others) to implementers of welfare state policies? Ritchie (1894: 46–7) had raised the question of rights in relation to needs, only to dismiss the issue on a minimalist interpretation of needs as natural instincts, incapable of bearing the full weight of natural rights. Hobson would have none of that restrictive view of needs. In line with his concern for the wholesome consumption of those material and non-material goods that contributed to human utility, he suggested that 'actual standards of consumption are moulded by the free pressure of healthy organic needs, evolving in a natural and rational order towards a higher human life' (Hobson, 1914: 113). True, human evolution was accompanied by a multiplication of wants, whose utility in terms of human development could occasionally be questioned. Nevertheless, human creativity, the exercise of human faculties, and labour were all capable of satisfying human needs – and abundance beyond needs – as well as capable of waste and malconsumption. In extending needs to include not only material ones, but 'housing, leisure, modes of recreation and intellectual consumption', Hobson (1914: 166–8) recognized both the unity and the diversity of human nature.

The desire to harmonize individual and social claims was central to this brand of welfare thought. By introducing the notion of incentives as a natural property without which human effort would not be drawn out, Hobson disavowed socialist formulas that relied wholly on an altruistic transformation in, or rediscovery of, true human nature; and he enabled the retention of an individualism that some socialisms lacked. By further acknowledging the pluralism of needs in parallel with their uniformity, Hobson departed from unsubtle approaches that simply detail universalistic needs guaranteed by identical rights. He expressed his view most fully in the 1920s:

> Wealth, the product of work, should be distributed according to the support it renders to the whole life of the recipients. It should give to each what each is capable of utilising for a full human life. Capacity of use or enjoyment, not 'needs' in its narrow sense of physical or even spiritual necessities of life, must be our humanist interpretation of the formula. It must cover three categories of payment, first, that required to maintain a member of society in the performance of his special economic function; secondly, a full, human maintenance fund for a member of a civilised society; and thirdly, an adequate economic provision for such education, travel, social intercourse, or other opportunities of personal development and human enjoyment as may raise his human value for himself and for society. (Hobson, 1929: 231)

This maximization and diversification of needs reflected a social utilitarian perspective that saw individual well-being as a prime basis of social welfare, and that refused to separate moral capacities from the total package of what constituted a human being. It comes as no surprise to see Hobson as early as 1909 advocating that 'each generation of Liberals will be required to translate a new set of needs and aspirations into facts' (1909: 93) and doing so himself by recommending a radical social welfare policy enshrining a wide range of rights. These were to include equal access to natural resources, effective liberty to travel through subsidized transport, easy access to industrial (electric) power, access to state credit, free and equal access to public justice, and free access to knowledge, education and culture (1909: 96–113) – and all these in addition to the policies for the underprivileged that welfare states are more commonly associated with.

Hobhouse, too, came to emphasize the importance of the social dimension of need. 'The common good', he asserted (1922: 108), 'supposes a differentiation between the conditions of social and those of an unsocial and imperfectly social life and personality, and is concerned to satisfy only the former which may be called in general the needs of its members.' Although the needs were those of individuals, a high premium was placed on personality components that catered for communal life. Hobhouse went on to define distributive justice as the satisfaction of equal needs of this nature, subject to the adequate maintenance of useful functions. But by introducing the concept of function, Hobhouse indicated the existence of *social* needs that had to be serviced in order for the whole social system to thrive. As he plainly stated (1922: 111; see also Tawney, 1921: 7–8), 'a function, however costly, is justified, if on the balance the community is better able to meet its needs with it than without it'. For both Hobhouse and Hobson, then, the idea of welfare diverged from its common contemporary association with public welfare programmes intended *solely* to redistribute resources to the disadvantaged (see Wellman, 1982), and was attached to opportunities and capacities that *no* individual could realize without communal assistance and rational direction.

The minimum standard: alternative arguments

It must repeatedly be stressed that thinking about welfare did not necessarily don the distinctive garb of the progressive theorists examined here. The conceptual paraphernalia employed by commentators on social policy, when not simply versed in language of contributory merit, were sometimes even more communitarian than those espoused by social philosophers. Many of these commentators, as noted earlier, did not suppose the language of needs and rights served their purposes optimally. They mainly appealed to considerations of national welfare and interests, rather than to the claims of classes or even individuals. This was evident in debates on minimum standards of living. Instead of appealing to individual need, a strong communitarian perspective was injected into the discussion on housing for the poor: 'it is to the interest and will conduce to the welfare of the community to protect and promote the common health by ensuring to every person a certain minimum amount of air, space, and household comfort . . . anything which lowers the general standard of healthiness impoverishes the community' (*Monthly Review*, 1901: 12–13). Rather than refer to individual right, many progressives thought the duty of the state lay in influencing the recipients of the redistributionary process so as to 'fit them to enjoy their new privileges'. Those 'privileges' were not conditional on specific behaviour; but they certainly suggested that the community was the benevolent agent of the individual, and hence that communal needs and interests had priority over individual claims. The aversion to rights language was particularly striking in an article in the influential liberal weekly *The Nation* (1912). It called eloquently for a claim to a share in life for every man – the nearest one could border on rights language without using it. Yet on the same page it insisted that 'the new conception of social health . . . [demands] the realisation of a living wage, not as an individual right, but as a social security'. Individual rights were an 'intellectual atavism' relating to individualistic contractarian notions. It was again left to the social philosophers to argue, as did Hobhouse (1911: 159), that 'the "right to work" and the right to a "living wage" are just as valid as the rights of person or property'.

Conclusion

The origins of modern welfare thought in Britain evinced a richness evocative of advanced humanitarian aspirations. They allowed for a conception of the individual, whose purposes could best be served within the wider context of the community. The welfare state was clearly a liberal product and it is erroneous to assert that liberalism can have no ready solutions to its problems. The present confusion surrounding the ideological implications of welfare arise in part from the introduction of an American, contractarian and philosophical liberalism which has little to do with the development of European social liberalism. In part it also emanates from a confusion between a revived libertarianism and liberalism, the former zealously clinging to a concept of liberty as non-intervention and forbearance, as preceding welfare rather than complementing it. The social liberalism, and liberal socialism, that nourished the welfare state were of a very different mould, permitting the retention of private ends, as long as those were compatible with communal ones, and enabling the parallel pursuit of social ends that ipso facto benefited individuals. Human welfare was thus the product of dual determination by public and private agencies.

Undoubtedly early welfare theorists carried with them an over-simplified faith in the rationality of the community. They were also far too sanguine as to the possibility of harmony among individuals; as well as between society, its representative the state, and the individual. As a result they were too comfortable with state regulation, and underestimated the dangers of paternalism. This confidence was sustained by a belief in participatory democracy – frequently linked to proportional representation and, occasionally, the referendum – and a genuine conviction that the state could act as an impartial agent for the common good. That holistic vision of the welfare state lacked any appreciation of the importance of interest groups and the need for power brokerage; indeed, its aversion to sectionalism blinded it to such possibilities.

On the other hand, the coupling of evolutionary theory to developmental models of human nature facilitated the emergence of non-static notions of need that could adapt to different times and places, though these were always anchored to a core of basic uniform needs. Thus needs could allow for diversity that was not socially injurious. It was possible to endorse wants unrelated directly to needs, though those wants themselves could be explained as psychological or emotional needs (Hobson, 1922: 671). A major weakness of such theories was their unawareness of the possibility of unlimited needs, but this was mitigated by the availability of social assessments of their utility.

Turn-of-the-century social thought shaped welfare theory in significant ways. It established a far greater scope of welfare claims and rights than had hitherto been accepted, and even when reluctant to use the language of rights, hinted at them as part of the new packaging of social utility. It attempted to overcome narrow welfare purviews that concentrated on residual groups and to broach instead a general formula of qualitative well-being for all, and needed even by the wealthy. It therefore expanded social membership to a notion of active citizenship that transcended the more rudimentary questions of resource redistribution. It espoused an 'altruism' that was not a feature of individual tendency, but of the socially oriented individual consciously embedded in a community educated in humanitarian perspectives. Though it encouraged voluntary action, it did so only within parameters set up by the state, and displayed deep suspicion towards private institutions that eschewed a communitarian viewpoint, such as the Charity Organization Society (Hobson, 1909: 192–217). And it retained some notion of purchased merit, though not so much in market exchange terms as in terms of contributions to the common good. Elements of this theory are worth salvaging (see Jordan, 1989). Its theoretical and historical successes and failures may assist in evaluating the problems of the welfare state towards the end of the century that produced it.

References

Bray, R. (1901) 'The children of the town', in C.F.G. Masterman (ed.), *The Heart of the Empire*. London: T. Fisher Unwin.

Churchill, W.S. (1911) *The People's Rights*. London: Hodder & Stoughton.

Ethical World (1898) 'The religious rights of children'. London, 3 December.

Freeden, M. (1978) *The New Liberalism: An Ideology of Social Reform*. Oxford: Clarendon Press.

Freeden, M. (1986) *Liberalism Divided: A Study in British Political Thought 1914–1939*. Oxford: Clarendon Press.

Freeden, M. (ed.) (1989) *Minutes of the Rainbow Circle, 1894–1924*. London: Royal Historical Society.

Freeden, M. (1990a) 'Hobson's evolving conceptions of human nature', in M. Freeden (ed.), *Reappraising J.A. Hobson: Humanism and Welfare*. London: Unwin Hyman.

Freeden, M. (1990b) 'Human rights and welfare: A communitarian view', *Ethics*, 100: 489–502.

Frey, R.G. (ed.) (1985) *Utility and Rights*. Oxford: Blackwell.

Gewirth, A. (1982) *Human Rights*. Chicago: University of Chicago Press.

Harris, D. (1987) *Justifying State Welfare*. Oxford: Blackwell.

Hobhouse, L.T. (1908) 'Old-age pensions: The principle', *Manchester Guardian*, 29 February.

Hobhouse, L.T. (1911) *Liberalism*. London: Williams & Norgate.

Hobhouse, L.T. (1913) 'The historical evolution of property, in fact and in idea', in C. Gore (ed.), *Property, Its Duties and Rights*. London: Macmillan & Co.

Hobhouse, L.T. (1922) *The Elements of Social Justice*. London: Allen & Unwin.

Hobson, J.A. (1893) 'Rights of property', *Free Review*, November: 130–49.

Hobson, J.A. (1900) 'The ethics of industrialism', in S. Coit (ed.), *Ethical Democracy: Essays in Social Dynamics*. London: Grant Richards.

Hobson, J.A. (1901) *The Social Problem*. London: J. Nisbet & Co.

Hobson, J.A. (1909) *The Crisis of Liberalism*. London: P.S. King.

Hobson, J.A. (1914) *Work and Wealth*. London: Macmillan & Co.

Hobson, J.A. (1922) 'The ethical movement and the natural man', *Hibbert Journal*, 20: 667–79.

Hobson, J.A. (1929) *Wealth and Life*. London: Macmillan & Co.

Holland, H.S. (1909) 'The right to work', *Commonwealth*, 14: 65–7.

Jordan, B. (1989) *The Common Good*. Oxford: Blackwell.

Monthly Review (1901) Editorial. 'The housing of the poor', February.

Nation (1912) 'The claim for a share in life', 28 September.

Plant, R., Lesser, H. and Taylor-Gooby, P. (1980) *Political Philosophy and Social Welfare*. London: Routledge & Kegan Paul.

Rae, J. (1890a) 'State socialism and popular right', *Contemporary Review*, 58: 876–90.

Rae, J. (1890b) 'State socialism and social reform', *Contemporary Review*, 58: 435–54.

Rashdall, H. (1896) 'The rights of the individual', *Economic Review*, 6: 317–33.

Ritchie, D.G. (1894) *Natural Rights*. London: Allen & Unwin.

Robertson, J.M. (1912) *The Meaning of Liberalism*. London: Methuen.

Tawney, R.H. (1921) *The Acquisitive Society*. London: G. Bell & Sons.

Wellman, C. (1982) *Welfare Rights*. Totowa, NJ: Rowman & Allanheld.

5

The Welfare State versus the Relief of Poverty

Brian Barry

My title has an air of paradox about it. Shouldn't any decent welfare state relieve poverty? Of course it should. But in a well-ordered welfare state almost all the job of relieving poverty will be done by policies whose objective and rationale are quite different. For all except a few unfortunates who fall between the cracks the relief of poverty is a by-product of a system of cash benefits founded upon principles that do not include the relief of poverty. Indeed, it is not even strictly accurate to speak of such policies as *relieving* poverty: we should rather say that they *prevent* it. They do this by providing money to people who qualify for it – on a variety of bases which it is our task here to explore – in such a way that poverty does not as a matter of fact arise. (Welfare states also provide their citizens with services such as education or medical care. My concern here, however, is with the moral basis of cash benefits.)

What I have just said about the proper function of the welfare state will occasion no surprise among social policy professionals, analysts, or historians. They take it for granted that, if the welfare state is to be identified with one objective, it is that of income maintenance rather than the relief of poverty. And they characteristically date the welfare state from the introduction of the principle of social insurance in Germany a century ago. The existence of means-tested benefits they regard as an anachronism, a hangover from the days of the poor law and a sign that the ideal of the welfare state is still incompletely realized.

On the continent of Europe, the poor law legacy is in every country a small one. In quantitative terms, means-tested benefits typically run at around 5 per cent of total cash disbursements, the balance being made up largely of payments made to people qua citizens (child allowances or old-age pensions) and beneficiaries of a system of compulsory social insurance. As a group the Anglophone countries present a more archaic picture, but even here the bulk of expenditures in Britain and the USA fall outside the scope of the poor law paradigm. What is more, in both countries the programmes that pay either universal benefits (child allowance in Britain) or social insurance benefits have proved more resistant to attack from right-wing governments than means-tested benefits.

All this makes it quite strange that, with very few exceptions, British and US philosophers who have written about the justification of the welfare state have in fact produced justifications of the poor law. This would, of course, be understandable enough in theorists who started from a basically Nozickian position and then watered it down (as both Friedman and Hayek are prepared to do) so as to allow the state a residual function in the alleviation of sheer destitution. But as far as I am aware none of the people I am now talking about falls under that description.[1] They have no principled objection to the state's taking money away from some people and giving it to others. Yet in their defence of the poor law they must be regarded as 'Conservative Liberals', as defined by Cornford (1906: 12) in his sardonic account of the parties in academic politics: 'A *Conservative Liberal* is a broad-minded man, who thinks that something ought to be done, only not anything that anyone now desires, but something which was not done in 1881–82.' In the present case, what is demanded is plugging the gaps in the poor law.

How can we account for this implicit or explicit repudiation of what would generally be thought of as one of the major achievements (and perhaps the one most likely to endure) of social democratic forces in the twentieth century? We might invoke the kind of cultural lag in interdisciplinary relations that in the other direction results in economics being the last hold-out of logical positivism. We might also point to the tendency of philosophers to take up only issues discussed by other philosophers – in this instance the barren question of whether or not there are such things as 'welfare rights'.[2] But there is, I think, a more respectable motive at work, and this is the idea that a poor law is redistributive in a way that a welfare state is not, and that this makes a poor law more defensible.

Now on a literal (and in my view entirely appropriate) understanding of the term 'redistribution' this claim is patently false. For a welfare state raises and hands out far more money per head of the population than a poor law. Obviously, those who say that the welfare state does not redistribute income must be using the term in some more restrictive way. In fact, what they mean is that the poor law by its nature brings about a net transfer between classes, whereas the welfare state has no inherent tendency to bring about such net transfers.

This charge, if charge it be, is perfectly correct. A classic poor law system raised the funds by a system of local property taxation and dispensed them to those – and only those – who met some official criterion of poverty. Surviving elements of the poor law have been largely shifted to a system of national financing in the course of the past 50 years, but here too, however attenuated the principle of progressivity may be in practice, we can discern a pattern of redistribution from the higher to the lower strata, defined by their lifetime market-derived incomes. By contrast, a welfare state characteristically transfers money within income strata: from those of working age to those of retirement age, from the childless to those with children, from the well to the sick, from the employed to the unemployed, and so on. The basic principle of social insurance, as it operates in almost all welfare states, is that contributions and benefits are both proportional to earnings. Any net transfers from higher to lower income strata (and there are usually some) derive from departures from strict proportionality: commonly, for example, there will be a floor below which benefits are not allowed to fall, and the percentage of earnings replaced may be shaved at the higher levels. Within any system that takes up a quarter or so of the Gross National Product, the cumulative effect of such deviations in creating net interclass transfers may not be insignificant. It would, however, betray a gross misunderstanding of the rationale of the welfare state to think of it as no more than a cumbersome way of bringing about a minor transfer of resources between income strata.

The case for or against compressing the distribution of income between strata defined by lifetime market-derived incomes is entirely independent of the case for a welfare state. A welfare state can take the system of net incomes as it finds them, however they may have been modified by trade union activity, minimum wage (or other) legislation, or taxation. This is not to denigrate the concern for vertical equity, but it is to say that one should not become obsessed by it to the extent of overlooking the great importance of horizontal equity.

The vocabulary of vertical and horizontal equity that I have just employed is in this context useful and perhaps indispensable. But it needs to be handled with care. Vertical equity is a reasonably simple notion. Once we have defined our income strata we ask whether, aggregating across each stratum, those in the higher strata are paying proportionally more than those in the lower, and if so whether the rate of progressivity is, in our view, adequate. But there is no correspondingly straightforward way of characterizing horizontal equity. On the contrary, my object in this chapter is to draw attention to the wide variety of reasons for providing cash benefits. Of all the bases for cash benefits that I shall analyse here, only the last entails any testing of income (or more generally of means) and I hope that by the time I get to this category its extremely modest role in a well-ordered welfare state will have become apparent.

It will perhaps be helpful to list the five categories under which I shall group cash benefits. Their precise signification will, of course, become clearer when I discuss them in detail. The five categories, which I shall take up in order, are as follows:

1 Payments made in anticipation or reimbursement of special expenses.
2 Payments made to compensate for some loss other than, or over and above, impairment of earning-capacity. (Payments in respect of special expenses are also excluded.)
3 Payments made to (or in respect of) those whose status entails that they are not expected (or permitted) to work full-time.
4 Payments made without regard to means or income to those whose earnings fall short of some norm.
5 Payments made to those whose means or incomes are insufficient to get them above some minimum income (the 'poverty line') set as the amount considered adequate for people in their situation.

It is important to make it clear that these categories distinguish different rationales for making cash payments. They do not necessarily map in any straightforward way on to any actual system of welfare benefits. We have no reason for expecting that to each rationale will correspond a specific benefit tied uniquely to that rationale. Nor should we be surprised if the criteria of eligibility are related only loosely to the rationale.

Let us take as an example a system of payments to the war-disabled where the amount paid is related to a percentage scale of disability (10 per cent for flat feet, and so on up). These payments are made according to the criteria of eligibility contained in the schedule that defines the percentage of disability corresponding to any given physical condition. But the rationale of the system is, as I shall suggest below, partly that those with the higher percentages of disability are expected to have impaired earning capacity (category 3) and partly that disabilities reduce the quality of life (category 4).

How can I assert this? To determine the rationale underlying such a system of payments, it is necessary to call upon a variety of techniques. One is simply to ask what is the most plausible rationale of each feature of the system. Another is to look at the discussion surrounding the introduction of the system and the way in which it has been defended when proposals have been made to change it.

In the end, ascribing a rationale (or more than one rationale) to a system of payments is a matter of judgement. Since this chapter is already long, I have not included any extensive discussion of the way in which rationales articulate with systems of payment. But my focus is, in any case, on the rationales themselves. I talk about actual systems of payment for illustrative purposes only.

Payments made in anticipation or reimbursement of special expenses

My first category has the advantage that it clearly has nothing to do with the relief of poverty but at the same time it equally does not fit the rationale of income replacement which it is easy to fix on as the alternative rationale for all cash benefits. It thus immediately forces into the open the point that horizontal equity is a diverse notion. The payments I intend to include here are aimed at equalization between those who (typically for reasons of sickness or disability) have to incur special expenses and those who are in other respects in the same economic position but do not have these special expenses. The rationale is that a condition giving rise to special expenses is a misfortune that should be compensated. The case for compensation is equally good whether the person affected is wealthy or poor: the relevant notion of equity is, as it were, local rather than global. Hence there is no place for means testing. The only thing that has to be established in order to qualify for benefit is the existence of the condition giving rise to the special expense.

It will be noticed that I distinguished in the heading between anticipation and reimbursement. I do not mean here to refer to the time of payment in relation to the time of the expense, which is of no analytic significance. Rather, I intend to mean by reimbursement a benefit corresponding to an actual cost: the claimant produces a receipt and payment is made on the basis of it. (Examples would be, in most systems, payments for some medical expenses, or payments made to cover the cost of converting a disabled person's car.) By 'anticipation', in contrast, I intend to refer to payments made in accordance with a standard tariff, such as a mobility allowance or a constant attendance allowance. Here the actual costs incurred are immaterial. The payment is made on the basis of the relevant conditions having been certified to exist, and it is then up to the recipient to deploy the money as he or she thinks fit.

My reason for mentioning this distinction is that payments of the second kind may create problems of categorization, in the following way. Where payments are made on a reimbursement basis, it is easy to establish that they are intended to cover expenses. But where payments are made to anyone in a certain condition, it may not be clear whether they are made in anticipation of special expenses or for some other reason. Thus, in the USA, one of the earliest forms of 'welfare' – existing in many states before the federal government became involved at all in the 1930s – consisted of payments made to the blind. These were not reduced if the recipient had earnings or income above some level, so they cannot be construed as falling under the fourth or fifth categories (earnings-replacement or alleviation of poverty) but they could perfectly plausibly fall under the second category (compensation for blindness itself), or the third category (possession of a status such that one is not expected to work full-time in an able-bodied job). This last may, incidentally, sound strange but I hope to show in a moment that it is quite typical of the earliest stratum of cash benefits, and still persists in the modern welfare state.

No doubt some light could be thrown on the motives of those who introduced these benefits by going back to the debates in the legislature surrounding them. But we would probably find that the benefits were overdetermined causally, and that many different sentiments supported the practical conclusion that the blind were electorally popular 'deserving' cases – in contrast to (at the opposite extreme) the able-bodied unemployed. This point is worth making because I can use it to emphasize that I am here trying to enumerate possible bases for cash benefits. I am not claiming that every actual cash benefit that has ever been provided anywhere can be unambiguously attributed to just one category.

Payments made to compensate for some loss other than, or over and above, impairment of earning-capacity (excluding payments in respect of special expenses)

In my discussion of the first category I pointed out that a particular payment may have more than one possible rationale. This observation will serve to introduce my second category. Thus in the 1970s a consortium of groups representing the disabled in Britain put forward a proposal for replacing existing ad hoc payments to the disabled with a consolidated Disablement Costs Allowance, graduated according to severity of disability. Although the name of this might be taken to suggest its purpose adequately, Brown (1984: 383), in her analysis of alternative disability

payment schemes, argued that the proposal could be construed in
either of two ways:

> The new Disablement Costs Allowance might be described as compen-
> sation for the fact of disability (in a manner similar to the equivalent
> benefits for the war and industrial disabled) or it might be seen as an
> equalisation benefit, enabling disabled people to maintain a similar
> standard of living to non-disabled people, in spite of higher costs
> related to the disability.

The first interpretation, compensation for the fact of disability,
falls within the second category that I am now discussing. And the
examples I shall take will be the two referred to by Brown:
compensation for disabilities incurred in the course of military
service and in the course of employment.

Although most societies seem to have had some provision for
widows and orphans, the earliest sources tended to be private
charity or the church. Probably the most widespread early involvement of the *state* in welfare lies in its making some sort of provision for those injured in war, or, in the case of those killed, their
dependants. The underlying idea here, evidently of universal
appeal, is that someone who has 'done the state some service' and
suffered for it has a just claim on the state for compensation.
States have gone about discharging their obligations in ways other
than providing cash benefits. It has been common for state agencies to be required to give preference in employment to the war-
injured. The state may also extend the requirement of preferential
treatment to other employers. (A parallel way of dealing with
widows was the biblical injunction to let them have the gleanings
after the harvest.) But cash benefits are now the standard form of
compensation for the disabled, perhaps in conjunction with these
other forms of provision.

The usual – as far as I know universal – way in which payments
to those injured in the course of military service are assessed is by
tying the amount paid to the gravity of the injury: so much for
the loss of an eye, an arm, a leg, and so on. Once established, the
payments stay at the same level so long as the person's physical
condition remains the same. If it deteriorates, in a way that
connects the deterioration with the original injury, the person can
claim more; if it improves, the payments should in principle be
reduced, though there seems to be a tendency to be generous here.
But the payments do not depend on the injury having lowered the
recipient's earning potential or actual earnings, or brought the
individual below the poverty threshold.

An attempt might be made to assimilate these disability

compensation payments to income maintenance by arguing that the disability scores (so much per cent disability for loss of a limb, for example) are intended as rough approximations of the loss of earning-potential. But then why not compensate actual loss of earnings? The answer might be offered that when such payments began the state did not have the apparatus for monitoring earnings, so a rough-and-ready substitute was all that was available, and that the system continues now under the force of inertia. More subtly, it might be suggested that the idea is to encourage the disabled to get the best job possible, without pushing up their marginal effective tax rate by adding the progressive withdrawal of disability benefit to their other taxes or losses of means-tested benefits, but that the compensation is still for expected loss of earning-potential.

The irrefutable evidence against any of this being the whole story about the basis of war-injury compensation is that the typical scheme clearly compensates injuries whose overwhelming ill-effect is on the person's quality of life rather than income potential. Serious disfigurement is unquestionably a grievous loss, and is compensatable, but does not close too many doors as far as employment is concerned. Even more demonstrably, impotence is a loss that I think any war compensation board would regard as worthy of substantial compensation, but I suppose the only careers it would blight would be those of gigolo or actor in pornographic movies.

Let me make it clear what I am saying here and what I am not. I am not committed to denying that part of the reason for compensating the war-disabled (and perhaps part of the way in which the scale of disabilities is constructed) is to make some allowance for the reduction in employment opportunities associated with most forms of disability. I am denying only that this, in any variant, can be the whole story. What I insist is that at any rate some part of the payment is made in virtue of the simple fact that somebody who has lost bodily tissue, is disfigured, or is functionally impaired, has a less good life than would have been the case if everything else were the same except for that loss. I should add that the logic of compensation would also suggest that continuous or recurrent pain should be compensated, in the absence of (or over and above) any loss of tissue or functional impairment. My impression is that this is in fact slighted, perhaps because it is regarded as too 'subjective' to fit into the tables of percentage disability.

Additional support for the view that war disability pensions are not simply compensation for anticipated loss of income can be drawn from a study carried out by the Congressional Budget Office (1982: 57–8) of the American system. This pointed out that benefits were being paid to many veterans with 'minor medical problems such as flat feet or an amputated finger' and considered the possibility of withdrawing benefits from those with low-rated disabilities (56 per cent of all beneficiaries) on the ground that 'it is doubtful that [these] actually cause large reductions in earning capacities, and therefore justify long-term periodic benefits'. But it added: 'Whether earning capacity is lost may be less important, however, than providing some compensation for illness and injury incurred while in service. Veterans' compensation payments are considered by some to be indemnity payments.'

After cash benefits for those injured in war, the next earliest cash payments found in western countries are cash benefits for those injured at work. (In Britain and most American states they came in during the last quarter of the nineteenth century.) What is the rationale for the special treatment of those injured in the course of employment? Why, to make it concrete, should someone who loses a leg at work be treated more favourably by the state than one who loses a leg in an accident at home, or from 'natural causes' – that is to say from a disease that is not considered as being causally related to the person's job?

If we ask for the historical origins of workers' compensation schemes, and for the explanation of their early appearance on the scene, the answer can easily be supplied. Under tort law, a worker injured on the job could in principle claim against his employer. But the workings of the tort law became increasingly capricious as large numbers of men in factories worked together: a worker would need to prove negligence by the employer and no negligence by himself, and even then, under the 'fellow servant' rule, his claim would fail if another worker had been at fault. (That he might succeed in a claim against an equally ill-paid fellow worker was little consolation.) Whether or not a worker would succeed became a lottery – and an expensive one to run, taking a half (in Britain) or two-thirds (in America) of the total amount spent.[3] Tort remedies were therefore in effect traded in for a scheme of workers' compensation paid for by a levy on employers in most countries before the First World War. As with contemporary mass out-of-court settlements (a recent and stark example being the Opren settlement in Britain) the level of benefits was less advantageous than would have been the result of winning a tort case, but it meant that a worker injured on the job could pretty much count on compensation, at any rate provided he fell off something or was mauled by a piece of machinery.

Since workers' compensation descends from tort law, it is quite understandable that it should retain some element of that law. Notionally, the tortfeasor is supposed to 'make whole' his victim, in so far as money can do that, so we may reasonably expect the employer, through contributing to a workers' compensation fund, to compensate for disability itself – for the loss of enjoyment of life inherent in the injury or disease sustained by the worker. But if we are rationalists rather than conservatives (as I am) we shall be unpersuaded that this explanation, couched in terms of origins, provides any good reason for continuing to make a distinction between work-induced disabilities and the general run of disabilities. Why should the source make a difference?

We can, I think, give an answer that retains much of the spirit of the previous one. This is that the worker has, after all, been harmed in the process of making profits for the employer, and it is only fair that the employer should compensate the worker, via the state workers' compensation scheme, for that harm. In assessing this argument we should not give it spurious plausibility by supposing that making the employers pay can be achieved only by giving special treatment to workers. There is every reason for making the employers pay, and for ensuring that the levy is adjusted to reflect the dangerousness of work in each industry – even for setting a rate for each firm where firms are large enough for experience-rating to make sense. There is a case in equity and also in economic efficiency in that employers will otherwise spend too little on safety (and research into improving safety), and the price of goods produced under hazardous conditions will not reflect the true cost of producing them (see Page, 1986). But this could be done without any differentiation on the receiving end. Indeed, the New Zealand Accident Compensation Scheme operates precisely in this way: all accidents are paid for on the same schedule, and the scheme collects money from employers (in lieu of workers' compensation) and drivers (in lieu of third party insurance), with some topping up from taxes (see Ison, 1980).

The rationale actually offered by the wartime coalition government in Britain for compensating 'disability as such' was, in fact, one which involved drawing an explicit analogy with compensation for war injuries. Rejecting the proposal in the Beveridge report for an earnings-related workers' compensation scheme (Beveridge's one exception to flat-subsistence payments, thus itself giving workers a special status), the government instead put forward a scheme for 'disablement pensions and other allowances as well as death benefits, closely modelled on the provision already made for private soldiers and civilian casualties of war' (Walley, 1972: 82).

As Sir John Walley expresses the mood: '"Soldiers of Industry" was the motto' (1972: 82). Unpacking this, the idea (no doubt fostered by the wartime drafting of civilian labour) was presumably that, just as soldiers contribute to the common weal, so do workers. Both deserve special treatment from their country if they suffer in the course of their duties.

How good is the case for making special payments in respect of the 'fact of disability' to those injured in the course of military service or work? This question can be decomposed into two others. First, should people with the same disability be treated differently by the state according to the source of their disability? And, secondly, if the answer to the first question is 'no', what implication should be drawn? Should compensation for disability as such be extended, or should it be withdrawn altogether (at any rate with respect to new cases)?

The obvious argument against making any differentiation in treatment is that what matters is the extent of disability, not its cause. Two people who have lost a leg, say, share a common misfortune. Both suffer the same limitations on the range of employment they can undertake, and both incur the same inconveniences in everyday life. Why should the source of the misfortune be considered relevant in deciding what cash benefits are appropriate?

The arbitrariness of such differential treatment comes out particularly sharply where compensation for disease is concerned. Workers' compensation statutes typically contain wording to the effect that a disease will be covered only if it is specific to the occupation. But most diseases – cancers, for example – brought about by exposure to toxic substances also occur in the general population. Even if there is no doubt that the incidence of some diseases is higher among some groups of workers, there is no way of showing that any particular worker would not have contracted the disease in the ordinary course of events. The same difficulties have been met by American servicemen seeking compensation for diseases consequent upon exposure to fallout from nuclear tests or to the defoliant Agent Orange used in Vietnam.

Where the predominant cause of some disease is occupational, the state can (as with Black Lung in the USA) bypass the process of proof in individual cases by establishing a presumption that anyone exposed to the hazard for a certain period of time who contracts the characteristic disease acquired it as the result of that exposure. This, however, merely shifts the zone of arbitrariness, creating one group of workers who receive compensation following exposure regardless of individual causation and another group who do not receive compensation following exposure regardless of individual causation.

My wider point, however, is not the difficulty of providing compensation to those and only those who actually contracted a disease as a result of exposure at work. It is, rather, that the more one thinks about the issue the less it seems to matter how the disease came about. To see this, imagine a disease which has an incidence of 5 per 1000 in the general population and 10 per 1000 among workers engaged in some industrial process. Since there is no way of compensating only the five 'excess' sufferers, either all those who contract the disease must be compensated or none. Now suppose that as a result of some advance in diagnostic technique it becomes possible to detect a subtle difference between the ordinary form of the disease (say, a kind of cancer) and the form it takes when produced by exposure to the occupational hazard. The sheep and goats can now be separated and only those with the second form of the disease compensated. Are we liable to feel that this is a giant step forward for social justice? Anyone who, like me, has no inclination to think so must conclude that justice does not require differentiation between sufferers from the same condition according to its source.

This still leaves open whether all disabilities should be assimilated to those incurred in the course of military service or employment or whether payments for the 'fact of disability' should disappear altogether. If we look at this question in a social insurance perspective, there need be no right or wrong answer. Assuming an adequate system of earnings replacement, it is up to those who have to foot the bill to decide whether or not they wish to pay additional contributions in order to provide compensation on top for the 'fact of disability'.

There are, however, three reasons for not expecting this kind of universal top-up to be popular. The first is that no country has introduced it, which suggests a lack of widespread support. The second is that private insurance against disabilities arising from accidents is available and not very expensive but not many people avail themselves of it. The third is that it is hard to see any rational basis for a willingness to pay premiums in order to guarantee disability payments over and above those necessary to cover special expenses (first category) and loss of earnings (fourth category). This is not in the least to deny that someone is worse off with a disability than without it, even if their economic position is entirely unaffected. But unless there is some reason for thinking that money would be worth more to you if you were disabled than it is now there is no good reason for giving up money now in order to have more if you become disabled. And, by the same token, if you do become disabled, you have no rational basis for regretting that you did not arrange things so as to be compensated for the disability as such.

Having said all this, I want to conclude this section by partially going back on my tracks. I have suggested that justice does not require special payments in virtue of the 'fact of disability' for those whose disability was incurred in the course of their occupation or military service. But can we go further and say that justice forbids it? I do not think so. Of course, it would be improper for a state to pay more to a white disabled person than to a black one in identical circumstances, or more to a man than a woman. But more advantageous treatment for some than others according to the source of their disability does not seem obnoxious in the same way. While not required by justice it is not contrary to it – provided, we must add, that the system of payments to those who do not obtain the more advantageous treatment is itself consistent with justice.

Although the analogy has to be treated with care, it is helpful to think for a moment about the outpouring of private donations that is attracted by any spectacular disaster. The result of this phenomenon is that those injured or bereaved in such a disaster may finish up far better off than those injured or bereaved in something mundane such as a house fire or a car accident. There is no justice in this, yet it would be hard to say that such generosity should be condemned, however capricious it may be in its choice of objects.

We cannot safely assume that any collective outcome of legitimate individual choices can legitimately be imitated by a state. States must act with a certain kind of impartiality which individuals are not held to, and this entails drawing up general categories of entitlement and sticking to them without fear or favour. But if the public is willing to tax itself to pay disability bonuses to those injured in war, or higher prices to cover the cost of disability bonuses for those injured at work, should this generous sentiment be deplored? I do not see why it should. What we have is in effect a supplementation of what justice calls for rather than a denial of justice.

This said, I should add that I do not think these bonuses should be really big: a lump-sum payment with a maximum in the tens rather than the hundreds of thousands would be the right kind of thing. There are two reasons for this. One is that, even if public discrimination of the kind envisaged is acceptable at all, it still seems inappropriate that it should place two people with the same degree of disablement in enormously different financial circumstances. The other is that, as I have shown, there is bound to be a good deal of arbitrariness in the administration of any scheme that gives more to those disabled in the course of military service or in the course of their occupation than to others with similar disabilities. This is a good reason for limiting the scale of the payments.

Payments made to (or in respect of) those whose status entails that they are not expected (or permitted) to work full-time

The significance of my first two categories is that neither can by any stretch of the imagination be fitted into the picture of cash benefits as earnings-replacement or as poverty-relief. The third category, however, actually includes in its definition a reference to work. On a hasty reading, this might be taken to entail that its rationale must be income-maintenance in some form or other. Such a reading would be too hasty because it ignores the crucial role of 'status' in the definition.

Earnings-replacement implies actual loss (total or partial) of earnings; the relief of poverty implies actual lack of income. But if someone receives a cash benefit by virtue of occupying a certain status and defies the expectations accompanying that status by earning a lot of money, the cash benefit is not withdrawn. This is enough to show that this third category cannot be collapsed into the fourth or fifth. If we try to deny its distinctness as a basis for cash benefits we shall seriously misread the past and also get a distorted view of the present.

By way of preface to this category I want to reconstruct a world-view which was dominant everywhere until this century, and still is prominent in debates about social policy, as well as playing a part (not always fully recognized) in shaping the actual system. In its strongest form, it took the following form: no public funds should be paid to an able-bodied man of working age, whatever his responsibilities. He should find work paying sufficient to meet his family obligations, and he should postpone marriage until he is in a position to earn enough in a steady job to meet those obligations.

We can trace this picture precisely in the provisions of the Elizabethan Poor Law of 1601 which came into being in response to the dissolution of the monasteries and the breakdown of ecclesiastical almsgiving. 'At its base stood the three traditional categories of the poor: the vagrant and "sturdy beggar", who must be ruthlessly repressed; the "impotent poor" (the aged, the blind, and the infirm), who were to be maintained in almshouses or "poor house", and the able-bodied paupers willing to work, who were to be given productive labor at public charge' (Furniss and Tilton, 1977: 96).

Where did women fit into this picture? It was assumed that the standard life-pattern of a woman was to be looked after by a man: until married she would stay at home and be kept by her father, though she might supplement the family income with some appropriate paid work at home (hence 'spinster'), and after she was married she would be kept by her husband. She might take paid employment but this would be for 'pin money': the obligation to support her rested on her husband.[4] The institution of divorce did not change the picture in any substantial way, since a man's obligation to support his wife would (in theory anyway) be carried out by maintenance payments. Widowhood did however pose a recognized problem, and widows were generally understood as deserving of support, especially if they had children. The final group recognized were the 'old maids' (the term itself suggesting an anomalous status) who would eventually have to move in with siblings (as 'maiden aunts') or find jobs to support them (preferably providing room and board) outside the family. Outside the scheme were the mothers of illegitimate children, who had incurred responsibilities without having secured a man to support them.

Without disturbing this general picture of the male 'breadwinner' as the keystone of the system by which income was provided for most members of the society, one could raise an obvious objection to the conclusion that able-bodied men of working age should not get anything from the state. This objection was that different men had different family responsibilities to discharge with their earnings from work. If it was felt too harsh to say that the low-paid should give up prospects of marriage and children, the implication seemed to be that the costs of a family should be partly shouldered by the collectivity. The earliest recognition that two men with the same pay might have different responsibilities which should be taken into account by the state arose not in the form of cash benefits but as income tax relief. A man received in both Britain and the USA an allowance for being married and for having dependent children which lowered his tax liability on any given earnings below what it would otherwise have been. It is significant that these allowances were not reduced if the wife in fact took paid employment, or if the children worked for up to the number of hours they could legally work while of school age. This shows that the basis of the allowance was the occupation of a certain status. That is to say, simply in virtue of his moral and legal responsibility for a wife and children a man received favourable tax treatment. His wife might be a brain surgeon and his children film stars, but that did not relieve him of his obligation to support them: their status as 'dependants' remained unchanged, and so did his reduced tax liability.[5]

Manifestly, however, tax reliefs were of no value to those who paid no income tax anyway, and these were precisely the people whose pay was most likely to be inadequate to meet their family obligations. Only cash payments could possibly meet the case. Now it is clear that, if the logic of the basic assumptions were carried through consistently, there should have been a married man's cash benefit as well as a children's cash benefit. To the best of my knowledge, however, no country has ever introduced a cash payment to men working full-time in virtue of their being married. A state contribution to the husband's marital obligations has remained everywhere a prerogative of the taxpayer – an illustration of the sheer pervasiveness of what Richard Titmuss (1969: 46) called the social division of welfare. By contrast, cash payments for children were introduced in some of the relatively wealthy countries after the First World War and in the rest (with the single exception of the USA) after the Second. These payments were clearly just like the child allowances offset against tax in being based on status – the status of being a child – in that they were also independent of the child's income. The payments I am thinking of here – universal child benefits – were also independent of family income. (Payments for children paid only to families that would otherwise fall below the poverty line will figure in my fifth category.) Their rationale was, fairly clearly, that raising children was an expensive business, the cost of which should be (at any rate to some extent) spread over the whole community. This meant a transfer over a whole lifetime from the childless to those with children and, within the lifetimes of those with children, from periods before and after child-rearing to the period of child-rearing.

The picture I began with, modified by the addition of child benefit, is essentially that underlying the Beveridge Report on which the post-war British settlement was founded. Earnings from work were to be the source of income for the able-bodied of working age, topped up by child benefits for the second and subsequent children. (The cost of the first child was to be absorbed by the parents.) Cash benefits should be paid on a long-term basis to the disabled (but not to married women who were disabled), to the retired (with an extra benefit of about 50 per cent for wives of retired men) and to widows. Beveridge's 'Assumption C', which underpinned the Report, took it as given that government would act in such a way as to ensure full employment, thus in effect putting on a national basis the duty of the local authorities under the legislation of 1601 to find work for the able-bodied who needed it. Beveridge did indeed propose a system of unemployment benefits, but these were to be of strictly limited duration in line with the presupposition that unemployment would be a phenomenon of gaps between jobs rather than persistent joblessness.

I have already said that the child benefit was paid in virtue of status. The extra payment to a retired man for a wife was also a status payment (thus providing an example of a cash benefit for a wife, though only paid in retirement), in that it was supposed to pay the extra cost of supporting a wife. It was clearly not compensation for loss of earnings, since two men with the same pre-retirement earnings, one single and one married, would get different pensions. The payment to a widow was also a status-related payment, in that it did not require as a condition of payment lack of previous or present earnings by the woman concerned. The underlying notion was, fairly clearly, that a married woman should not have to earn a living, and this should not be changed by the death of her husband.

In looking for status-based payments, we should also think back to the previous category. I said that an element in compensation for injuries incurred in the course of employment or military service must be for the fact of disability itself, and that that part fell into the second category. But I also acknowledged that an important element (especially in the higher ratings of percentage disability) was recognition of the tendency of disability to reduce earning capacity. That element in disability compensation must, I suggest, be brought under this third category of status-based payments. It does not, as I have emphasized, tie the level of payments to actual loss of earnings as a result of the disability. It therefore does not fit in my next category of income-replacement. The rationale can only be that the seriously disabled are not *expected* to be able to hold down a well-paying job, and their level of benefit is tied to that. If they defy the expectation, that does not make any difference to their entitlement, any more than a film star child loses child benefit or a working widow the widow's pension.

I have made a good deal of the distinctive rationale for benefits that fall under the present category because it is easy to dismiss them as mere 'anomalies'. We should instead see them as logical implications of a certain picture of society. To the extent, however, that the underlying picture fails to correspond to social reality, or even more to widespread expectations, the system of status-based payments will inevitably come in for criticism. We can see this happening easily enough today. In Britain, there are, every time the budget comes around, recommendations in the newspapers to abolish the marriage allowance. In the USA, the provisions of the social security retirement pension have come under fire for continuing to be based on the assumption that women will be taken care of by an extra 50 per cent on their husbands' pensions rather than by a pension in their own right, which has the effect that a woman whose earnings do not exceed half of her husband's gets nothing extra in return for her insurance contributions. Universal child benefit, which also comes under periodic attack in Britain as 'wasteful', has in fact been reduced in real terms and may well, it seems, be eliminated in favour of an extension of means-tested benefits (my fifth category). I suspect that if the other status-based benefits were more salient, they would also be attacked, and that they escape only because they affect relatively small numbers of people.

My own view, I may say, is that the criticisms are largely justified. The presuppositions of status-based benefits are archaic. The legitimate concerns with which they deal would, I think, be better dealt with by forms of benefit falling in my next category. People should, in other words, be paid for loss of earnings, not according to some status. The one exception seems to me to be child benefit, where the status of limited-earner is more or less imposed by law. Ideally, no doubt, child film stars should not get children's benefit, but there are so few children who can (legally) earn a significant amount while of school age that it is hardly worth the administrative bother of shifting from a status-based system of payments to one based on lack of earnings.

Payments made without regard to means or income to those whose earnings fall short of some norm

With this category, we finally arrive at what is indubitably a form of income-maintenance but one which is not directed at the relief of poverty. That it is so can be seen by observing that at no point in this section shall I discuss any scheme of cash benefits involving a test of income or means. The basis of a claim here is the deficiency of earnings, in relation to one of a variety of criteria. Such a claim is not invalidated by the existence of a large bank account or a highly paid spouse, for example.

The great bulk of payments falling within this fourth category are made to people who are not employed full-time. I shall take up this case first and then go on to discuss other payments. Before doing either, however, I must dispose briefly of the definition of full-time employment. Plainly, there is no God-given number of hours in a week that constitutes full-time employment. The standard of a full week's work changes over time, and even at one time will differ between jobs. Fortunately, however, there is in most occupations an idea of what the job pays on a full-time basis from which short-time working or part-time employment can be defined as departures by virtue of paying less. For my purposes that is good enough as a way of characterizing full-time employment. What matters is not how long someone works but how long he or she is paid for working.

The normal way in which earnings-replacement works is that the level of payments is related to the size of the earnings lost. If the object is to replace work income that is no longer coming in due to unemployment, disability or retirement this is, as I have already remarked, the logical approach. The system of flat-rate earnings-replacement proposed by Beveridge and implemented after the Second World War in Britain is one whose logic is hard to fathom. One might think that there are only two intelligible rationales for a system of payments to those who have lost earnings: to replace their earnings on a proportional basis or to help them out if, and only if, the loss of earnings pushes their household below the poverty line. And in practice we see that flat-rate earnings replacement is an unstable arrangement. Either the move is made to earnings-related payments (as in Britain with the retirement pension and for a time unemployment benefit) or the pressure builds up to 'target resources' on those below the poverty line.

In what follows I shall ignore the anomalous case of flat-rate earnings replacement. From now on when I talk about payments to replace lost earnings I shall mean payments whose size is related to the size of the earnings lost. It may be wondered why I speak of lost earnings instead of, more simply, previous earnings. The answer is that taking previous earnings as the baseline is only one way of operationalizing the criterion of replacing lost income. To assume that earnings-replacement is equivalent to replacement of previous earnings skews the analysis. It drives us towards the conclusion that the rationale of earnings-replacement must be the utilitarian one that once someone has got used to a certain standard of living, and made arrangements based on the assumption that the income to support it will continue, it will cause hardship to drop far below that income. But that is not the only rationale for earnings-replacement, and alternative rationales imply alternative bases of calculation for the payments to be made.

Stated in general terms, the concept of earnings-replacement entails a counterfactual conditional. That is to say, the payment is made in order to close or narrow the gap between actual earnings and earnings in some hypothetical situation. The 'loss of earnings' referred to in the definition of the fourth category is, then, the gap between actual and hypothetical earnings. And the way in which the loss is conceived will depend on the nature of the hypothetical situation that is considered relevant.

In the case of involuntary unemployment, the amount earned in the job previously held is a natural baseline. But in the case of disability, an alternative baseline that presents itself is the amount that would have been earned if the disability had not occurred. The rationale for choosing the hypothetical situation in this way is that the insurable risk is loss of earning capacity, and loss of earning capacity can be assessed only by asking what earnings would have been without the disability. If we ask why earning capacity should be insured, we may conclude that the underlying notion is a Lockean one of each human being having a 'property in his person' and that the risk of damage to this property is one that any prudent man or woman should wish to be covered against.

In the short run, we may reasonably expect that the two ways of conceiving income loss will yield the same answer. Over time, however, there is a good deal of room for them to diverge. A young professional disabled at the beginning of his career, for example, would presumably have enjoyed much greater earnings in later years than those he was receiving at the time when he was struck down. He would therefore over the rest of his lifetime be a lot better off under this conception of earnings-replacement than under the one that equated loss with the shortfall from previous employment.

The special hardship allowance (SHA) payable in Britain to some workers' compensation claimants is in principle an award based on what the income would have been in the absence of the disability. It supplements the payment based on degree of disability (already discussed under the second and third categories) in cases where the loss of earnings is in excess of the degree of disability. In the parliamentary debates that led in 1946 to the addition of the SHA to payments based on degree of disablement, the typical example of someone for whom the scheme was intended was taken to be 'a skilled man who as a result of a minor injury (say loss of a finger) might be wholly prevented from pursuing his craft and yet receive only trivial compensation' (Brown, 1982: 217). In practice, however, the most common claimants have turned out to be men previously engaged in heavy manual work (especially mining) where 'a relatively minor injury may prevent a man from carrying on his normal work'.[6]

In calculating eligibility for the SHA 'the benchmark is the regular occupation, since the allowance is given if, as a result of the relevant loss of faculty, the injured worker is incapable of following his regular occupation and is incapable of employment of equivalent standard' (1982: 237). The loss of earnings is the gap between actual earnings and those that would have been achieved in the regular occupation – and in estimating this 'the loss of possible promotion opportunities within the regular occupation must also be taken into account' (1982: 237).

In practice, however, because the SHA and the disability allowance cannot exceed in total the maximum disability allowance and the SHA has a low maximum itself, payment of SHA at the highest rate is in most cases inadequate to fill the gap between current earnings (if any) and previous earnings. The higher flights of fancy that would be required to estimate what earnings *would* have been under the counterfactual conditional that the worker had not been disabled are for this reason rarely called into play. 'The situation is apparently only made workable by the fact that ninety per cent of awards are made at the maximum rate – that is, it works because it does not actually cover wages in full' (Brown, 1982: 238). Nevertheless, officials of the Department of Health and Social Security (DHSS) wrote at heartfelt length to the Pearson Commission (on disability compensation) about the problems of implementing SHA. The longer the worker has been out of the job on which his or her benchmark claim is based, the greater the problems involved. Among those mentioned in the DHSS submission were the following:

1 The allowance may derive from a regular occupation which has ceased to exist.
2 Entitlement may cease or be reduced, or be increased because the value of the regular occupation has increased or fallen, years or decades after the injury.
3 It is assumed that the level of earnings in the claimant's regular occupation is a valid benchmark forever afterwards. But the

level then achieved might only have been possible for a limited time.

4 Claims to the allowance may be disallowed because of the existence of occupations of which the claimants are regarded as capable but which they may never have an opportunity to take up. (Brown, 1982: 237)

These objections seem to me cogent, and suggest that the estimation of earnings in the 'regular occupation' is not a workable basis for compensating loss of earning capacity. This does not, however, entail that there is no alternative to projecting forward previous earnings. Thus, it would surely be possible to construct a few standard kinds of earnings trajectories (e.g. unskilled labour, skilled labour, clerical and professional) and place people on one of these according to the nature of the occupation they are prevented by disablement from pursuing. There are, I suggest, two independent rationales for this arrangement. The first is that it might be thought of as an approximation of the Lockean condition under which what is insured by the system of social insurance is earning capacity. (I should perhaps add that even those who, like myself, have severe reservations about the Lockean principle as a basis for earnings differentials may quite reasonably hold that, in any economy of unequal earnings, relative equity is better served by a regime of proportional contributions and benefits than by any alternative.) The second rationale is that, when we are dealing with the permanently disabled, the utilitarian criterion is not fully satisfied by the indefinite continuation of whatever was the real income enjoyed at the time when the disability occurred. What is important to people is not just their incomes in absolute terms but their incomes in relation to those of their associates. This implies that the monetary value of benefits should be adjusted not by the cost of living index but by the index of earnings; and a further quite natural refinement of this is that professionals who are disabled young should stay within the income range for professionals over the rest of their lives, and so on.

In the remainder of this section I shall turn my attention to payments that supplement the earnings of those who are in full-time employment. Obviously, of the three cases so far considered – the retired, the unemployed and the disabled – the first two must drop out here. It is, however, quite possible for those who are disabled and in full-time employment to qualify at the same time for a disability benefit if their earning capacity has been impaired by the disability so that they are earning less than they would have been able to do otherwise. In fact, the special hardship allowance to which I referred earlier in this section is most often paid to those in full-time employment, for the simple reason that combined payments under SHA and disability allowance cannot exceed the maximum disability allowance. This means that those on a high disability allowance will be ineligible for SHA, so recipients of SHA may well be able to work full-time, though not at their original occupations.

It may perhaps seem strange at first glance that there can be two men sweeping the floor and taking round the tea one of whom is paid extra because he could once do heavy work while the other gets nothing extra because he has never been able to do anything else. If it is bad luck to have been disabled at some point in your life so that you can do only a low-paid job thenceforward, isn't it even worse luck to be born that way? Why, then, should the disabled person be made better off than the one who has never been able to hold a more attractive job?

Once again, the argument lies in an appeal to relative equity, and here it is, I believe, of overwhelming strength within any system that relates the benefits of those unable to work full-time to their previous or hypothetical earnings. For it would surely be odd if those who are partially disabled, so that they can work full-time but at a lower category of work than before, finish up with a lower income than those whose disability prevents them from working at all or restricts them to part-time work.

Before leaving the subject of the disabled in full-time work, I want to bring up a question that has actually arisen in the calculation of benefits. This is whether someone who, as a result of disability, makes less per hour than before, has a legitimate claim to benefit if he works longer hours than he did before and thus eliminates any shortfall of total earnings. The question has been litigated in the UK, where the Court of Appeal ruled in 1971 that 'a man who has to take a lower grade of work but needs or chooses to maintain his previous level of earnings by working longer hours does not receive the allowance' (Brown, 1982: 237).

This question might well appear to be a mere curiosity, and it is no doubt one of minor importance in itself. But it has great theoretical significance because it unambiguously forces apart the utilitarian and Lockean justifications for relating entitlements to previous or hypothetical earnings. On the utilitarian criterion, according to which the loss of previous income causes hardship, there is apparently no case for dissenting from the judgment of the Court of Appeals. If what matters is the maintenance of previous earnings, then that has been achieved so there is no call for any supplementation. On the Lockean approach, however, the case for supplementation looks strong. The earning capacity of the claimant has undeniably been impaired if he can hold only a job that pays less per hour than he could obtain before. That he can make up the loss by working longer hours scarcely seems relevant to this. If he would unquestionably be eligible for benefit if he worked the same number of hours as before, why should he not get some reward for the extra hours worked? The pull of this Lockean approach may be gauged by its reception among those charged with administering the scheme: 'the former Chief Commissioner has stigmatized this decision [of the Court of Appeals] as "completely unjust"' (Atiyah, 1970: 396).

I have been discussing the supplementation of the earnings of those who are in full-time employment on the basis of some disability that reduces their earning capacity. We can imagine a system, however, that would supplement low earnings even where no question of disability arose. Full-time earnings falling below some level might be increased by a payment of, say, 50 cents for every dollar by which they fell below that level. As far as I am aware no country has such a scheme for the systematic supplementation of low earnings – as against the supplementation of low household *incomes*. Not every country, it should immediately be added, has any necessity for one. Some countries (for example Sweden and West Germany) have a high minimum wage – for our present purpose it does not matter whether this is state-mandated or maintained by trade union action – and then seek to give the workforce sufficient training to make its members profitably employable at that wage. In such a set-up, nobody in full-time employment will have an unacceptably low income, provided that there is an adequate scheme of child benefit. For then full-time pay will be enough for everyone to live on.

This approach has much to commend it. To insist that every full-time job should pay a 'living wage' makes eminently good sense economically as a way of forcing firms to make efficient use of labour. It is also, I believe, morally obnoxious that people in full-time employment should require their pay to be supplemented to bring it up to a level that is regarded in their society as constituting a decent amount to live on. By the same token, it is also, I suggest, morally obnoxious that firms that pay low wages should in effect be publicly subsidized.

Nevertheless, some countries, such as Britain and the USA, have gone down the low-wage path. Thus, in the past 10 years in Britain, the minimum wage legislation covering traditionally low-wage areas (e.g. catering) has been abolished, and the new jobs that have been created have been in precisely such low-wage service occupations, while the jobs that have been lost have tended to be semi-skilled ones with adequate rates of pay. Faced with an economy in which a substantial proportion of jobs fails to pay enough to live on, a government that accepts an obligation to avoid stark poverty (and wishes to ensure that being employed compares favourably with being unemployed) has only two choices. One is the poor law approach of making up household income where it falls short of the official poverty level, and this is the approach that has been followed in Britain and (less systematically through the food stamp program) in the USA. The alternative is precisely the general supplementation of earnings that I discussed above.

In the case of a person living alone, the implications of the two schemes would be the same, unless he or she had some income not derived from earnings – from investments, for example. In the case of a married couple, however, the first model would make payments depend on the joint income of the couple, the idea being that the state steps in only as a last resort to alleviate household poverty. Thus, a woman (and it usually is a woman) in a low-paid job will be ruled out if her husband has a well-paid job, but will be eligible otherwise for means-tested benefits such as income support and housing allowance.

It should be apparent from everything said so far in this chapter that the welfare state solution to low pay – if low pay is to be tolerated at all – is to supplement the pay itself according to a fixed scale without regard to household income or means. Just as unemployment benefit should replace lost earnings, and be unaffected by the earnings of a spouse or other sources of household income, so, if low pay is to be supplemented, this should be done not only when this is necessary to relieve poverty but across the board. There is no good reason for transferring to spouses part of the burden of subsidizing low-wage employers.

Payments made to those whose means or incomes are insufficient to get them above some minimum income (the 'poverty line') set as the amount considered adequate for people in their situation

Let us imagine a system that provides for the special personal expenses covered by the first category; that takes from the third category a universal child benefit set at a level sufficient to meet the actual marginal cost of raising a child (at the standard of the 'poverty' level or above it), and an income for those of working age not expected to work because they are looking after young children or adults who need constant care; and, finally, in line with the third category, that provides a continuing income (again at least at the 'poverty' level) for the unemployed, the sick and disabled, and the retired. Then, with one proviso, we can make a strong assertion: that there is no need for any additional payments to be made under the fifth head of means-tested or income-tested benefits. For everyone will either have an income from being employed full-time or will be provided for otherwise. The proviso is implicit in what was said at the end of the previous section. It is simply that anyone in full-time employment will be above the poverty line with the aid of the other benefits already listed. This means in effect that full-time pay should be adequate to keep a single adult above the poverty line. For then presumably households consisting of two or more adults in full-time work will also be above the poverty line. And households including one or more persons not in full-time employment will be eligible for payments that will get them above the poverty line by virtue of unemployment, sickness or disability, retirement, or caring for young children or others needing constant care.

The ideal underlying the modern welfare state is precisely the elimination of any need for means-tested or income-tested benefits. Beveridge's system of flat-rate income-replacement was designed with this in mind. Thus, in 1948,

> Aneurin Bevan, the Minister of Health introducing the Bill which set up the N[ational] A[ssistance] B[oard], told Parliament that the work 'to be left to the Assistance Board [the body set up to administer social assistance] after the whole of the needs have been met by all the other measures – insurance allowances, old age pensions, sickness benefits – will be very small indeed. Only the residual categories will be left'. (Donnison, 1982: 14)

The existence of this residual element is unavoidable to the extent that payments are based on a prior record of social insurance contributions, since those who have never worked (due to disability or lack of jobs) will be excluded from coverage, as will immigrants. In addition, insurance-based unemployment benefits normally have a fixed term, so those who (in defiance of the underlying assumptions of the system) are out of work for long periods of time will cease to be covered by the earnings-replacement part of the system. In spite of these limitations to the universal adequacy of citizenship-based and insurance-based benefits, the continental European welfare states do succeed in allotting only a genuinely residual role to social assistance.

To give a few examples, the French have until now done

without any general system of means-tested benefits, which has undoubtedly caused serious hardship to those outside the social insurance system, such as immigrants and agricultural workers (see Atkinson, 1975: 210). No interest in any such scheme was in evidence during the previous socialist administration (Jallade, 1985), though it is on the agenda now. Germany is more typical in spending about 5 per cent of its total social security budget on means-tested assistance (Heidenheimer, 1981: 293).

Against this background, Britain and the USA stand out as the oddities among economically developed countries in relying heavily on means-tested assistance. There are three reasons for this. The first is that even programmes that are not means-tested fail to provide payments that save all their recipients from falling below the poverty line. The second is that universal child allowances are non-existent in the USA and vastly inadequate to support the cost of raising a child in the UK. And the third is (as already observed) that in both countries it is possible to be in full-time employment and still be below the poverty line. Thus, the experience of these two countries does nothing to impugn the analysis with which I began this section. That as many as one in seven of the British population are dependent on means-tested benefits, in cruel contradiction of the hopes expressed by Bevan, is an easily traceable result of the failure to get things right; in particular 'the failure of insurance benefits and child benefits to grow as they had been intended to' (Donnison, 1982: 40–41).

This chapter has not been very 'philosophical', in the sense that it has left on one side any question about the deep justification for the institutions of the welfare state and the reasons for considering them as morally superior to those of the poor law. The explanation is, in the words of Sherlock Holmes, that 'it is a capital mistake to theorise before one has data' (Conan Doyle, 1967: 349). The data here are, obviously, the variety of conditions under which eligibility for cash payments is in fact established in contemporary welfare states. Of these the presence of household income below some official line is not even a universally present trigger of payments, as the case of France attests; and in almost all other welfare states it plays a very minor residual role, taking care of those who for some reason (typically inadequate attachment to the workforce to generate social insurance entitlements) fall between the cracks. We get a better grip on the phenomena with the more sophisticated suggestion that the essence of the welfare state is income maintenance for those who are unable to derive an income from work as a result of sickness or disability, unemployment, or old age.[7] But I believe that the analysis offered here shows that this too is inadequate as an account of the basis of benefits in a modern welfare state. It excludes, to be precise (in addition to the fifth category) the first three: payments to cover special expenses, compensation for the 'fact of disability', and status-based cash benefits, of which the most important are those given to those raising children.

The beginning of wisdom, then, is to recognize that there is no reason for expecting the welfare state to have a simple structure or a single rationale. To assume in advance that there is, or ought to be, a single objective underlying all cash payments is to guarantee that one will be baffled by a host of so-called anomalies that in fact have a distinctive rationale. Thus, child allowances have always been understood on the continent of Europe as a way of, in effect, collectivizing the costs of feeding, clothing and housing children in exactly the same way that free schooling collectivizes the cost of educating them. As Lee Rainwater (n.d.: 197) put it, 'family allowances existed to compensate families who chose to rear children and thus made more equitable the distribution of income between parents and nonparents'. In Britain and the USA, with their greater legacy of poor law thinking, this way of looking at child benefit has never become firmly established, in spite of the fact that tax relief for parents (which has the same effect but benefits only taxpayers and then is worth more to higher-rate taxpayers) has been widely regarded as uncontroversial. On the strength of the assumption that the exclusive role of cash benefits must be to relieve poverty, universal child benefit thus comes under attack in Britain as an 'uneconomic' use of resources, in comparison with 'targeted' means-tested benefits, and in the USA the policy intellectuals who backed the Nixon administration's so-called Family Assistance Plan similarly preferred it to a system of universal child benefit on the ground that it would be more efficient at relieving poverty. In this context, it is significant that in Britain those who have recently come to the defence of universal child benefit have tended to do so not on the basis of the principle that it is an instrument of equity between those with children and those without (whether rich or poor) but on the basis of the purely practical argument that means-tested child benefits are expensive to administer and are far from being taken up by all those who qualify. The grip exerted by poor law thinking could hardly be better illustrated.

Once we get away from the idea that there must be a single rationale for every aspect of the welfare state, we can quite readily see how the different kinds of payment that I have listed can be justified. Although I have not developed these justifications systematically, they have been presented in passing. The only point I would like to make here is that we must be careful not to conflate questions that operate at different levels. Thus, if we ask why some particular person should be paid a certain benefit, we must refer to the actual rules (concerning previous social insurance payments, say) that establish eligibility. If we ask why there should be such a system (say of social insurance) we should look for a different sort of answer. We can invoke two complementary lines of justification. One is that ex ante everyone has good reason for wanting insurance against loss of earnings, and for technical reasons of an impeccably neoclassical kind private insurance cannot do the job.[8] The other, which is synchronic rather than diachronic, is that it is just for undeserved misfortunes to be compensated. The notion put about by some people that the welfare state runs contrary to the principle of desert is entirely false. On the contrary, its central features (each of my first four categories in one way or another) are applications of the notion of desert in its negative form: that those who suffer through no fault of their own have a valid claim against the more fortunate.

Notes

I am grateful to my commentator at the Welfare State conference, Rudolf Klein, for his painstaking and very helpful reconstruction of my analysis. Thanks are also due to Robert Goodin for editorial suggestions. A substantially similar version of the chapter appears in *Ethics* 100 (1990) 503–29.

1. Wellman (1982) is so besotted by the poor law paradigm that he explicitly condemns all 'categorical' programmes; for him the ideal welfare system is AFDC and he proposes it as the model for all cash benefits. Other recent writers do not explicitly reject anything that goes beyond the poor law, but they do not argue in favour of it either. These include Goodin (1988), Held (1984: esp. 184–5) and Plant et al. (1980: ch. 4).

2. If this question is taken to be one of legal rights, the answer is uninterestingly 'yes', since any system that creates entitlements according to some formula may be said to create rights. This was equally so under the poor law as in any contemporary welfare state. If it is understood in any other way it is merely a way of asking about the reasons for having some system of legal rights to cash benefits, but one that carries with it the misleading impression that the answer lies in discovering some system of ghostly entitlements on which real entitlements should be modelled.

3. When workers had to pursue claims through the tort system, it was estimated that they got 36 cents in the dollar, the remaining 64 cents being dissipated in legal expenses (Tishler, 1971: 117). A recent estimate is that in the USA 'only 37.5 cents of each premium dollar of products liability insurance ever reaches the pockets of claimants. Lawyers, insurance companies, expert witnesses, and courts retain the remaining 62.5 cents' (Anon, 1980: 916). In Britain the administrative cost of the tort system was estimated at 48 per cent of the total costs in 1923, while Beveridge

put it at 46.5 per cent 20 years later (see Brown, 1984: 129–30). A more recent estimate puts the claimant's share as 54p in the pound (Atiyah, 1970: 511).

4. William Beveridge expressed the classical conception in his Report as follows: 'On marriage a woman gains a legal right by her husband as a first line of defence against the risks which fall directly on the solitary woman. The attitude of the housewife to gainful employment outside the home is not and should not be the same as the single woman. She has other duties' (quoted by Donnison, 1982: 117).

5. As Richard Titmuss (1969: 46) pointed out, the history of the system of tax allowances 'shows the growth in public concern and responsibility of "states of dependency", family and kinship relationships, individual "self-improvement" and standards of "minimum subsistence" among income taxpayers . . . and that, for the purposes of social policy, [taxation] can no longer be thought of simply as a way of benefiting the poor at the expense of the rich.'

6. Here Brown (1982: 234) is quoting the Ministry of Social Security (1952: 29).

7. The thesis that the alternative to the poor law is income maintenance is encapsulated in the subtitle of Hugh Heclo's (1974) study – *From Relief to Income Maintenance*.

8. For a lucid discussion of this see Barr (1987).

References

Anon (1980) 'Note: Compensating victims of occupational disease', *Harvard Law Review*, 93: 916–37.

Atiyah, P.S. (1970) *Accidents, Compensation and the Law*. London: Weidenfeld and Nicolson.

Atkinson, A.B. (1975) *The Economics of Inequality*. Oxford: Clarendon Press.

Barr, Nicholas (1987) *The Economics of the Welfare State*. London: Weidenfeld and Nicolson.

Brown, Joan C. (1982) *Disability Income Part 1: Industrial Injuries*. London: Policy Studies Institute.

Brown, Joan C. (1984) *Disability Income Part 2: The Disability System*. London: Policy Studies Institute.

Conan Doyle, A. (1967) 'A scandal in Bohemia', pp. 346–57 in W.S. Baring-Gould (ed.), *The Annotated Sherlock Holmes*. New York: Clarkson N. Potter.

Congressional Budget Office (1982) *Disability Compensation: Current Issues and Options for Change*. Washington, DC: Government Printing Office.

Cornford, F.M. (1906) *Microcosmographia Academica*. London: Bowes and Bowes.

Donnison, David (1982) *The Politics of Poverty*. Oxford: Martin Robertson.

Furniss, Norman and Tilton, Timothy (1977) *The Case for the Welfare State: From Social Security to Social Equality*. Bloomington: Indiana University Press.

Goodin, Robert E. (1988) *Reasons for Welfare*. Princeton, NJ: Princeton University Press.

Heclo, Hugh (1974) *Modern Social Politics in Britain and Sweden: From Relief to Income Maintenance*. New Haven, Conn.: Yale University Press.

Heidenheimer, Arnold J. (1981) 'Education and social security entitlements in Europe and America', pp. 269–304 in Peter Flora and Arnold J. Heidenheimer (eds), *The Development of Welfare States in Europe and America*. New Brunswick, NJ: Transaction Books.

Held, Virginia (1984) *Rights and Goods: Justifying Social Action*. New York: Free Press.

Ison, Terence G. (1980) *Accident Compensation: A Commentary on the New Zealand Scheme*. London: Croom Helm.

Jallade, Jean-Pierre (1985) 'Redistribution and the welfare state: An assessment of the French socialists' performance', *Government and Opposition*, 20: 343–55.

Ministry of Social Security (1952) *Annual Report*. London: HMSO.

Page, Talbot (1986) 'Responsibility, liability and incentive compatibility', *Ethics*, 97: 240–62.

Plant, Raymond, Lesser, Harry and Taylor-Gooby, Peter (1980) *Political Philosophy and Social Welfare: Essays on the Normative Basis of Welfare Provision*. London: Routledge & Kegan Paul.

Rainwater, Lee (n.d.) 'A sociologist's view of the income maintenance experiments', pp. 194–201 in Alicia H. Munnell (ed.), *Lessons from the Income Maintenance Experiments*. Boston: Federal Reserve Bank of Boston Conference Series, No. 30.

Tishler, Hace Sorel (1971) *Self-reliance and Social Security 1870–1917*. Port Washington, NY: Kennikat Press.

Titmuss, Richard H. (1969) *Essays on 'The Welfare State'*. Boston: Beacon Press (first published 1958).

Walley, Sir John (1972) *Social Security: Another British Failure?* London: Charles Knight and Co.

Wellman, Carl (1982) *Welfare Rights*. Totowa, NJ: Rowman and Allanheld.

6
Models of Old-age Pensions

Joakim Palme

There seems to be a growing awareness among comparative researchers that institutional aspects of the welfare state are important for a wide range of issues, not only for the consequences of welfare state expansion but also for understanding the factors behind its growth. But empirical studies of the welfare state have mostly used published social expenditure data to identify sources of cross-national commonality and variation,[1] and these data do not capture institutional differences, at least not directly. There is therefore a need, as has recently been emphasized by a number of scholars, to reorient the comparative analysis of social policy.[2]

Behind the common concern for a better understanding of institutional differences, however, are rather divergent perspectives and hypotheses. One strategy, going back to Titmuss's (1974) notion of 'models of social policy', has been to distinguish between different 'models' or 'policy regimes'. A closer look at Titmuss's and later attempts to classify social policies reveals that a number of issues are involved, that researchers have different aims with their classifications and that, as a consequence, the character of the models which have been distinguished varies substantially.

An underlying hypothesis in the present chapter is that social policy institutions differ across nations, and that they change over time, because they are outcomes of political processes involving different and contradictory values, principles, ideologies and class interests (Esping-Andersen and Korpi, 1984). Outcomes have been patterned by the relative strength of the 'social actors' involved, by the pressure of demographic changes, and by economic opportunities and constraints facing the actors. Moreover, it must be recognized that social policy institutions in each country have been subject to influence from different and contradictory interests and ideologies. In order not to confuse the concepts it is thus important to define what the classifications are aiming at, and to which analytical level they refer.

In this chapter, the old-age pension will be used as a test case.

This is a strategy of getting closer to welfare state institutions and away from the aggregate study of the welfare state. The case of pensions is interesting for various reasons. With education and health care, they constitute the largest part of social welfare expenditures. Furthermore, the study of pension systems can be expected to have important consequences for poverty, inequality, labour supply, savings and so on.

The purpose here is to arrive at a system classification of old-age pensions in 18 OECD countries (see below) that reflects the more institutional aspects of pension entitlements. The general idea is to simplify a complex pattern of similarities and differences, and 'classification' is a way of handling both commonality and variation without neglecting fundamental aspects (Everitt, 1981). It is also a purpose of this chapter, and indeed a necessary precondition for classifying the countries, to conceptualize and measure different aspects of old-age pension entitlements across nations and over time.

The chapter is organized in the following way: first is a section on how to conceptualize different aspects of welfare state variations in pension entitlements. Secondly, the general development trends on some of these aspects are delineated. Thirdly, the role of different principles for benefit provisions are depicted. Fourthly, a reformulated set of models of pensions are confronted with empirical data on pensions in 18 OECD countries. Finally, the implications of the findings are discussed.

Welfare state variation in social entitlements

The rise of modern social security legislation marked an important break with the earlier poor law systems, at least as regards the responsibilities of the state. Starting with Bismarck's social security legislation in the 1880s, economic support from the state was tied to a number of rather broadly defined situations of work incapacity, such as sickness and old age, and not to poverty alone. But entitlements to support have also been dependent on additional criteria. These additional criteria, I would argue, are important for understanding the differences between welfare state institutions, and very much so in the case of pensions.

In this regard, an interesting point of departure for the study of the institutional aspects of social entitlements, or social rights, is provided by T.H. Marshall (1950). According to his analytic scheme, the welfare state is the third stage in the development of citizenship, the first two being the attainment of civil rights (equality before the courts) and political rights (universal suffrage). Marshall saw welfare state provisions as a set of rights aimed at securing a decent living for every citizen. Contrary to the traditional poor laws which deprived beneficiaries of their citizenship rights, the new kinds of social security legislation which have appeared in the last century could be seen as an extension of these rights.[3]

Public old-age pensions can no doubt be seen as a set of social *citizenship* rights and thus well suited as a test case. However, it is vital to recognize that social entitlements are often not based solely on citizenship. Two other important principles behind the provision of benefits are *need*[4] and *work merit*. Together, these three principles will guide the discussion of old-age pension entitlements in this chapter.[5]

Citizenship is the basis for citizenship-right pensions, or 'people's pensions' as they have been called in the Scandinavian countries. Need is the guiding principle in means- or income-tested pension programmes, while work merit is the underlying principle in work- and earnings-related programmes. Thus, an underlying dimension of public old-age pension rights is the *qualifying conditions*[6] for benefit entitlement. Citizenship, or permanent residence, is in a way the most unambiguous condition for acquiring a right to a pension; once pension age is reached the benefit is paid more or less automatically.[7] It is more complicated to qualify for a pension on the basis of need. Means- or income-testing automatically excludes the well-to-do and, because of ignorance and the stigma of testing, not all of those who in principle would be entitled to benefits will claim them. Eligibility criteria based on work merit is another way of sharpening the qualifying conditions. The right to most work-merit pensions is based on contributions and is related to the size of these contributions, i.e. to the size of previous income. These dimensions of the qualifying aspects determine the conditions of eligibility and the size of pensions.

Although there are and have been social policy systems that rest on a single qualification principle, in practice most of the systems represent mixes of two or all three of the principles; citizenship, need and work merit. The prominence of these principles have consequences for the distribution of social entitlements in several respects, not least on the size and structure of benefits. Before we turn to these relationships it might be useful to examine which dimensions of public pension entitlements we can distinguish.

The outcomes of the conditions outlined above are reflected along two dimensions, the *coverage* and *adequacy* of old-age pensions. There are two aspects of the coverage of pensions (a) the formal *entitlement* to pensions among those of working age, i.e. the proportion of people that have formal rights to a future pension; and (b) the actual recipience rate among those above pension age, i.e. the proportion of those above normal pension age who actually receive some sort of public old-age pension.

Citizenship-based pensions imply both a universal entitlement and recipience rates. With such pension programmes, all those who are citizens in a country automatically have the right to a future benefit; and, among the elderly, everyone will receive a pension regardless of the size of his or her income and wealth. With the purely needs-tested programmes, entitlements among those of working age can be considered to be zero since the right to receive a future pension is dependent on the person's future income and wealth, which are not known. For reasons outlined above, the recipience of needs-based pensions will not be complete. The coverage of work-merit-based programmes will be dependent on the current and past labour force participation rates, as well as on the existence of exclusions from insurance of any segments of the labour force. Also, rules for contribution will vary across nations, some demanding longer contribution periods than others, thus in the end lowering the recipience (and benefit levels, for that matter).

The adequacy of benefits is not easy to predict from the principles of citizenship, need and work merit. However, a few things can be noted, especially concerning the structure of benefits. Here it is fruitful to distinguish between two sub-dimensions of adequacy: (a) *basic security* and (b) *income security* (Myles, 1984). Citizenship and needs-based pension programmes typically aim at providing an adequate minimum, leaving it open, however, at what level an adequate minimum is reached. Work-merit pensions are typically tied to contributions and the level of previous earnings, thus aiming at some degree of income security. To sum up: citizenship pensions are paid at a flat rate; needs-tested pensions are in practice flat-rate for those with no other income but reduced for others; and work-merit pensions will in principle follow the structure of earnings.[8]

Trends in the development of pension entitlements

The focus in this chapter will be on the scope and adequacy of benefits since the underlying interest is in the welfare outcomes of the pension systems.[9] Since the basic interest is in the quality of pensions as social citizenship rights, it also seems fruitful to restrict the analysis to legislated programmes, despite the fact that individual and collective private pensions can be very important as a source of income and are subject to substantial cross-national variation. Therefore, the only pensions included are those which have been created through national legislation, the conditions concerning entitlements of which are regulated by the state and/or which are financed by the state.[10]

Data on pension rights have been compiled for 11 time-points (1930, 1933, 1939, 1947, 1950, 1955, 1960, 1965, 1970, 1975 and 1980) and for 18 countries (Australia, Austria, Belgium, Canada, Denmark, Finland, France, Germany, Ireland, Italy, Japan, the Netherlands, New Zealand, Norway, Sweden, Switzerland, the United Kingdom and the United States). The following indicators of pension rights have been used in the analysis that will be presented below: (1) entitlements, (2) recipience (3) citizenship-based pension, (4) minimum pension, (5) worker's minimum pension, (6) standard worker pension, (7) maximum pension (see appendix for a more detailed definition of these indicators).

The first legislated pension programmes, for other than very limited occupational groups such as civil servants and miners, can be classified roughly into two categories: on the one hand, pensions based primarily on means or income testing (in the following referred to as needs-testing) and, on the other, pensions that were primarily based on the insurance principle. Some countries had both kinds of programmes very early while in other countries the insurance system had a needs-tested component. About half of the countries fall into the first category where needs-tested programmes were introduced first (the date within parentheses indicates the year of legislation): Australia (1908), Canada (1927), Denmark (1891), France (1905), Ireland 1908; 1924), New Zealand (1898), Norway (1936) and the UK (1908). Of these countries, France (1910) and the UK (1925) had introduced social insurance pensions before 1930. Austria (1906), Belgium (1924, wage-labourers; and 1925, salaried), Finland (1937), Germany (1889), Italy (1919), Japan (1941), the Netherlands (1913), Sweden (1913), Switzerland (1946), and the United States (1935) legislated for insurance pensions first.

In Austria the first insurance system only covered salaried employees and needs-tested pensions were in the end introduced (1927) before insurance pensions were implemented for wage-labourers (1938). In Finland and Sweden the insurance-based benefits did not achieve any importance; instead the means-tested 'supplements' constituted the major part of the pension for those who retired. The difference between the latter two countries was that all citizens above pension age in Sweden could claim the pension, whereas eligibility in Finland was restricted to previous contributors according to the 1937 law. Switzerland and the United States introduced two-tiered systems from the very start, with insurance pensions for those on the labour market complemented by needs-tested benefits for those with insufficient income in old age. Some of the other countries with insurance pensions had needs-tested supplements during the 'transitional periods'.[11]

Thus, by 1930, 13 out of our 18 countries had already legislated about some sort of public old-age pension programmes. By 1950, all of the countries paid out some sort of public old-age pensions. Since the early 1930s the expansion of both the scope and adequacy of pensions has been pervasive. On average, entitlement and recipience as well as replacement rates have more than doubled between 1930 and 1980.

In 1930, just above 20 per cent of those aged 15 to 64 were on average (across 18 countries) covered by old-age pension insurance. Entitlements increased during the second half of the 1930s and growth continued during the Second World War. In the late 1940s and early 1950s growth remained high, but the real boom came between 1955 and 1960. The growth since then has been less rapid, though continuing even in the late 1970s. In 1980 the average entitlement rate reached almost 80 per cent. Countries with work-related programmes have had a rather gradual extension of entitlements with increasing labour force participation and growing importance of wage labour. In some countries, entitlements have been widened with the inclusion of previously excluded occupational groups.[12] When work-related programmes have been introduced in countries with no existing pension programmes the entitlement rate was increased sharply in connection with the implementation of the laws – but only gradually thereafter. In countries where universal pensions based on citizenship have been introduced, entitlements have often changed very dramatically, often from 0 to 100 per cent.

The average recipience rate tripled from 30 per cent in 1930 to about 90 per cent in 1980, i.e. the recipience is near-universal in all the 18 countries. It is not surprising, due to the existence of needs-tested pensions, that the recipience rate is higher than the entitlement rate. Turning to the adequacy of benefits, and here the discussion will be limited to two of the indicators, worker's minimum and standard worker pensions (both for single householders), it can first be noted that their averages tripled (or more) over the 50 years from 1930 to 1980. The net replacement rate for the standard worker averaged 14 per cent in 1930; fifty years later, it had increased to 55 per cent. For worker's minimum the corresponding averages of net replacement rates were 10 and 30 per cent respectively. There is a tendency towards differentiating the levels of standard worker pensions from the worker's minimum benefits, and fewer countries have identical levels for the two kinds of benefits in 1980 than in 1955, for example.

Among these 18 countries there is also a trend towards increased commonality in entitlement and replacement levels as measured by the coefficient of variation (the standard deviation divided by the mean). This convergence trend was less rapid in the 1970s but did in fact continue at least up to 1980.

Citizenship, need and work merit

If we look on the qualifying conditions behind the benefit provisions, the variation is greater than if benefit levels alone are considered. The presentation of the results started with the distinction between countries that had legislated work-related pensions and countries that had legislated needs-tested pensions. This illustrates how different principles, of work merit and of need, were guiding the early legislation. Since the first laws were implemented, the citizenship principle has been introduced and most countries have developed mixes of the three principles. By 1980, only a few of the 18 countries (see below) relied on a single one of the three principles. The development has been gradual and complex and in the following only a few comments can be offered about the extension of the different principles.

A few main paths of development can be delineated. First, countries with work-merit pensions have introduced complementary needs-tested 'basic' pensions, leaving only the Federal Republic of Germany with a purely work-merit system in 1980 (and social assistance for those who did not qualify). Secondly, countries with primarily means-tested programmes have introduced citizenship pensions, and then some of these latter countries have introduced work-merit pensions as a third component.

The first path has been followed by Austria (1955),[13] Belgium (1969), Italy (1965) and Japan (1959). Switzerland and the USA had, from the beginning, introduced two-tiered systems where the needs-tested programme clearly constituted the second tier. The Swiss system implied universal entitlement for all citizens since the government paid contributions for citizens outside the labour force (such as housewives and students). However, the basic pensions were – in the end – tied to needs-testing. The work-merit programmes in Finland, the Netherlands, and Sweden were either discontinued or never of any significance. By the early post-

Second World War period, needs-tested pensions dominated in all three countries, and (with the possible exception of the Netherlands) it would not be too far-fetched to consider these latter three countries in a post-war perspective as 'needs-testing starters'.

The second path has been followed by Australia (1974), Canada (1951), Denmark (1960), New Zealand (1938,[14] 1976), and Norway (1957) and, in a slightly different way, by Finland (1955), the Netherlands (see below) and Sweden (1946). Later, Canada (1956), Denmark (1964), Finland (1961), Norway (1966) and Sweden (1959) brought in work-related benefits, thus following an extension of the second path. After the war, the Netherlands introduced needs-tested 'emergency pensions', preparing the ground for the 1956 law which reformed the pension system by introducing contributory pensions for all residents. The government pays contributions for those with low incomes, resulting in universal coverage.[15] Ultimately, the entitlement to pensions is dependent only on residence and not on contributions. For those who do not fulfil the residence requirements, pensions are paid at a reduced rate but without needs-testing. The full pensions are not income-related, only related to years of contributions like the Danish work-merit pensions.

France, Ireland, and the UK have followed a different path when first legislating needs-tested pensions and later, work-related benefits. France and the UK had done this by 1930. The needs-tested benefits in France were marginal from the start and remained so with the introduction of work-related programmes. New laws in France were implemented on needs-tested benefits during the 1940s but their character has remained complementary, even if the level of minimum pensions was raised sharply in the beginning of the 1980s. The first (1925) work-related pensions in Britain were integrated with the needs-tested programme from 1908. After the Second World War, the work-merit system became pre-eminent and needs-tested pensions were relegated to supplementing work-related benefits. In Britain, two attempts have been made at instituting income-related pensions. The first programme, legislated in 1959, has failed to provide adequate pensions and the second, implemented in 1978 (SERPS), has yet to prove its viability. By 1980 the benefits paid under this scheme were still insignificant as the system was not mature. Ireland legislated work-merit but flat-rate pensions as late as 1960 and 1971. The level of benefits by 1980 still did not differ much between the work-merit system(s) and the needs-testing programme in Ireland.[16]

To sum up, it seems as if the early development of pension

institutions was important for their later development. Countries which introduced work-merit programmes early seem to have stuck to this principle, introducing needs-tested programmes as complements, while countries with needs-tested systems have introduced the citizenship principle. It seems fruitful to speak about institutional effects in these terms.

Turning to the level and structure of benefits, we can first state that there is no deterministic relationship between the qualifying conditions and the size of benefits. Although there is a clear tendency for work-merit pensions to be aimed at giving income security and thus to be higher, the observed cross-national differences cannot be fully explained in these terms. Neither is there a clear ranking over time between, on the one hand, countries relying on the citizenship principle, and, on the other, countries relying on needs-testing. As noted above, however, there has in the post-war years been a growing tendency for differentiation of benefit levels. On average, minimum pensions tend to get smaller in relation to standard worker pensions.

If we start by looking at standard worker pensions in 1930, it turns out that German pensions replaced 37 per cent of an average production worker's wage, at that time the highest rate among the 18 countries. Most of the other countries had replacement rates below 20 per cent and there was no clear ranking between work-merit and needs-tested pensions. By 1955 a more distinct pattern was emerging. France, Germany, Italy and the USA all had standard worker pensions replacing about 40 per cent of previous earnings and in Austria this rate was 71 per cent! In Denmark, the Netherlands and New Zealand, needs-tested pensions replaced about a third of an average production worker's wage. Even if both work-merit and needs-tested systems are found among the rest of the countries, replacing less of lost earnings, a tendency towards differentiation between replacement levels of different kinds of systems is clear. This tendency is more pronounced in 1980, though exceptions are still at hand, and, as noted above, the differentiation of benefit levels within countries is still even more striking.

In figure 6.1, three different kinds of replacement rates are delineated for the 18 OECD countries in 1980. The rates are expressed as percentages of an average production worker's wage (APWW), benefits and wages net of taxes. The size of the *standard worker pension*, assuming 35 years of full-time work with an APWW before retirement, is indicated by the entire bars, i.e. when the different portions are added. If the darkest portions are excluded, the bars indicate the size of the *minimum pension*, i.e.

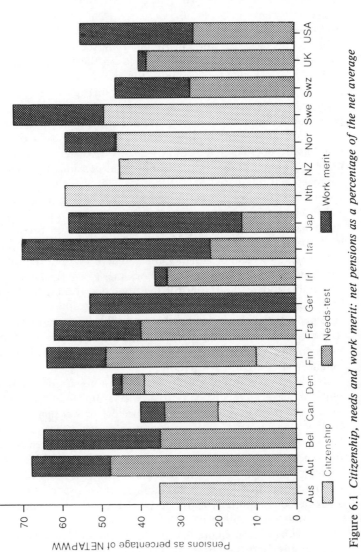

Figure 6.1 *Citizenship, needs and work merit: net pensions as a percentage of the net average production worker's wage (NETAPWW)*

the size of benefits after needs-testing but also including benefits paid on the basis of citizenship. The lightest portions of the bars indicate the size of the third kind of replacement rate, the *citizenship-based pension*. It should perhaps be noted that the darkest portion of the bars does not indicate the size of the whole benefit paid on the basis of work merit but only the difference between work-merit pensions and pensions paid on the basis of citizenship and/or need. Thus, for example, the standard worker in France received a pension entirely based on work merit, and in Finland the standard worker did not get the needs-tested part of the minimum pension but still arrived at a replacement rate of about 65 per cent.

By 1980 about half of the countries had some kind of citizenship-based benefits. Some countries paid needs-tested pensions on top of those pensions, while the minimum pensions in other countries were entirely based on needs-testing. As was noted earlier, the Federal Republic of Germany had no such basic pensions.

The highest replacement rates for the standard worker appear in countries like Austria, Belgium, Finland, Italy and Sweden. The highest minimum pensions are to be found in Austria, Denmark, Finland, New Zealand, Norway and Sweden. Figure 6.1 shows that only countries with some kind of work-merit benefits have replacement rates above 50 per cent for the standard worker. On the other hand, citizenship- and needs-based pensions in some countries exceeded the levels of work-merit pensions in some of the other countries. The citizenship pensions in the Scandinavian countries, for example, were higher than the work-merit pensions in Canada, Ireland and the United Kingdom.

When it comes to citizenship-based pensions versus needs-tested pensions, levels are difficult to predict from what principle lies behind the provision of benefits. Figure 6.1 shows that there are a number of countries with comparatively low needs-tested minimums, such as Italy, Japan, Switzerland and the United States. It also shows that citizenship benefits were low in Canada and Finland, although the needs-tested supplements granted a fairly high minimum pension in these countries too. Austria paid out high needs-tested minimums, at the level of the citizenship pensions in the Scandinavian countries.

It is evident from figure 6.1 that the structure of benefits varies considerably both in terms of levels and in terms of differences between minimum and standard worker pensions. A majority of the countries seem to provide for adequate income security, what Myles (1988) has labelled 'the retirement wage'. Most countries pay minimum pensions at a third of the APWW after tax (NETAPWW), which might be considered as adequate, but this is in many cases only thanks to the needs-tested benefits. Some countries provide for both basic security and income security, while it is doubtful if either of these goals is achieved in other cases. This is something to which we will return in the following section where also entitlement, take-up, and maximum pensions will be taken into consideration.

Models of pensions

The different attempts to model social policy development reflect differences in perspectives and purposes. Drawing on the recent work of, inter alia, Titmuss (1974), Korpi (1980) and Esping-Andersen (1982, 1985) I suggest that the models of social policy would have to satisfy the following four criteria. First, if social policy is best understood in a class-political perspective, then the classification has to reflect class-political differences. Secondly, the classification should reflect the relative importance of different principles for benefit provisions, i.e. citizenship, need, and work merit. Thirdly, since perhaps the most profound aspect of welfare state benefits is that they provide a source of income independent from the market, and thus more or less violate the market principle, the classification has to capture the degree of market independence provided by the benefits. Fourthly, since, in addition to simplifying complex patterns, the classification of systems is supposed to serve as a starting-point for the study of the effects of institutional variation, the classification should be relevant for investigating issues such as the size of public and private pension expenditure, poverty and inequality among the elderly, savings, and labour supply.

The system of classification that will be suggested for these purposes includes four categories. There are important and evident similarities with the previously defined models. The categories are defined to be applied, more or less exclusively, in the case of old-age pensions even though it might also be possible to elaborate the classification to encompass other branches of social policy. The empirical analysis of models will focus on the situation in 1980. This is not just for reasons of simplification. It was only by that date that pension systems in most of our 18 countries began to mature. If we want to compare institutions it seems more fruitful to do that by the time they really are 'institutionalized'.[17]

The first model is labelled *the work-merit model*.[18] Here the intention is for adequate pensions for those who are working for wages, to give compensation for loss of income. In several countries classified in this category, pensions are still separated by occupation, thus emphasizing the status-maintaining aspect of the benefit provisions. Pensions in this model should also provide income security for occupational groups other than industrial workers. Classification into this model requires the following characteristics in terms of our indicators: the net standard worker pension should at least replace half of the average production worker's wage after tax *and* the maximum pension replace more than 100 per cent of the average production worker's wage *and* minimum benefits should not be granted as citizenship rights.

The second model is labelled *the citizenship model* and is in a way the outcome of the chronologically second type of pension that was instituted, for example, in Denmark as early as 1891. This type of pension gave all the elderly a right, in principle, to a pension. However, through needs-testing, those who had 'adequate' incomes were excluded. Later, the principle of needs-testing was abolished in a number of countries, thereby bringing the citizenship principle to the fore. The introduction of the citizenship principle meant that the family and the market were abandoned as the primary channels of welfare. It is also a requirement that the pensions in this model provide for an adequate minimum. In terms of our indicators the following conditions have to be fulfilled for classification into this model: the entitlement rate is 100 per cent *and* the right to the pension is based on citizenship *and* minimum pensions should replace at least one-third of the NETAPWW; benefits based on work merit should not increase the replacement rate by more than 10 per cent.

In the third model both universalism based on citizenship and adequate benefits have been realized. It has been labelled *the institutional model* since the need for both basic security and income security has been provided for, thus crowding out the scope of market-based solutions for social security. In this model the entitlement rate is 100 per cent *and* based on the citizenship principle *and* the minimum pension replaces at least one-third *and* the standard worker pension replaces at least half of the average production worker's wage after tax.

The countries classified into the fourth *residual model* have public pensions that give neither basic security nor income security, i.e. pensions are not adequate and/or they do not cover all the elderly. This model has been labelled residual since it in practice assumes a heavy reliance on market solutions. Thus, in the residual model, standard worker pensions replace less than half of the average production worker's wage *or* the maximum pension replaces less than 100 per cent of the average production worker's wage *and* minimum pensions are not adequate nor granted as citizenship rights. (All replacements refer to benefits and wages after tax.)

Table 6.1 *Models of old-age pensions in 18 OECD countries,
and benefit levels in 1980 (mean, minimum and maximum of
minimum pensions and standard worker pensions of the
countries in the respective models)*

	Institutional	Citizenship	Work-merit	Residual
	Finland	Australia	Austria	France
	Netherlands	Canada	Belgium	Ireland
	Norway	Denmark	Germany	UK
	Sweden	New Zealand	Italy	USA
			Japan	Switzerland
Minimum pension				
mean	51	40	22[1]	33
min	46	33	0	27
max	59	45	48	41
Standard worker pension				
mean	64	42	63	48
min	59	35	53	36
max	72	47	70	62

[1] Excluding Germany where the minimum pension, according to the definition used here, is zero, yielded a mean of 28 per cent.

Using the criteria defined above yields the classification of countries as displayed in table 6.1. It should first be noted that all the countries have started in the residual model, i.e. no country met the qualifications for any of the other models as early as the 1930s. Starting with Austria moving into the work-merit model, and Denmark into the citizenship model,[19] most of the countries have qualified into either the work-merit, citizenship, or institutional models. In 1980 Austria, Belgium, Germany, Italy and Japan were classified into the work-merit model; Australia, Canada, Denmark and New Zealand into the citizenship model; Finland, the Netherlands, Norway and Sweden into the institutional model; France, Ireland, Switzerland, the UK and the USA remained in the residual model.

The definition of categories is naturally somewhat arbitrary at the margin. It is evident that some of the countries are close to categories that they have not been classified into. France and the United States come close to the work-merit model.[20] Switzerland and the United Kingdom are fairly close to both the citizenship and the work-merit models.[21] Australia and Canada are near the residual model due to their reliance on needs-testing.[22] In 1980, Finland is rather close to the work-merit model and the

Netherlands a little problematic when it comes to pension rights among married women.[23]

Nevertheless, the four models capture fundamental differences in the scope, adequacy and structure of old-age pensions in these 18 countries. This is to some degree also illustrated in table 6.1 where the average replacement levels of the minimum and standard worker pensions are given for the respective models. On average, the benefit levels follow the expected pattern with the highest minimum pensions in the institutional and citizenship models, and the highest standard worker pensions in the work-merit and institutional models. The residual model lags behind somewhat in both cases, although standard worker pensions are, on average, higher than in the citizenship model.

Conclusion

A massive growth of public old-age pension entitlements and expenditures is a common feature of all the most developed welfare capitalist nations. However, the results presented in this chapter show, in the case of old-age pensions, that there are substantial differences in qualifying conditions behind benefit provisions, in the scope of the programmes, and in the level and structure of benefits. We thus need data and methods that can handle both commonality and variation along different dimensions.

But comparative studies of welfare state provisions have largely relied on expenditure rates. We have tried in this chapter to conceptualize pensions as social rights and then to distinguish between different aspects of these rights. By looking for different patterns in the structure of benefits we have also attempted to reorient the focus of the comparative study of pensions towards the more institutional aspects of the systems. A rather complex pattern of cross-national similarities and differences has emerged.

Four different pension models were identified, each representing a unique combination of scope, level and structure of benefits; the citizenship model, the work-merit model, the institutional model and the residual model. Even if old-age pensions are multidimensional, and every system has its own peculiarities, there appears to be enough common ground to make it fruitful to talk about models of pensions. Classification seems to be a way of handling both commonality and variation without disregarding vital aspects of the phenomena under study.

Although I believe that there is merit in accurate description, which is often lacking in comparative welfare state research, the usefulness of the classification should also be tested in analysing, for example, the effects of old-age pensions on poverty and inequality among the elderly. Needs and contributions, however defined, apparently have very different impacts on the entitlements to pensions. The relative importance of these principles varies across nations and the consequences of these differences for the variation in economic welfare in the elderly populations are likely to be substantial (Kohl, 1988; Palme, 1989). The welfare state as a system of stratification certainly deserves our attention in future research. It also remains to explain the observed differences in pension entitlements. For this purpose a multi-factorial approach seems to be most fruitful. Beside economic and demographic factors, political and institutional conditions can be expected to be important (Palme, 1988).

Appendix

Old-age pension variables

The preparation of the database that has been utilized in the present chapter has involved a major effort on the part of a number of country experts. The result is a data-set (SSIB data) that in several respects is superior to what has earlier been used in the comparative research on, for example, pensions. First, a large number of countries have been studied and this over a comparatively long time-period. Secondly, data is organized in variable form to allow for the use of quantitative methods. Thirdly, the comparability of the statistics has been improved with the use of ideal-type cases and standardized definitions. Fourthly, benefit-levels are more comparable since the effect of income-taxation has been calculated.

The variables used for the purposes of this chapter have been calculated as indicated below. The following should be noted concerning all the replacement rates; (a) they are expressed as percentages of an average production worker's wage (APWW), (b) benefits and wages have been taxed when subject to income taxation, (c) benefits have been calculated for single householders.

Entitlement refers to the number of people that have the right to a future pension. It is expressed as a percentage of the population aged 15 to 64. In insurance schemes entitlement is equal to the percentage of that population contributing to legislated pension programmes. Those covered by public employers' pensions have also been included. In countries with only needs-tested pensions, the entitlement rate is set to zero since the entitlement to a future pension is dependent on the person's future income and wealth, which are not known. Entitlement rates are 100 per cent in countries with citizenship-based pensions.

Recipience is the number of recipients of (legislated) pensions and is expressed as a percentage of the population above normal pension age. Recipients of means-tested pensions have been included. It should again be noted that the normal pension age varies across nations, and over time, and that low pension age can be seen as a matter of pension generosity, or pension-quality, though this has not been accounted for here.

Citizenship-based pension is the benefit for a single person provided on the basis of citizenship, i.e. without needs-testing.

Minimum pension is the pension provided for a single person after needs-testing (but also including benefits based on citizenship).

Worker's minimum pension reflects the pension of a worker with low earnings who only meets the minimum, rather than the 'full', contribution conditions. Benefit provision involves needs-testing in some countries. In reality, the worker's minimum pensions in the different countries have rather different characters: citizenship-based, needs-tested pensions, and/or work-merit.

Standard worker pension has been calculated assuming that the 'standard worker' has worked 35 years before retirement with the average earnings of a production worker in manufacturing and that he retires at the end of the year of measurement. This means that this variable measures the replacement rate for a newly retired 'ideal-type worker'. It is not an average for all retired people with a similar work record.

Maximum pension is the maximum benefit paid to a single householder within the major public pension system. Benefits have been calculated assuming that the beneficiary has fulfilled the maximum contribution period and has had earnings at the maximum level for benefit purposes, and that he retires at the end of the year of measurement.

Notes

This chapter is part of a study on old-age pensions in a comparative perspective that I am working on with support from the Swedish Commission for Social Research. The data on pensions that is presented is part of a larger data-set on the development of social policy in 18 OECD countries (SSIB data) that has been compiled at the Swedish Institute for Social Research in Stockholm. In revising the first draft of the chapter I have benefited from comments from the participants of the ECPR workshop in Paris, especially Stein Kuhnle, my colleagues at the Swedish Institute for Social Research, and Olli Kangas. I wish to thank Bob Goodin for providing me with very useful editorial and other suggestions in preparing the manuscript, and Alan Ware for his excellent work in organizing the ECPR workshop.

1. Cutright (1967), Wilensky (1975), Castles (1982), Pampel and Williamson (1985, 1988).

2. Alber (1988), Esping-Andersen (1987), Korpi (1989), Therborn (1986).

3. However, a problem is that Marshall himself did not elaborate how, for example, the distribution of welfare provisions could be expected to vary, nor did he develop a comparative perspective on these matters. Yet it is apparent that there are important distributional differences between individuals within countries, and that the distributional pattern varies in a cross-national perspective.

4. In this chapter the principle of need is rather narrowly defined and refers to situations when the individual household's economic circumstances demand support. An alternative would be, in the case of pensions, to consider age per se to be a sufficient criterion for economic support. Needs-testing will be used as a common denomination for means- and income-testing disregarding the differences in the testing rules actually applied in the various countries over time.

5. It goes without saying that *age* is a crucial condition for qualifying for old-age pensions. The question of retirement age will, however, be treated very briefly in the discussion even if it is subject to interesting cross-national differences (see Tracy, 1979). But the question of retirement age is intricate and brings the

questions of early retirement, long-term unemployment, and disability among the older workers into the discussion (see Laczko and Walker, 1986) and here that would lead too far. It is a subject that deserves a chapter of its own.

6. Apart from the conditions discussed below there are also other qualifications of relevance, e.g. income ceilings, residence tests, the treatment of married women, and minority discrimination. Income ceilings excluded high earners from entitlement to pensions in work-merit programmes. Residence tests can disqualify those who have not been permanently living in the country from either citizenship or needs-tested pensions. Married women are in some instances excluded from pension rights of their own. Minorities such as Australian Aborigines have been excluded from insurance.

7. In reality, so-called citizenship pensions are in some cases tied to contributions, as in Norway, although those with no income get automatic credit in Norway.

8. Another important dimension of social security pensions is the financing of the pensions. A few predictions can be made. First, work-merit pensions are generally financed via contributions, from the insured person and/or his/her employer. Secondly, needs-tested pensions are typically financed via taxation. Thirdly, while citizenship-based pensions are in reality financed in very different ways, individual contributions are never an ultimate condition for the receipt of benefit since low income earners and those without income get automatic credit by the state. Since many countries exhibit a mix of the different principles, the picture of the distribution of the financial burden is not so clear-cut.

9. The question of financing is of course vital for the understanding of what kind of redistribution occurs in the welfare state. But to capture these kinds of effects another type of approach, not taken up in this study, must be applied (Kohl, 1987; Ståhlberg, 1989).

10. The exclusion of individual and collective private pensions from this study is problematic since these pensions tend to be larger in countries with low public pensions (Esping-Andersen, 1987). But comparative research in this field has shown that the rank order between countries does not change when private pension spending is added to public pension spending (Rein and Rainwater, 1985). However, the relation between public and private pensions, and the effects of this mix on economic well-being and inequality among the elderly, falls outside the framework of this chapter (see however Kangas and Palme, 1989).

11. Sources for information about the first pension laws have been derived from: *Non-contributory Pensions* (ILO, 1933), *International Report of Social Services* (ILO, 1933), *International Report of Social Services* (ILO, 1936), *Social Security Legislation throughout the World 1949* (US Department of Health, 1949), and SSIB data.

12. In France, for example, the self-employed in agriculture were included in 1952 (SSIB data).

13. Austria's old needs-tested programme, which was tied to unemployment benefit, had by then been abolished.

14. In New Zealand, the 1938 Social Security Act introduced an old-age pension without needs-testing. However, this pension has remained very small. By 1950, it was only a quarter the size of the needs-tested pension and less than a tenth of the APWW.

15. The recipience was not universal, however, until 1985 when married women also got the entitlement independent of their husbands.

16. It should be mentioned that Finland and Canada by 1980 had needs-tested supplements to their citizenship pensions. It can also be noted that Australia re-introduced needs-testing in its pension programme in 1984, and Denmark introduced needs-testing for those below 70 years of age – a system previously applied in e.g. Australia. Finland abolished the income test for supplements to citizen-based pensions in 1985, and the size of the supplements is now only dependent on other pension income.

17. It is also possible that 1980 marks some kind of historical turning-point. With the 'golden years of economic growth' behind them, most OECD countries faced severe budget deficits and mass unemployment by that time and the merits of the welfare state were questioned. Comparative research on what happened to the modern welfare states during the 1980s has only just begun (see e.g. Alber, 1988).

18. This is not to say that welfare provisions are organized outside the public sector by occupational groups or on the firm level. Titmuss (1974) made the distinction between welfare provisions of a social, occupational or fiscal character. The work-merit model refers to pensions provided within the social (public and legislated) sphere and not in the occupational. Benefits in this model are occupational in the sense that they compensate for loss of earned income, not in the sense that they are organized outside the public social sector.

19. New Zealand introduced the citizenship principle as early as 1938, Sweden in the late 1940s, but benefit levels were too low in both countries (especially in New Zealand) for meeting the requirements of the *citizenship model* as defined above.

20. France and the United States would have qualified for the work-merit model in 1980 if standard worker pensions alone were considered (replacing 62 per cent and 55 per cent respectively), but they do not meet the criterion that net maximum pensions should be at least 100 per cent of the NETAPWW. Without the latter criterion France would have been classified as work merit in 1965, 1970 and 1980 and the United States as work merit in 1970 and 1980. But in 1975 standard worker pensions in neither of the two countries reached 50 per cent of NETAPWW, since the maximum benefit limits had not followed the growth in nominal wages and pressed down the standard worker benefits. Thus, the classification of France and the United States seems appropriate since their pension systems have failed to provide income security over time.

21. Social security in the United Kingdom is often thought of as universal (e.g. Baldwin, 1988), and although more than 90 per cent of those who are above normal pension age do get some form of public old-age pension, pensions are still either based on work merit or needs-testing. This means that every old person will not get a benefit in the British system, so the system is not universal. The high take-up rate is not unique to the UK but shared by most of the other countries. The Swiss case is close to the citizenship model, as indicated above. Entitlement is based on contributions but the government pays the contribution (e.g. for students and housewives), thus implying a universal entitlement. However, the basic pensions are in the end needs-tested and too low for providing an adequate minimum, i.e. they replace less than one-third of the NETAPWW. Also, both Switzerland and the UK are getting closer to the work-merit model with increased levels of standard worker pensions: preliminary data for 1985 suggest that they now reach about 50 per cent of the NETAPWW (although maximum pensions are still rather low).

22. Australia is fairly close to the residual model because those below 70 years of age got their pensions needs-tested and, as of 1978, increases in the rates of benefits were also needs-tested. Classifying Canada into the citizenship model is straightforward according to the operationalizations, although it is only thanks to the needs-tested supplements that the minimum pensions reach one-third of the NETAPWW.

23. About the cases in the institutional category a couple of points may be noted. The recipience rate in the Netherlands was not 100 per cent in 1980 since married women did not have a separate entitlement to old-age pensions; the right to benefits for them was tied to the age of her husband and the timing of marriage (in relation to when the woman gained entitlement). In Finland the supplements to the citizenship pensions were needs-tested in 1980 and the 'pure' citizenship pension did not replace as much as a third of the NETAPWW. Changing the criteria so that citizenship pensions, and not the minimum pension, should replace a third of the NETAPWW would thus move Finland into the work-merit model.

References

Alber, Jens (1988) 'Is there a crisis of the welfare state? Cross-national evidence from Europe, North America, and Japan', *European Sociological Review*, 4(3): 181–206.

Baldwin, Peter (1988) 'How socialist is solidaristic social policy? Swedish postwar reform as a case in point', *International Review of Social History*, 33: 121–47.

Castles, Francis G. (1982) 'The impact of parties on public expenditures', pp. 21–96 in F.G. Castles (ed.), *The Impact of Parties*. Beverly Hills: Sage.

Cutright, Philips (1967) 'Political structure, economic development, and national social programs', *American Journal of Sociology*, 70: 550–57.

Esping-Andersen, Gösta (1982) 'The welfare state as a system of stratification'. Mimeo: Harvard University.

Esping-Andersen, Gösta (1985) *Politics against Markets: The Social Democratic Road to Power*. Princeton, NJ: Princeton University Press.

Esping-Andersen, Gösta (1987) *State and the Market in the Formation of Social Security Regimes. A Political Economy Approach*. European University Institute. Working Paper 87/281.

Esping-Andersen, Gösta and Korpi, Walter (1984) 'Social policy as class politics in post war capitalism: Scandinavia, Austria, and Germany', pp. 179–208 in John H. Goldthorpe (ed.), *Order and Conflict in Contemporary Capitalism*. Oxford: Clarendon Press.

Everitt, Brian (1981) *Cluster Analysis*. London: Heinemann Educational.

International Labour Office (1933) *Non-contributory Pensions*. Studies and Reports M:9. Geneva: ILO.

International Labour Office (1933) *International Report of Social Services*. Studies and Reports M:11 Geneva: ILO.

International Labour Office (1936) *International Report of Social Services*. Studies and Reports M:13. Geneva: ILO.

Kangas, Olli and Palme, Joakim (1989) *Public and Private Pensions: The Scandinavian Countries in a Comparative Perspective*. Working paper 3/1989, Swedish Institute for Social Research.

124   *Needs and welfare*

Kohl, Jürgen (1987) 'Which guarantees can the system of social security offer? A concept for old age security'. Paper prepared for the colloquium of the European Institute of Social Security on Structural Problems of Social Security: Today and Tomorrow, Krems (Austria), 1–3 October 1987.

Kohl, Jürgen (1988) 'Inequality and poverty in old-age: A comparison between West Germany, the United Kingdom, Sweden, and Switzerland'. Paper prepared for the Workshop on Comparative Research in Social Policy, Labour Markets, Inequality, and Distributional Conflict (ISA Research Committee 19), Hässelby Slott, Stockholm, 25–28 August 1988.

Korpi, Walter (1980) 'Social policy and distributional conflict in the capitalist democracies: A preliminary comparative framework', *European Politics*, 3(3), October (ed. A.S. Heidenheimer).

Korpi, Walter (1989) 'Power, politics and state autonomy in the development of social citizenship: Social rights during sickness in 18 OECD countries since 1930', *American Sociological Review*, 54: 309–28.

Laczko, Frank and Walker, Alan (1986) 'Excluding older workers from the labour market: Early retirement policies in Britain, France and Sweden', *The Year Book of Social Policy in Britain 1984–5*. London.

Marklund, Staffan (1988) *Paradise Lost? The Nordic Welfare State and the Recession 1975–1985*. Lund: Arkiv.

Marshall, T.H. (1950) *Citizenship and Social Class*. Cambridge: Cambridge University Press.

Myles, John (1984) *Old Age in the Welfare State. The Political Economy of Public Pensions*. Boston: Little, Brown.

Myles, John (1988) 'Postwar capitalism and the extension of social security into a retirement wage', in M. Weir, A.S. Orloff and T. Skocpol (eds), *The Politics of Social Policy in the United States*. Princeton, NJ: Princeton University Press.

Palme, Joakim (1988) 'The determinants of old-age pensions in 18 OECD-countries 1930 to 1980'. Working paper for the Workshop on Comparative Research in Social Policy, Labour Markets, Inequality, and Distributional Conflict (ISA Research Committee 19), Hässelby Slott, Stockholm, 25–28 August 1988.

Palme, Joakim (1989) 'Models of pensions and income inequality: A comparative analysis'. Paper prepared for the Conference on the Welfare State in Transition, Solstrand Fjord Hotel, Bergen, 24–27 August 1989.

Pampel, Fred C. and Williamson, John B. (1985) 'Age structure, politics and cross-national patterns of public pension expenditures', *American Sociological Review*, 50: 782–99.

Pampel, Fred C. and Williamson, John B. (1988) 'Welfare spending in advanced industrial democracies, 1950–1980', *American Journal of Sociology*, 93: 1424–56.

Rein, Martin and Rainwater, Lee (eds) (1985) *Public/Private Interplay in Social Protection*. New York: M.E. Sharpe.

SSIB data *Database on the development of social security in 18 OECD-countries 1930–1980*. Swedish Institute for Social Research, University of Stockholm.

Ståhlberg, Ann-Charlotte (1989) 'Redistribution effect of social policy in a lifetime analytical framework', in B.A. Gustafsson and N.A. Klevmarken (eds), *The Political Economy of Social Security*. North-Holland: Elsevier.

Therborn, Göran (1986) *Why Some People Are More Unemployed than Others*. London: Verso.

Titmuss, Richard A. (1974) *Social Policy*. London: George Allen & Unwin.

Tracy, Martin (1979) *Retirement Age Practices in Ten Industrial Societies, 1960–1976*. Geneva: ILO.

US Department of Health (1949) *Social Security Legislation throughout the World 1949*. Washington DC: US Federal Security Agency, Social Security Administration.

Wilensky, Harold (1975) *The Welfare State and Equality, Structural and Ideological Roots of Public Expenditures*. Berkeley and Los Angeles: University of California Press.

7

Needs, Services and Political Success under the British Conservatives

Richard Parry

The primary need of every government is to remain in office. The vocabulary of politics concentrates on the needs and demands of the electorate, but for governments a much cruder notion of political survival soon becomes the preoccupation. A successful government will develop a strategy that has both a philosophical element and a command of the techniques of securing voter allegiance. Political science, too, needs to develop the connection between theory and action, and strategy – the application of the resources of government to long-run political objectives – is one concept that can help to make the link.

Governments may have a philosophical orientation; a set of interests or groups to be satisfied; ties of obligation or sentiment to corporate interests; and an economic framework to be managed. Ultimately, these must conform to a strategy that convinces voters by arranging the distribution of gainers and losers in an optimal way. In the process, attitude structures favourable to a party may be formed, and even new types of political personality. Coalition governments and rapid alternation of parties in office frustrate the pursuit of strategy; examples of successful long-run single party government are rare, and tend to be confined to countries with a clearly dominant political party such as the Social Democrats in Sweden and Fianna Fáil in Ireland.

One of the most outstanding examples of political management in recent European politics is the success of the Conservative government in the United Kingdom. Elected in 1979, it was returned in 1983 and 1987 with an almost identical percentage of the popular vote. After the 1987 general election, it led in all opinion polls until February 1989; only time will tell whether the subsequent onset of a mid-term dip, with a defeat by Labour of 40 to 35 per cent in the European elections of June 1989, is of a different character to those of 1982 and 1986. Moreover, it has not done this by tending towards the centre of electoral politics, as have governments in Germany and Sweden. It has pursued, almost to the point of indulging itself in, many of the policies that previous Conservative governments had hesitated to become involved in. High unemployment and a less progressive structure of taxation have left substantial sections of the population relatively worse off.

There is a major phenomenon here that requires explanation. During its first term, the Thatcher government seemed to be heading down the familiar British path of instability and ungovernability that had resulted in no government since 1964 serving two full terms. There were by-election losses, especially to a new alliance of Liberals and Social Democrats; a failure to control public expenditure; industrial unrest; and disputes between 'wets' and 'dries' in the cabinet. Added to this was the impact of a major economic recession, and unfavourable demographic trends, with more teenagers and elderly imposing an expensive burden on public policy.

Then events happened which saw the crystallization of 'Thatcherism' as a byword for robust government. The less 'heavyweight' of Mrs Thatcher's political opponents were removed from the Cabinet in 1981. Despite recession, a deflationary budget was introduced in 1981. The Falklands War of 1982 gave a rare chance to a western conservative party to fight a winnable, limited war and achieve a demonstrable success on a ground where it was stronger than its opponents. The British electoral system, and opposition disarray, allowed a consolidation of Conservative rule on a minority of the popular vote and without a reshaping of the attitude profile of the electorate. British conservatism found the trick of 'statecraft' (Bulpitt, 1986) which enabled it to balance its own philosophy with the needs of voters: an important element of this is securing a hegemony of public discourse, something that started to happen when Britain emerged from recession in 1982 and the government began its privatization policy with conviction.

Conservative statecraft has gained a further economic underpinning since Bulpitt wrote in 1986. Steady economic growth since 1983 has enabled the government to contract the shares of national income and employment occupied by the public sector. It has solved the 'crisis' of the welfare state in an old-fashioned way – by buoyant growth in employment, income and taxation which has floated state revenue above the cost of public policy. In 1988–9 the ratio of public expenditure to GDP fell below 40 per cent for the first time since 1966–7. The general government budget surplus for 1988–9 is estimated at £12bn on top of expenditure of £179bn (including £7bn from privatization proceeds); it is projected to remain at least £9bn annually until 1993. In 1987 public employment was 26 per cent of the workforce, less than in Germany and down from 31 per cent in 1979 (Parry and Schmidt, 1987). Almost the entire state-owned industrial sector has been, or is in the process of being, transferred to private shareholding – the major aspect of the government's privatization programme.

One important aspect of Conservative statecraft consists of their management of public resources – public expenditure, tax expenditures and regulation of the private sector – in social policies delivered to individuals. This is examined in the following four sections. In the first we look at the contribution of social policy to Conservative strategy in the 1980s. The second relates the policies to some of the theoretical perspectives of 'New Right' thinkers. The third looks at the record on aggregate spending and in each service area on the dimension of public and private provision. The conclusion assesses the part played by recent British conservatism in the development of our understanding of needs, contributions and welfare.

Political strategy of the Conservative government in social policy

It is not clear how far we can speak of the 'social policy' of a government that is essentially unsocial in its philosophy and denies the validity of social entities in a way that would disturb Christian Democrats as well as socialists. The Beveridgean tradition of universal benefits allocated by public bureaucracies to its fellow-citizens is deeply inimical to Thatcherism. One could scarcely find a greater philosophical distance from the present government than in the network of educators and practitioners in what used to be called 'social administration'. Conservatives often display a factual ignorance of social needs and circumstances and a reluctance to promote social investigation. The general absolute rise in living standards makes it possible to attack notions of poverty expressed in terms of relative maldistribution or inequality, notably in a notorious speech in May 1989 by Social Security Secretary John Moore, who lost his job in July 1989 (Moore, 1989).

The Conservatives have found that the groups from which most of the clients of the welfare state are drawn (such as those in manual employment, and the elderly without a home or pension) are contracting as a proportion of the electorate. In their place is an electorate with assets (houses, shares, pensions) whose value can be affected by political and economic confidence. The concentration of Conservative electoral support in the south and

Midlands of England provides territorial reinforcement in these areas; in the 1987 General Election, the Conservatives polled 50 per cent in these areas but 37 per cent in the north, 30 per cent in Wales and 24 per cent in Scotland.

The Conservative distaste for protracted expert inquiries is well known: they have not appointed a single Royal Commission, and are unreceptive to research and consultation exercises (Davidson and White, 1988). The model of scientific investigation in the Rowntree–Townsend tradition is replaced by the use of market research and advertising to put the best construction on policies. Initiatives like Action for Cities on inner-city decline (March 1988), the Employment Training scheme for the adult unemployed (September 1988) and the National Health Service review (February 1989) were launched with careful design and advertising. Action for Cities was a repackaging of existing policies, and the latter two White Papers concealed a rather sketchy notion of how the policies were to be implemented (Department of Employment, 1988; Department of Health, 1989). Social states are characterized not as needs, but as products. This is consonant with the value-free emphasis on 'presentation' in the British civil service, which expresses its non-partisanship by putting the best construction on the policies of whichever party is in office.

The unifying theme driving policy is that of privatization. This involves the development of instruments to overcome the problems of the welfare state by shifting the public–private balance within it. It is naturally easier to apply in industrial fields where there are assets to be sold (Veljanovski, 1987), but in social policy areas there are several instruments which can induce or compel private supply of welfare, and in the process reduce the extent to which the state must take a view on social needs. These techniques include:

1 Mandated private provision, in which services are social (available to all) but not public – typically these are employment-related, like sickness and maternity pay, and may involve government subsidy to business (O'Higgins, 1989).
2 Giving the opportunity for private investment funded by borrowing on the capital market (housing, hospitals, often with American investment (Higgins, 1988), private residential homes, and now even roads).
3 Purchase of services (from voluntary and private producers, especially in the social services), which is reinforced by thinking on the 'mixed economy of welfare', an unsatisfactory conceptualization of the options available to public agencies to finance services rather than produce them directly.

4 Compulsory competitive tendering (of support services like cleaning, catering and maintenance in the National Health Service and, from August 1989, in local government, but liable to be extended to service provision). It provides the employers' dream of requiring their workforce to reapply for their own jobs and is the key element in weakening the power of public sector trade unions (Ascher, 1987).

5 Consumerist marketing, in which public institutions have to justify themselves in terms comparable to the private. This extends from trivial matters such as annual reports by schools to elaborate plans and statements in order to attract clientele and continued government support.

6 Positional advantage – the notion developed by Fred Hirsch (1977) that many publicly supplied services are, in economic terms, private goods and that there will be competition for the privileged positions they may confer. In effect this has been exploited by the Conservatives in their proposals to allow schools and hospitals to become self-governing and outside the managerial control of local and health authorities. This will create a positional differentiation within the public sector in which the opted-out establishments may gain higher prestige and, controlling access on ill-defined criteria, are liable to become enclaves of middle-class privilege.

What these techniques have in common is the leverage they allow policies to exert over social and political outcomes. Using the business analogy of leveraged buyouts, where a small investment can induce a major change of ownership by the issue of high-yielding but high-risk 'junk bonds', we can see them as an exploitation of the power of government to create both threat and opportunity. This intensifies with length of office-holding and extent to which disparate policies take on a consistent colour. Many policies – especially contracting-out – have been developed experimentally over a number of years in office.

The Conservative approach seeks to differentiate the various social and economic roles played by individuals. It distrusts the kind of 'all-through' provision by the state that encompasses both the definition of needs and the production of services. Instead, a variety of modes of production on the supply side is matched by a variety of consumer demands. The theoretical basis of this remains incomplete, but it does suggest a contraction of the sphere in which services are public goods (marked by indivisibility of output, non-excludability and positive externalities). The monolithic nature of the public sector (in terms of output, production technology and especially employment structures) no longer seems so inevitable or desirable. In contrast, private sector supply (or public production that mimics private styles) seems better equipped to deal with the demands of the 1980s, and has consequently been prominent in the philosophy of recent Conservatism in Britain.

Philosophical adaptations

Conservative strategy has derived an impetus from the recent intellectual climate about needs and rights. This involves scepticism about traditional notions of needs as having an objective validity established by research and observation. It is outside the scope of this chapter to elaborate theoretical points, but in a sense this is not necessary, because Conservative policy is based on some oversimplified theses about the corrupting effects of access to the public purse. The theses contend that:

1 needs are unknowable and constantly shifting, especially once economic growth makes minimal subsistence an obsolete notion;
2 lack of normative public provision can be liberating (the near-anarchic theme implicit in much writing by Milton Friedman and Robert Nozick);
3 rational choice theory correctly predicts government failure and bureaucratic pathology;
4 the market is the most accurate means of intelligence about wants, and that needs are not capable of experimental discovery;
5 location of production in the public sector under democratic accountability facilitates producer self-interest.

Public opinion data do not suggest any general support for these theses. Public sector social services (especially health and provision for the elderly) are endorsed by most of the electorate, and there has been a hardening of this support since 1983, especially among Conservatives (Taylor-Gooby, 1987: 3–5) and it is shared by both middle and working class (Heath and Evans, 1988: 55). But this is not necessarily incompatible with support for a mixed economy of welfare: middle positions, involving a tolerance of choice but good state provision, tend to be supported (Taylor-Gooby, 1985, 1987). It was only a temporary phenomenon of 1979 that a plurality of British voters preferred tax cuts to improved services (Crewe, 1988: 38).

In the 1980s, there has been a discrepancy between government-specific and issue-specific attitudes. Opinion on most social policy issues is very sceptical about Conservative strategy (especially on health, which by 1988 had risen to challenge unemployment as the issue of greatest concern to the public). But on the 'hard', 'fear' issues like defence and taxation the Conservatives continue to be seen as the party with the best policies and, even though these are no longer regarded as the most important issues, Conservative credentials on them underpin a general sense of capability for government. American experience shows the electoral potency of a consistently firm line on the 'fear' issues. The slightest equivocation as we read the candidate's lips can undermine a party's position. Once the salience of these issues weakened in 1989 with international reductions in defence forces and a greater preoccupation with green issues, the Conservatives faltered.

The question remains as to whether the Conservatives can sustain their position as the leading party in the light of a consistently low consent to their social policies. As Ivor Crewe says (1988: 44), 'Conservative success remains a puzzle. Voters oppose the government on a vast array of its specific policy initiatives.' He sees the main factor as being the perception of constancy and fitness to govern, but 'whether a distinctive statecraft can form the basis of an enduring party realignment, however, seems doubtful' (1988: 48).

In the long term the Conservatives are indeed unlikely to keep pulling off the same electoral trick, especially if Labour regains its position as the only credible opposition party, as began to seem likely in 1988–89. But the Conservatives overcame similar signs of weakness in the mid-term of the 1983 parliament, and we should not underestimate the extent to which traditional concepts of need, welfare and personal autonomy have been reappraised in the Thatcher era. What we can see is a new balance between three variables:

1 Political success – the short-term management of the political agenda and the building-up of a longer-term hegemony in discourse and office-holding; it includes electoral success, achieved in Thatcher's Britain through a greater fragmentation of the opposition parties than had occurred in any previous post-war period, but also image and competence to govern and the locking-in of policies to consumption patterns.

2 Satisfaction of needs – the 'pure', 'improving' function of politics, applying the resources of government to individual and social welfare. The Conservatives have redefined it to mean the protection of the material interests of a plurality of voters; it means not just a high level of service but also the emerging

notion of 'affordability' (especially prominent in housing) which comprises adequacy of supply as well as price.
3 Modes of policy – the instruments through which policies are implemented effectively and without side-effects, based on the calculus of maximum political return from the minimum of policy effort. This involves overcoming the amply documented problems of implementing public policies.

The Conservative art is to optimize this triangle of needs, policies and electoral success with a pragmatism denied to parties of the left. The government does not seek to construct the state on its philosophical principles; that would be unlikely to succeed, for even the most conservative administrations have to carry a dead weight of welfare programmes sustained by status and precedent, not need. But the principles may be used to justify policies that seem harsh in terms of the previous standards of the British welfare state. The generation of Conservatives formed by the two-party context of the 1940s is no longer in office, and electoral success has become an end in itself.

The evidence on change by service area

What is the evidence of change? In the early 1980s it was fashionable to suggest that the Conservatives would leave the welfare state largely intact. This was not because the Conservatives liked it, but because it was too much trouble to tackle it. Now the issue is not so clear, because in practice very few doors of the British polity have been resistant to a Thatcher initiative. This 'searchlight technique' of policy making includes the social security reviews of 1983–5 (which had some public hearings and outside experts and so was a transition from old-style Royal Commissions to the new internalized reviews), the device of opting out of local authority management in education and housing (devised for the 1987 election manifesto) and the National Health Service review of 1988–9. This last policy was conducted within the Cabinet system, within an ideological perspective provided by the Prime Minister's Policy Unit and influenced by right-wing 'think tanks'.

The underlying themes may be seen as an attack on the trades unions (in the first Thatcher term, through controls on calling strikes without a ballot, picketing and the closed shop), local government (in the second term, through controlling their discretion over spending and taxation) and the professions (in the third term, through loss of monopoly rights and self-regulation). All three were seen as unduly privileged corporate interests, with a guaranteed source of income – the closed shop, the rates (property tax), fixed fees – who, to put it crudely, no longer needed to hustle in the market-place. Privatization suggests the idea of a periodical market test in terms which mobilizes the competitive instinct and sense of alternative possibilities on the part of individual consumers.

How have these changes affected the public–private balance in the social policy field? Table 7.1 is an attempt to use national income statistics to provide a measure of the sources of expenditure. Investment has been excluded; the data in the table have been set at constant prices; transport has been included though it is not unequivocally social in character. For social security, of course, final consumption is largely by private individuals and the public–private distinction is in the source of the transfer

Table 7.1   *Public and private current social expenditure 1979–87 (£m at 1985 prices)*

| | Public | | Private | |
	1979	1987	1979	1987
Social security	34,581	47,441	16,266	31,000
Transport	3,466	2,867	27,073	36,067
Housing	4,220	3,525	28,625	34,547
Health	16,070	17,679	1,799	2,917
Education	16,604	17,370	1,682	1,710
Total	74,941	88,882	75,445	106,241
Percentage change 1979–87		+ 18.6		+ 40.8
Percentage of total	49.8	45.6	50.2	54.4

Source: National Income and Expenditure, 1988 edition, calculated as follows (where data at 1985 prices are not published, current price data have been deflated by the average figure for general government final consumption (derived from T9.2 and 9.3) or consumers' expenditure (T4.7 and 4.8) as appropriate to the economic category):

Social security – public T9.4, non-capital expenditure deflated by GGFC (goods and services), CE (remainder); private T4.10 (payments, transfers and costs from life assurance and pension schemes) deflated by CE.

Transport – public T9.4 deflated by GGFC (goods and services), CE (remainder); private T4.8.

Housing – public T8.5, income of local authority housing operating accounts not paid by tenants, deflated by GGFC; private T4.8 (rent, rates, maintenance, imputed rent of owner-occupied housing).

Health – public T9.3; private T4.8 (NHS fees, medical expenses, pharmaceuticals).

Education – public T9.3 (local authority final consumption) + T9.4 current grants deflated by CE; private T4.8 (fees).

payment (the state, or insurance companies and pension funds).

The finding is that in 1979 there was almost equality of public and private financing, but by 1987 private had become 54.4 per cent of the total. In constant price terms, private finance had grown over twice as fast – 41 as against 19 per cent – though this is a reminder that public social spending has not in any sense been cut. In 1987, it was 23.2 per cent of GDP, while private financing was 27.8 per cent of GDP. Two-thirds of private spending was on housing and transport, two areas important in determining economic and social status and with high potential for political manipulation.

The record of change in particular services shows that two services – housing and transport – are more than 90 per cent privately financed, and have become decisively so under the Conservatives. Two – health and education – are at least 85 per cent publicly financed, and show no prospect of becoming anything else. In the former pair, real markets can operate, but with a high degree of imperfection in price and supply. In the latter, the Conservative strategy is to create 'internal markets', in which resource costing and comparison is important but the consumer is not charged. An intermediate position is occupied by social security, where the value of private pensions and life insurance raises the privately financed proportion to 40 per cent of the total in 1987, up from 32 per cent in 1979.

Changes in the market shares of public and private sectors are traced in table 7.2. Two services – residential social care and retirement pensions – have a fairly even public–private balance: the market is unwilling to provide complete coverage. Housing is becoming decisively private (owner-occupation is up from 55 to 65 per cent of dwellings, but the decline in the private rented sector moderates the rise in the overall private share). Two services – health and education – show a rising but still small private share, with a doubling of the coverage of private medical insurance since 1979.

Probably the best way of moving from a needs-based approach is to divert public policy effort from direct public expenditure to tax expenditures. This is a response to consumer demand and is a kind of black hole in the budget whose size is difficult to estimate (Wilkinson, 1986). Two categories are important: tax relief on the interest payments on mortgages taken out to purchase a principal residence, and on contributions to, and the investment income of, a recognized pension fund and on lump sum payments at retirement. Table 7.3 estimates the cost of these reliefs, using methodology that does not exaggerate their extent (tax foregone

Table 7.2 *Private sector market shares*

	1979	1983	1987
Pensions (% workforce covered)	50	52	n/a
Health (% population insured)	5	8	9
Housing (% dwellings)	67	70	72
Education (% pupils)	5.5	6.0	6.6
Social services (% of residential places for the elderly)	33	39	48

Source: pensions *Employment Gazette*, December 1985: 434–7; housing *Housing and Construction Statistics 1977–87*: T9.3; remainder *Social Trends*, various editions

Table 7.3 *Tax expenditures and public expenditures (£ '000s)*

	1980–81		1988–89	
	Public	Tax	Public	Tax
Pensions	11,357	1,650	20,483	6,525
est. at 1988–89 prices	17,870	2,600		
Housing	6,260	1,960	6,747	5,500
est. at 1988–89 prices	9,850	3,080		

Tax expenditures defined as relief for employees' contributions to occupational pension schemes; investment income of schemes; lump sum payments to pensioners (pensions); qualifying interest on loans for the purchase or improvement of owner-occupied property (housing). The published pensions figure for 1980–81 (£940m) has been adjusted in the light of new methodology introduced in 1983 (see Cmnd 9428-II: 25). Public expenditures defined as pension benefits and war pensions; housing excluding local authority receipts.

Source: The Government's Expenditure Plans 1981–2 to 1983–4 (Cmnd 8175, 1981) T4.14 [for pensions tax 1980–81]; 1985–6 to 1987–8 (Cmnd 9428, 1985) T2.5 and 3.17.20 [for public 1980–81]; 1989–90 to 1991–2 (Cm 621, 1989) T21.1.7 [for public 1988–9] 21.1.25 [for tax 1988–9] T21.4.1 [for GDP deflator]; *Inland Revenue Statistics* 1988 T5.2 [for housing tax 1980–81]

on capital gains from housing sales and employers' pension contributions is excluded, as it is difficult to estimate and unlikely to be recouped were the relief ended, as are public capital receipts from housing).

In these two fields tax foregone is £12bn in 1989–90. Tax expenditure has more than doubled as a percentage of public expenditure in the two services: in pensions from 15 to 32, in housing from 31 to 82. The Treasury would like to restrict tax expenditures, and has had some success: relief on new life insurance policies was withdrawn in 1984, and the limit on mortgage relief has risen only from £25,000 to £30,000, well below the average house price. Any further restriction has proved unacceptable politically. The costs of other tax reliefs are much smaller. Private schools which are charities received tax concessions to the tune of £42m in 1986–7 (Papadakis and Taylor-Gooby, 1987: table 3.2). Two groups receive tax relief on private health insurance premiums: from 1981 those earning less than £8500 a year (now less than average earnings) and, from April 1990, the over-60s, at an estimated annual cost of £40m.

A brief examination of some of the policy instruments used by the Conservatives illustrates their approach. In *pensions*, the state contribution to the National Insurance fund was phased out by 1988. An important change was the linking of pension increases to prices rather than earnings in 1980, which meant that all benefit recipients would fall behind general economic growth. The coverage of occupational schemes has not increased, but their flexibility has, with portability between employers in 1986 and tax-subsidized personal pensions in 1988. For the rest of the workforce, the State Earnings-Related Pension Scheme (SERPS) was not abolished as the Conservatives wished in 1985 because employers could not be induced to make even minimal such provision for all their employees. Instead, SERPS has been reduced in cost by making the earnings calculation less generous.

In other aspects of *income maintenance*, reforms in 1982 and 1988 redistributed spending within the benefit-claiming population through the notion of 'targeting' at no net overall cost. The 1988 changes followed the 'Fowler' reviews of 1984–5, and were a bolder attempt to reshape the system on Conservative lines. Families with children were left better off at the expense of the single unemployed and the elderly; a 'social fund' provides interest-free loans for major expenditure items. As with pensions, when changes have been unacceptable to business interests, they have tended to be modified: sick pay has been transferred to employers, but at full state subsidy of the cost; a similar principle was followed in Statutory Maternity Pay.

In *health*, a similar, and equally inappropriate, principle of maintaining expenditure in real terms has been adopted. This has posed political problems for the Conservatives, because increases at or near the level of general price inflation elicit a perception of severe resource shortage to producers and consumers. The proportion of health spending in GDP is under 6 per cent, little more than half the US level. The growth of private medicine relies on the pooling of medical personnel between sectors (most senior doctors do both NHS and private work) and on the provision of medical insurance as an occupational benefit. The health service review of 1988–9 proposes a major move to an internal market; it is not yet clear what extent of disturbance to the previous principles of the National Health Service this involves.

In *education*, private fee-paying education has been relatively flourishing under the Conservatives, with the number of pupils in private schools remaining constant and so rising as a proportion of the total (table 7.2). Tax expenditures are difficult to estimate but pre-date the Thatcher government (they involve the charitable status of some private schools and, until 1988, the tax-deductibility of covenanted help towards school fees by relatives other than parents). The main Conservative initiative has been the 'assisted places scheme' (1981) which subsidizes the fees paid by low-income parents. Total public support in 1986–7 is estimated at £288m (Papadakis and Taylor-Gooby, 1987: 98). More important are the 'grant-maintained schools', which from 1988 can opt out of local authority control after a ballot of parents, so creating a superior tier of publicly financed schools on the initiative of a majority of parents.

Housing is the policy area where the instruments of privatization are most potent. The Conservatives have come close to ending public sector house building (only 12 per cent of all 'starts' in 1988) and the 'right-to-buy' policy introduced in 1980 has resulted in over 15 per cent of the public stock being sold to tenants. This is a natural area of political recruitment for the Conservatives, though evidence suggests that the Conservative political allegiance of those who purchase council houses pre-dates their decision to buy (Heath et al. 1985: table 4.4).

Public spending on housing has fallen in real terms even when (as in table 7.1) the proceeds from the sale of public housing are excluded. Policies have tried to make the private rented sector more attractive to landlords in an attempt to arrest its long-term decline. Tax expenditure on mortgages has increased (table 7.3): the value to the individual has more than doubled in real terms and the numbers receiving have increased from 5.9 to 8.8 million (Board of Inland Revenue, 1989: table 5.2). The financial implications of home ownership involve a combination of interest rates, tax relief and capital appreciation, and so are susceptible to political manipulation and volatility: the sharp rise in interest rates in 1988–9 thus represents a political risk for the Conservatives.

Personal social services (advice and care not involving medical treatment) are a mix of public and private elements. In the residential care of the elderly, over half the places are provided by the private or voluntary sectors, but with many residents' fees financed by social security payments. Conservative ambivalence on the matter is illustrated by their failure until July 1989 to accept an eminently technocratic report of March 1988 on community care (the Griffiths Report). This calls for local social services departments to be the arrangers and purchasers of care they would not necessarily provide themselves.

Transport, although not seen explicitly as a social policy, is an example of how social needs can be marginalized by free market approaches. Economic growth is relied on by the Conservatives to allow public subsidies to be withdrawn, and on the whole this has happened. Competition has been promoted by the deregulation of bus transport by 1986, most state-owned bus companies have been privatized, and the railways too are being prepared for self-financing and some form of privatization.

For an estimate of the cumulative impact of these policies on the individual, we may look at the estimates in table 7.4 of the equality of distribution of income and wealth. Inequality of original income has increased by 7 per cent, and the tendency in

Table 7.4 *The distribution of income and wealth*

| | | Gini coefficients | | |
	1979	1983	1986	Change
Income				
Original	45	49	52	+ 7
After adding in (cumulatively):				
Cash benefits	35	36	40	+ 5
Direct taxes	33	33	36	+ 3
Indirect taxes	35	36	40	+ 5
Benefits in kind	32	33	36	+ 4
Wealth				
Marketable wealth	76	69	68	− 8
After adding in (cumulatively):				
Occupational pension rights	62–68	61–67	59–65	− 3
State pension rights	45–50	47–52	48–53	+ 3

Gini coefficient = index of equality of distribution (0 = complete equality, 100 = complete inequality); some wealth estimates have upper and lower boundaries.

Sources: income, Family Expenditure Survey (*n* = 7000) reported in 'The effects of taxes and benefits on household income 1986', *Economic Trends* 422 (December 1988), table 11; wealth, *Inland Revenue Statistics* 1985 tables 4.8–4.9 and appendix D2, 1988 tables 10.5–10.7

the 1979–83 term for it to be moderated by tax and benefits is no longer evident. Cash benefits have a substantial impact on inequality but taxes, taken as a whole, none at all. The inequality of private wealth has reduced, but it is now diminished to a smaller extent by state pension rights. Even though the base of national wealth and income has increased (in Conservative eyes, the greatest need of all), various policies, especially the linking of benefit increases to prices not earnings, have reinforced the marginal position of consumers dependent on public benefits.

How far does a conception of need underlie these policies? Implicitly, it must be there, especially when there are discrepancies in the rate of expenditure growth of the various social policies and social security benefits. The Conservative approach has three elements:

1 it is inimical to notions of relative poverty which imply that equality of income will produce social cohesion, and hence benefits do not attempt to keep pace with the resources of wage-earners;
2 it is resistant to a cushioning of the individual from the labour and political markets; hence the test of availability for work has become more rigorous (the period of loss of benefit when leaving work voluntarily has increased from six weeks to six months) and every taxpayer must now pay at least 20 per cent of local taxes (property tax being replaced in 1989–90 by a flat-rate poll tax abated for those on low incomes);
3 some goods are redefined as non-welfare (notably housing, transport and the training element of education)

Need becomes less of an operational principle for public policy and more of sentimental stimulus for charity. The point for Conservatives is that the meeting of need cannot be allowed to inflate the size of the public sector, and therefore it cannot be an absolute call on the resources of the state. With this premise, need cannot be an absolute philosophical principle either.

Conclusion: the contribution of British evidence to international theory

The identification of needs was never a primary characteristic of the Conservative view of the British welfare state. Rather, social insurance was a desirable technical means of averaging risks and legitimating the social concerns of right-wing governments. Conservative attitudes to needs and altruism derive from the notion of private welfare consumption as prudent and defensive.

They have little sympathy with the rationalist social democratic tradition, because this recognized the limitations of individual action to deal with socially caused (even though individually borne) contingencies. Its idea of altruism was a collectively experienced one: in Richard Titmuss's idea of the 'gift relationship' (illustrated by the system of voluntary blood donation in Britain), his 'gifts' were subscriptions rather than donations, reinforcing reciprocity with unseen fellow-citizens. The technical inefficiency of having a multitude of private sector producers was also very close to Titmuss's mind.

Two propositions of the Conservative government require more scrutiny. One is that individuals will naturally devote some discretionary income beyond their needs to charity and influence the agenda of social concern through this invisible hand. The other is that private preferences for welfare can be satisfied by the privately financed topping-up of public expenditure held constant in real terms and so declining as a proportion of national income.

Both have tended to be disproved empirically. Charitable giving has risen but to attractive projects like hospital care for children rather than to the core needs of the welfare state. Private topping-up has not solved the problem of security of provision in health and pensions, where it might seem most applicable: the contingencies involved are long term and hard to predict. Personal pensions are an aspect of labour mobility but are likely to remain a marginal element in total pensions provision.

The propositions have an important place in the explanatory discourse of Conservatives, but they neglect the historical experience that altruism can seldom be institutionalized except through political collectivities; to cite blood donation or lifeboats is to isolate exceptions, not models. The idea of a minimum or floor provision by the state has a long history of operational inadequacy in Britain. The slow extension of access to higher education, of earnings-related occupational pensions and of the use of medical services suggest that the withdrawal of the state reinforces inequalities of consumption – even if much of the previous growth had flowed disproportionately to the middle class, on the thesis of the book *Not Only the Poor* (Goodin and Le Grand, 1987).

In Britain the contributory principle is weak: in pensions it became a minimal bar to entitlement after 1958 (when all who retired after 1948 became eligible) and in unemployment after 1982 when earnings-related supplement ended and payment became linked to family circumstances, not a contribution record. Now, only working wives and those with high savings are left

Table 7.5   *Income tax and national insurance contributions*

	May 1979 (%)	March 1989 (%)
Income tax		
Rates	25–83	25–40
Standard rate	33	25
National Insurance contributions		
Standard rate for employees	6.5	9

	1979–80 Yield (£'000s)	1979–80 % of GDP	1987–88 Yield (£'000s)	1987–88 % of GDP
Income tax	20,610	9.9	41,402	9.8
at 1987–88 prices	36,158			
National insurance	12,026	5.8	28,992	6.8
at 1987–88 prices	21,098			
Total taxation	71,214	34.3	156,965	37.0
at 1987–88 prices	124,937			

Source: Financial Statistics January 1985 and January 1989, tables 2.1 and 3.13

better off by an entitlement to unemployment benefit rather than to means-tested Income Support. Very similar numbers pay income tax and national insurance contributions; liability for income tax starts at 20 per cent of earnings for a single man, 31 per cent for a married man with children (Board of Inland Revenue, 1989: appendix C). Table 7.5 shows that national insurance contributions have increased as a ratio of GDP and income tax, to 6.8 and 70 per cent respectively in 1987–8.

National insurance contributions have only a fragile existence separate from income tax, but have a curiously regressive structure which is a vestige of the flat-rate Beveridge design. Until 1989, they were not payable at all by those earning less than £43 a week, then at 5 per cent up to £75, 7 per cent up to £115, and 9 per cent by those earning more (those contracted-out of SERPS pay 2 percentage points less). But these percentage rates were levied on all the earnings up to £325 a week (average earnings in 1988 were £218). A reform introduced in the March 1989 budget makes the rate 2 per cent of the first £43 of income and 9 per cent of the rest without altering the limits. Contributions, for Conservatives, are suspect because they legitimize universal benefits on a basis unrelated to means or needs. The common argument of paying national insurance and so being entitled to benefit is a political threat to a welfare-cutting government. Contributions only take on reality for British Conservatives when they are based on the actuarial insurance of the private sector.

Alternatives of the basic income or negative income tax kind seem much less attractive than privatization to a non-technocratic government. Conservatives are especially sensitive to leaving some of the middle mass of earners worse off and so, for instance, have not removed the upper earnings limit at which employees cease to make national insurance contributions. They prefer to explore private sector instruments within a consumerist orientation which simplifies the task of producers to one of keeping the customer happy.

To return to the triangle of success, needs and instruments: what is the nature of Conservative political success? It involves the flattening of the class gradient of Conservative voting, so the skilled working class have swung Conservative faster than any other group. But it is too much to speak of a locking-in of support. Share-ownership, though doubled to 20 per cent of the population and a political issue should the value of the shares be threatened, is basically trivial in substance. For most people, private consumption means a house and a car, matters where other parties should be equally able to offer policies of political appeal.

Conservative policies have turned out to be effective and successful, but they hardly reshape theory. They neither introduce a politically stable minimal welfare, nor move away completely from status-determined entitlements (concepts explored by Robert Goodin and Brian Barry respectively in other chapters of this book). They try to force a reliance on private consumption as a defensive reaction to the diversion of economic growth away from public social expenditure. The various instruments of policy – tax inducements, restriction of the generosity of state benefits, greater freedom for the private sector to operate – have a cumulative effect. The Conservatives have exploited the fact that by the 1980s the post-war Beveridgean concepts had lost their resonance. Even though state welfare provision was not rejected – and public support for it has been a consistent theme of survey evidence in the 1980s – it has not so far been the determining factor in electoral outcomes. By recognizing that its perceived fitness to govern can survive unpopular social policies, the Thatcher government has moved the political analysis of needs and welfare on to new ground.

144 *Needs and welfare*

References

Ascher, Kate (1987) *The Politics of Privatisation*. London: Macmillan.

Board of Inland Revenue (1989) *Inland Revenue Statistics 1988*. London: HMSO.

Bulpitt, Jim (1986) 'The discipline of the new democracy: Mrs Thatcher's domestic statecraft', *Political Studies*, 34(1).

Crewe, Ivor (1988) 'Has the electorate become Thatcherite?', in Robert Skidelsky (ed.), *Thatcherism*. London: Chatto and Windus.

Davidson, Roger and White, Phil (1988) *Information and Government: Studies in the Dynamics of Policy-Making*. Edinburgh: Edinburgh University Press.

Department of Employment (1988) *Employment for the 1990s* (Cmnd 540). London: HMSO.

Department of Health (1989) *Working for Patients* (Cm 555). London: HMSO.

Goodin, Robert and Le Grand, Julian (1987) *Not Only the Poor: the Middle Classes and the Welfare State*. London: George Allen & Unwin.

Heath, Anthony, Jowell, Roger and Curtice, John (1985) *How Britain Votes*. Oxford: Pergamon.

Heath, Anthony and Evans, Geoff (1988) 'Working-class Conservatives and middle-class Socialists', in Roger Jowell, Sharon Witherspoon and Lindsay Brook (eds), *British Social Attitudes: The Fifth Report*. Aldershot: Gower.

Higgins, Joan (1988) *The Business of Medicine: Private Health Care in Britain*. London: Macmillan.

Hirsch, Fred (1977) *Social Limits to Growth*. London: Routledge & Kegan Paul.

Moore, John (1989) 'The end of the line for poverty', 11 May. Mimeo. London: Conservative Central Office.

O'Higgins, Michael (1989) 'Privatisation and social welfare: Concepts, analysis and the British experience', in Sheila Kammerman and Alfred Kahn (eds), *Privatization and Welfare*. Princeton, NJ: Princeton University Press.

Papadakis, Elim and Taylor-Gooby, Peter (1987) *The Private Provision of Public Welfare*. Brighton: Wheatsheaf.

Parry, Richard and Schmidt, Klaus-Dieter (1987) *Public Employment in Britain and Germany*. Glasgow: University of Strathclyde, Studies in Public Policy 157.

Taylor-Gooby, Peter (1985). *Public Opinion, Ideology and State Welfare*. London: Routledge & Kegan Paul.

Taylor-Gooby, Peter (1987) 'Citizenship and welfare', in Roger Jowell, Sharon Witherspoon and Lindsay Brook (eds), *British Social Attitudes: The 1987 Report*. Aldershot: Gower.

Veljanovski, Cento (1987) *Selling the State: Privatisation in Britain*. London: Weidenfeld and Nicolson.

Wilkinson, Margaret (1986) 'Tax expenditure and public expenditure in the UK', *Journal of Social Policy*, 15(1): 23–49.

8

Problems for the Mixed Economy of Welfare

Norman Johnson

At its simplest, the mixed economy of welfare means the provision of health and welfare services by a variety of suppliers. Four sectors are usually identified as being concerned with welfare: the state sector, the commercial sector, the voluntary sector and the informal sector of families, friends and neighbours.

In Britain, as in other welfare states, the mixed economy of welfare has a history as long as that of the welfare state itself. Of course, the precise proportions of the mixture have varied from time to time, from country to country, and even from service to service within a single country. For example, cross-nationally, it is clear that the mixture in the Scandinavian countries differs markedly from that in the United States.

Changes in the mixture can occur over a relatively short period. Since the mid-1970s there have been changes in most countries of Western Europe in the balance between the sectors, most notably in the greater size and significance of private welfare markets. From a very different starting-point, similar developments occurred under the Reagan administration in the United States.

Variations from service to service can be seen in most welfare states but, if we take Britain as an example, then housing may be contrasted with health services and education. In housing the state sector has diminished so that it now operates as a welfare service alongside a very powerful private housing market. In health and education, on the other hand, private markets, although growing, are still relatively small.

This chapter focuses on the capacity of the informal, voluntary and commercial sectors to substitute for the state in the sphere of welfare. For reasons of space, the analysis will be restricted largely to the position in Britain, with only brief references to other countries, although many of the arguments are capable of broader application. An important distinction must be made, however, between those countries, such as Britain and the Scandinavian countries, in which the state is extensively involved in direct service provision, and those countries, such as France and West

Germany, which rely more heavily on income transfers. Income transfers leave welfare consumers to decide their own mix of services (Kohl, 1981). Obviously, it is in the former group of countries that the problem of the substitutability of one sector for another is more pressing.

My contention is that those eagerly pursuing a reduction in the welfare role of the state have paid insufficient attention to the problems facing the mixed economy of welfare. I do not examine the ethical issues raised by the transfer of responsibility from the state to the other three sectors but, rather, focus upon the practical constraints. The question to be addressed is not whether the other three sectors *should* substitute for the state but whether they are *able* to do so without adverse consequences for welfare provision.

Many of the problems identified arise from economic and social change and would have to be faced irrespective of whether the role of the state was reduced. Yet some of the discussion surrounding the alleged crisis in the welfare state ignores the pressures already being experienced by the informal and voluntary sectors and assumes that they are capable of doing more.

Later in the chapter the particular problems associated with trying to encourage the informal, voluntary and commercial sectors to do more will be discussed; but first we must examine the role of the state, since it is a proposed reduction in the state's direct involvement in welfare which is at the heart of the debate. The state interconnects with each of the other sectors and consideration of some of these linkages will serve as a unifying theme.

The state sector

After 1945 a stable welfare mix was established in which the state played a major role in the meeting of people's needs. With slight modifications from time to time this welfare mix persisted throughout the 1950s and 1960s and into the early 1970s. The whole of this period has been characterized as one of consensus in which there was broad agreement over a range of political issues (Bell, 1960; Marshall, 1965; Hadley and Hatch, 1981). Though there is probably some truth in Taylor-Gooby's (1985) argument that the degree of welfare consensus has been exaggerated, criticism of the welfare state was relatively muted until the mid-1970s.

The oil crisis and the world recession which followed gave its critics the opportunity to intensify their attack on the welfare state. The lower rate of growth, falling profits and investment and rising levels of unemployment were said to be a consequence of continually rising government expenditure, especially social expenditure. Furthermore, the critics argued, the vastly increased social expenditure had not solved the problems the welfare state was established to combat (Hadley and Hatch, 1981; Le Grand, 1982). Allegedly benefits were inadequate, services were of poor quality and the whole welfare state apparatus was over-centralized, over-bureaucratic, over-authoritarian and unresponsive to people's needs.

Welfare states everywhere were said to be in crisis. The opening sentence of Mishra's *The Welfare State in Crisis* (1984: xiii) is indicative of the tenor of much of the writing: 'In varying degrees and forms, the welfare state throughout the industrialised West is in disarray'. Whether or not there was such a crisis is debatable, but governments reacted as though there were indeed a crisis and they may have actively encouraged the idea in order to make cuts in social expenditure and services more acceptable.

One response to the alleged crisis was an attempt to change the balance in the welfare mix by reducing the role of the state and relying more heavily on the other three sectors. However, as Le Grand and Robinson (1984) demonstrate, the state does not have a single role in relation to welfare. In a study of privatization, these authors use a threefold classification of state involvement in welfare: provision, finance and regulation. A service provided mainly by the state may depend on both public and private finance. Commercial enterprises, voluntary agencies and informal carers may be subsidized and regulated by the state which may withdraw wholly or partly from direct provision.

The New Right, of course, would wish to see a diminution of the state's role in all three areas. On the other hand, Hadley and Hatch (1981) may be taken as representative of a widely held, more moderate view which argues for a reduction of the state's role in welfare provision, but with the state retaining its financing and regulatory functions. As will be seen, however, there are good reasons for doubting the capacity of the informal, voluntary and commercial sectors to substitute effectively for the state in the welfare field.

The informal sector

Informal care is provided mainly in the recipients' own homes by families, friends and neighbours. This is easily the most important source of care for certain dependent groups. The Family Policy

Studies Centre (1989) has estimated that the value of informal care ranges from £15 to £24 billion a year. In no way, however, does this reflect the true cost of such care: it is based on an hourly rate of pay of only £4 and takes no account of additional expenditures and opportunity costs in terms of wages foregone by carers. The figures also take no account of child care and, when it is remembered that there are over 11 million children under sixteen in Britain, it can be appreciated by just how much this would inflate the estimates. For purposes of comparison with the cost of caring, it may be noted that total government current expenditure on personal social services was £3.34 billion in 1987–8 (HM Treasury, 1987). Again, if the figure of £4 an hour is used, the work of volunteers in personal social services amounts to just over £2.2 billion.[1] (In addition, the voluntary sector employs many full-time, paid workers.)

Of course, the state makes a substantial contribution through the provision of education and health services and, in relation to families, it has important regulatory and financial functions. There is a whole body of family and child care law covering such areas as marriage, divorce, separation, property rights, parental rights and duties, wardship, adoption and fostering, custodianship and child protection. The state imposes obligations on parents to achieve certain minimum standards, and there are sanctions available if these standards are not met. The most obvious example is in cases of child abuse and neglect. It should be noted, however, that there are strong sentiments relating to the family as a private institution in Britain, and this renders detailed regulation difficult.

The government's emphasis on family care might be more acceptable if its financial support for families were more generous. There is a wide range of benefits available to families, but they are ill-coordinated and inadequate. Indeed, families on income support are actually worse off as a consequence of the social security changes introduced in 1988. The Benefits Research Unit (MacPherson and Svenson, 1988) claims that 81 per cent of couples with children and 74 per cent of lone parents are worse off. Family Credit is means-tested and the universal child benefit has been frozen for three consecutive years. Again, the invalid care allowance certainly does not compensate people for giving up work to care for a sick or frail elderly relative.

It is impossible to estimate how far the low levels of financial support affect the amount of care being provided by families. Probably the number of people being cared for is unaffected, but the quality of care they receive does suffer.

There is little doubt that the informal sector provides a wide variety of services for large numbers of the population. Willmott (1986) identifies five categories of informal caring:

1 Personal care, which includes washing, bathing, dressing, feeding and toileting – general attention to bodily needs and comforts corresponding to Parker's (1981) notion of 'tending'.
2 Domestic care – cooking, cleaning and laundering.
3 Auxiliary care – mainly less onerous tasks including baby-sitting, child-minding, shopping, transport, odd-jobbing, gardening, borrowing and lending.
4 Social support – visiting and companionship.
5 Surveillance – keeping an eye on vulnerable people.

Of the three sources of informal care, families are overwhelmingly more significant than the other two. The more personal the care, the more the emotional commitment involved and the longer the care continues, then the more likely it is that care will be provided by families rather than by friends and neighbours. Thus, the first two categories in Willmott's classification are predominantly provided by families. This is also true of two services not covered by Willmott: accommodation and financial help.

While the significance of families in the provision of care is unquestionable, those supporting the privatization of welfare suggest that families are capable of taking on *extra* responsibilities. However, there are several reasons for questioning this.

In all advanced industrial societies the number and proportion of dependent people in the population is increasing. Every country in Western Europe, for example, has an ageing population. In Italy and France 19 per cent of the population is over 60, in the Federal Republic of Germany, Belgium and Denmark the proportion is 20 per cent and the United Kingdom has the highest proportion with 21 per cent (Family Policy Studies Centre, 1988). Only a very small proportion of these people will require care, of course, but the very elderly (80+) are increasing at a faster rate than the younger age groups among the elderly population. Furthermore, improved health care means that more disabled children are now surviving into adulthood, thereby further increasing the number of people who require care.

At the same time as the number of dependants is increasing, social changes are reducing the capacity of families to provide the necessary care. Three changes are of particular significance in this respect: declining family size, the increasing participation of women in the labour market and rising divorce rates.

General fertility rates have been declining for several decades in all advanced industrial nations (United Nations, 1981). Falling fertility rates are reflected in reduced family size, which means that there will be fewer potential carers when the present generation of parents reaches old age or when a sibling becomes disabled.

Women's greater participation in the labour market will also have an impact on caring. An OECD study published in 1984 notes that between 1950 and 1980 the number of economically active women in the twenty-one member countries increased by 74 per cent whereas the number of economically active men increased by only 25 per cent (Paukert, 1984). It is true, of course, that many women, especially those with young children, work part-time. Nevertheless it seems probable that in future an increasing number of women will want full-time jobs. There can be no guarantee that women 'will continue to accept their cultural designation as carers' (Finch and Groves, 1980: 506) or that they will always be willing to sacrifice work opportunities in order to care for a dependent relative. In relation to children, female participation in the labour force has created both a market for child care facilities and a demand for the state to increase provision in this area.

The higher divorce rates in all advanced industrial nations affects the family's capacity for caring in two ways. First, divorce is the single most common cause of lone parenthood. In Britain, for example, 21 per cent of all lone parents in 1971 were divorced mothers, but by 1984 this proportion had risen to 40 per cent and a further 18 per cent were separated mothers (University of York, 1988). It is noteworthy that 91 per cent of lone parents are women. Lone parents usually have fewer financial resources than other families and the lack of a partner with whom one can share child-rearing responsibilities limits the capacity to provide other forms of care.

Secondly, divorce complicates relationships and kinship networks – especially if divorce is followed by remarriage. Finch and Groves (1980: 506) argue that we know too little about: '. . . which people count as "family"; what kind of obligations are attached to given relationships; who endorses these obligations and who does not; how such obligations are reinforced; and whether they depend upon a legal relationship such as marriage.' Does a divorced spouse feel any binding obligations towards former in-laws? What obligations do remarried people have towards new in-laws? If obligations to former and new in-laws are both acknowledged, what implications does this have for the amount of caring each will receive?

With all these problems, it appears that the question we should ask is not whether the informal sector can provide more care in the future, but whether it will even be able to maintain its current level of provision.

The wholesale transfer of responsibility from the state to informal carers, which some New Right theorists advocate, is likely to lead to falling standards of care and intolerable pressure on carers. There are limits to the extra work which families can absorb, and those limits may already have been reached. The informal sector is in no position to compensate for a reduction in the state sector's role. Indeed, if informal care is to continue at its present level, state support of the family will have to be increased.

The voluntary sector

The voluntary sector encompasses a great variety of organizations. There are variations in size from small, entirely local groups to large national organizations employing paid staff and with branches throughout the country. These variations in size are related to differences in financial and other resources. There are differences, too, in ethos: a self-help group, for example, is very different from a service-providing organization, and neighbourhood groups and campaigning groups are different again. However, it is not the purpose of this chapter to enter into a general discussion of the voluntary sector, but to examine the problems associated with the transfer of functions and responsibilities from the state to voluntary organizations.

Berger and Neuhaus (1977) characterize voluntary organizations as 'mediating structures' standing between the state and the individual. Such structures are more easily understood, they claim, by those who use them. By bridging the gap between the governed and those who govern them, mediating structures make alienation less likely and result in the 'empowerment of people'.

It is significant that many of those who argue the case for the replacement of state *provision* by voluntary provision of services (Gladstone, 1979; Hadley and Hatch, 1981) continue to insist upon state *finance*. It is clear that without statutory finance the voluntary sector would be unable to meet the wishes of its supporters by becoming the major provider of welfare.

Government finance or subsidy of voluntary organizations may take several forms; grants for general purposes, grants for specific items of expenditure (e.g. staff costs), grants related to a particular aspect of an organization's work, fees for the use of voluntary facilities by local authorities (such as places in residential homes or day centres), the provision of equipment or premises and tax concessions.

In Britain, although statutory funding of the voluntary sector has increased substantially over the last decade or more, the combined contributions of local and central government in 1985–6 accounted for only 8.9 per cent of the voluntary sector's total income of £12.65 billion (Campling, 1988: 229). If the voluntary sector were to become the chief provider of welfare, its income would need to be increased massively and the government might have to provide as much as 95 per cent of the total (as happens at present in the Netherlands).

Even the present level of government funding has given rise to fears about the threat this may pose to the independence of voluntary organizations. Brenton (1985: 93), writing about Britain, has claimed that 'it must be acknowledged that government control and influence over the future development of the voluntary sector is more than marginal, and that for some kinds of agency it may be decisive'. In the United States the Reagan administration used financial pressure to curb the lobbying activities of the more radical organizations. The government in the Netherlands has increasingly made the disbursement of funds to voluntary organizations dependent on two main factors: the acceptance of rationalization, and the provision of information which allows the government to introduce a measure of quality control.

Although control is sometimes direct and overt, there are more subtle ways in which funding bodies may seek to influence the activities of voluntary organizations. If the funders are known to favour particular kinds of programmes, those applying for funds may tailor their claims accordingly. Billis and Harris (1986) have identified the conflicting goals of funders and agencies as a major concern in the British voluntary sector.

Participation in government schemes may be even more restrictive. In Britain, the Manpower Services Commission was a major source of funds for voluntary agencies participating in its programmes until its demise in 1988. Several studies have been critical of the Commission's excessive influence and one study (Addy and Scott, 1988) has claimed that the MSC's real political agenda was the privatization and deprofessionalization of the welfare state.

While the government has at its disposal the means to control voluntary agencies, especially those dependent on government funds, it has no overall strategy for regulating the voluntary sector. The Charity Commission, which is almost totally ineffective, has recently been the subject of a highly critical report by the Public Accounts Committee (1988). The report identified serious short-comings in virtually every aspect of the Commission's work.

Although the Voluntary Services Unit was established in 1973 to provide a focal point both for voluntary organizations in their relationships with government and for the diverse departmental interests and involvement in the voluntary sector, it too has not been particularly influential. The relationships of government departments with the voluntary sector remain as diverse and uncoordinated as ever.

The problems with regard to regulation are related to the more general issue of accountability in the voluntary sector. Indeed one of the most serious problems that would arise from a transfer of responsibility from the state to the voluntary sector would be the loss of accountability. This is particularly serious because large sums of public money would be involved. How would it be possible to ensure the provision of high quality services in sufficient amounts and in the right places?

In an interesting and closely argued paper Leat (1987) identifies four forms of accountability applying to voluntary organizations:

1 fiscal accountability – accountability for the proper use of public money;
2 process accountability – accountability for following proper procedures;
3 programme accountability – accountability for quality of work;
4 accountability for priorities – accountability for the relevance or appropriateness of the agency's work.

It is difficult to see, however, how these different forms of accountability are to be enforced. Voluntary organizations are not accountable either directly to the electorate or indirectly to an elected body. The political and hierarchical accountability which is a feature (albeit an imperfect one) of state services is absent in the case of voluntary organizations. This problem is exacerbated by the complete lack of any internal democracy in many voluntary bodies. It is true that contractual accountability and contract compliance may be viewed as an alternative to political account-ability, but much of what the voluntary sector does is not capable of precise measurement for inclusion in a contract.

There are, then, considerable difficulties in attempting to ensure accountability, and Leat (1987: 43) comments that 'problems are likely to increase if a policy of pluralism and closer relationships between the voluntary and statutory sectors is pursued'.

One advantage which the state has over the voluntary sector is that its resources are more certain and less subject to sharp fluctuations. This, together with the pervasiveness of the state, facilitates long-term planning over broad areas. Potentially, at least, the state is in a better position to ensure greater uniformity of provision. There is ample evidence to show that uniformity of provision is very far from being realized, but voluntary provision is almost certainly more uneven – both territorially and between one client group and another.

The territorial distribution of voluntary provision is related very closely to social class. Although their research was done some years ago, the conclusions of Hatch and Mocroft (1983: 66) still hold: 'On the whole, towns low in voluntary organisations tended to be the ones that were low in social class'. If low social class is equated with greater social need, then voluntary organizations are distributed in such a way that the areas of greatest need are the least well served. Brenton (1985: 79), in a study looking at the feasibility of the voluntary sector replacing the state sector *to some degree* in the provision of personal social services, concludes: 'Asking what is the capacity for such an expansion, in practical terms, we must conclude that the available evidence suggests that it would require a transformation that would be nothing short of miraculous. Voluntary organisations are thinly and unevenly distributed, and where the need is greatest, they do not exist.' It is interesting to note that Sosin (1986) found a similar discrepancy between levels of need and voluntary action in the United States.

There is also uneven distribution among different client groups, whether this is measured by the number of voluntary workers or by resources. Children, the physically disabled and the elderly tend to be well-served by voluntary agencies, whereas the mentally ill, alcohol and drug abusers and the single homeless are poorly served. Uneven and incomplete coverage leads to overlapping, duplication and waste in some spheres of activity and gaps and shortages in others. Even with tight government control, it is doubtful whether a system that is so fragmented and poorly coordinated could ever ensure an equitable distribution of resources.

The problems associated with voluntary provision cannot be dismissed lightly, nor can they be easily solved. They may be tolerable so long as the voluntary sector continues to play a subsidiary role to that of the state, but they would become much less acceptable if the voluntary sector were to develop into the major provider. A modest expansion of the voluntary sector might be attempted, but the sector's shortcomings are simply too many and too serious for major transfers from the state to be contemplated.

The commercial sector

The mixed economy implies a role in welfare provision for private markets, although there is little agreement about how powerful and extensive the commercial sector should be. In many welfare states the commercial sector has been growing rapidly during the 1980s, sometimes with the direct encouragement of governments.

For example, between 1981 and 1986 the number of beds in registered nursing homes and private hospitals in Britain increased from 33,500 to 65,100. In this same period the number of private outpatient attendances increased from 181,800 to 261,600. At the beginning of 1981 3.5 million people were covered by private health insurance, but by the end of 1987 the number covered had increased to 5.3 million. These figures must be put into perspective, however; in 1986 only 16 per cent of all beds in health care institutions in England and Wales were in private hospitals and nursing homes, and by the end of 1987 slightly less than 10 per cent of the population of the UK was covered by private medical insurance (Central Statistical Office, 1989: 131).

Britain has also witnessed quite dramatic growth in private residential (and nursing) homes, principally for elderly people. Between 1979 and 1986 the number of places in private residential homes more than tripled – an annual average increase of more than 17 per cent. The number of places in local authority homes increased only marginally with an average annual increase of less than 1 per cent. More than 52 per cent of all homes are now in private ownership (Phillips et al., 1988: 8).

This unrestricted and unplanned growth has led to distortions in the distribution of welfare facilities. It is obvious that markets respond to demand, not need, and there may very well be over-provision in some areas. In Britain the development of private hospitals has produced too many beds in London and in the West Midlands and Wessex regions. This has resulted in falling bed occupancy rates: an average of 65 per cent in private hospitals in 1984 as compared with an average of 77 per cent in National Health Service Hospitals (Higgins, 1988: 118–19). The south coast of England has seen the most rapid expansion of residential homes, and signs of over-provision are appearing now with homes beginning to close down in quite large numbers.

The commercial sector poses something of a dilemma for those advocating a mixed economy of welfare and a reduced role for the state. Clearly, without a commercial sector the mixed economy of welfare lacks a basic ingredient. On the other hand, the more moderate welfare pluralists recognize some of the limitations and dangers of commercial services.

Faced with this dilemma, a common reaction is to accept the usefulness of a commercial sector, but to qualify this acceptance and make it conditional on adequate safeguards and regulation. Hadley and Hatch (1981: 100) typify this approach:

> A system of social services dominated by the commercial sector . . . in important respects negates some of the objectives for which the social services are established. Hence the criticisms levelled at the statutory services in this book should not be taken as arguments for patterns of provision that are predominantly commercial. But there are likely to be situations in which commercial provision, when subject to safeguards to maintain the quality of service and when it does not have a detrimental effect on other sources of services, can contribute usefully to a plural system of services.

Once the commercial welfare sector has been legitimated, however, it may prove difficult to limit its growth. In commenting on Hadley and Hatch's guarded acceptance of a regulated commercial sector, Beresford and Croft (1984: 25) state:

> The problem is that welfare pluralists seem to overestimate the capacity of the state to regulate the slice of the welfare market the commercial sector takes . . . More fundamentally . . . welfare pluralists cannot escape opening wider the door to privatisation by the support for the commercial sector inherent in their advocacy of a plurality of sources of welfare.

Problems of control, of course, relate not only to the total size of the commercial sector, but also to the quality of its provision. The market's potential for abuse and exploitation of vulnerable clients implies extensive and detailed regulation.

This creates two problems for the mixed economy of welfare. First, one of the advantages claimed for private markets is that they tap reserves of entrepreneurial flair. Supposing this to be true, entrepreneurs are likely to be frustrated by the necessary amount of regulation, and flair may be stifled.

The second problem is the cost and difficulty of devising effective systems of regulation. This problem is highlighted by Phillips et al. (1988: 11) in a study of private residential accommodation for elderly people in Britain:

> An essential role of government in a mixed economy should be to supervise the regulation of the market sector, especially insofar as this is providing surrogate services or facilities for the public sector. The 1984 Residential Homes Act was intended to provide new substantive and procedural controls. . . . However, the powers available to the social services and health authorities under the Act are limited and they

can claim that they have not been given the money for adequate monitoring . . . A report from the social services inspectorate accepts that the 1984 Act is presenting difficulties of implementation and standards vary between authorities.

There are problems in the original vetting procedures, which are far from rigorous. The sheer volume of applications during the early 1980s meant that local authorities were hard-pressed to keep pace. Once homes are opened, monitoring is perfunctory. The number of instances of abuse of patients that have been coming to light seems to indicate that some homes are run by totally unsuitable people.

There are similar problems of regulation in relation to private hospitals, highlighted in Britain by the recent case involving the sale of kidneys for transplants at the Humana Wellington Hospital. Higgins (1988: 135) argues that:

> The best means of controlling private sector developments fairly and efficiently are by no means self-evident and the experience of different countries reveals flaws in many of the possible options . . . attention must be given not only to the control of planned developments but also to monitoring standards of care and accreditation procedures in both institutional and non-institutional settings.

One reason for attempting to control private welfare markets in a mixed economy of welfare is that powerful private suppliers might damage the voluntary, non-profit sector. This could happen either through direct takeover or through diversion of funds. In the American context, Gilbert (1984: 64) writes, 'Once an almost exclusive preserve of voluntary nonprofit organizations . . . the private sector of social welfare has been penetrated by an increasing number of proprietary agencies dedicated to service at a profit'. Higgins (1988: 120) reports that in Britain rising costs brought about the closure of thirteen non-profit hospitals between 1980 and 1985. Several others had been bought up by the larger chains. In addition, the promotion of private welfare markets might encourage values inimical to those on which voluntarism depends. Ware, in another chapter in this book, argues that 'the general effect of the expansion of the market system has been to corrode altruism' (see p. 204).

We have seen how the state contributes to the finance of informal and voluntary providers of welfare. State financing of commercial provision raises ethical issues about using public money to increase private profits. A full discussion of these issues is beyond the scope of this chapter, but what can be said is that the problems of regulating private organizations become even more significant when public funds are used to support private ventures. It is clear that private health and welfare depend very heavily on state support which may take several forms.

1 Fiscal support: for example, tax relief on private pensions, mortgage repayments and health insurance contributions. According to Wilkinson (1986) the cost of tax relief to private pension schemes in Britain increased by 106 per cent between 1979–80 and 1983–4, whereas the cost of state retirement and supplementary pensions increased by only 12.3 and 22.8 per cent respectively. In this same period, public sector housing subsidies declined by 21.5 per cent, but tax relief on mortgage interest payments increased by 28.6 per cent.

2 Subsidies: probably the most significant subsidy is the acceptance by the state of the costs of training. Most of the cost of training doctors, nurses, teachers and social workers is met out of public expenditure, with the private sector providing very little.

3 The payment of fees for services and facilities: a good example of this in Britain is the Supplementary Benefit/Income Support payment for the provision of places in private residential and nursing homes. This has undoubtedly encouraged and sustained the rapid growth of private facilities, and without these state payments (a total of £500 million in 1986) many homes would be forced to close. Another British example is the financial support given to private hospitals. Regional and District Health Authorities pay private hospitals to perform minor operations on National Health Service patients. (This kind of arrangement is, of course, very common in the American Medicare and Medicaid programmes. Vendorism – the purchase of services by public bodies from either non-profit or profit-making organizations – is also very common in the personal social services in the United States. Kramer (1981: 69) estimates that such arrangements account for over one-third of governmentally financed personal social services.)

If the market is left to grow unchecked, and even more if it is nurtured by government subsidies, then the state sector may be reduced to a residual role in which it is left to provide poor services for poor and dependent people. The choice for some – those with the ability to pay – might be increased, but others would have no choice but to rely upon a reduced range and quality of stigmatizing state services. In this way, notions of integration and community may be weakened. Thus, Wilding (1986: 129–30) writes of 'the corrosive effect of the market system on social cohesion' and claims that 'the market . . . is responsible for the crucial divisions and conflicts of our society – between capital and labour, rich and poor, employed and unemployed'.

Conclusion

There can be little doubt that in most welfare states the current trend is towards a mixed economy of welfare in which the state plays a less dominant role. This is a direct reversal of the trends in the 1960s. The attraction of this from the point of view of governments is that it legitimates state disengagement from and cuts in welfare provision.

The role of the state has been central to the debate about the mixed economy of welfare. The welfare mix established in the 1950s and 1960s – a mix in which the state was dominant – has been under threat since the mid-1970s. The New Right wish to see a new mix established with the state retaining no more than a residual role. Although the Conservative government in Britain would not go quite that far, it clearly does wish to push back the state and it continually stresses the central role of the voluntary and informal sectors in meeting need. Webb and Wistow (1987: 92–5) show how speeches made by Mrs Thatcher and former Secretaries of State for Social Services, Mr Jenkin and Mr Fowler, posit a view of welfare provision in which the personal social services provided by local authorities were seen as merely filling the gaps or acting as a back-up to the informal and voluntary sectors.

More moderate still are those policy analysts (Gladstone, 1979; Hatch, 1980; Hadley and Hatch, 1981; Hatch and Mocroft, 1983; Gilbert, 1983) who wish to see the retention of the state's role in finance and regulation, but a reduction in its role in the direct *provision* of services.

However, the policy of shifting the balance in provision decisively away from the state and towards the commercial, voluntary and informal sectors is not based on extensive research. In Britain and elsewhere there have been small-scale demonstration projects, mainly neighbourhood schemes of one kind or another. But well-resourced, specially designed projects with a highly committed management willing to give a great deal of time to them, scarcely provide a credible model for general implementation.

The most extensively and carefully researched scheme is the Kent Community Care Scheme. The Personal Social Services Research Unit at the University of Kent was involved in this scheme at every stage, advising and evaluating. What the scheme demonstrates is that community care can be successfully implemented to provide a satisfactory alternative to institutional care, even in the case of frail elderly people whose circumstances place them on the verge of admission to residential care. The Kent scheme makes use of volunteers, but it cannot be used to justify the conclusion that a wholesale shift towards voluntary provision, and still less to commercial provision, is possible.

The arguments presented in this chapter cast doubts on the capacity of the informal, commercial and voluntary sectors to substitute for the state. The problems associated with each sector have been identified.

The family, already providing a great deal of care, is undergoing changes which is reducing its capacity to care at the very moment when the number of people requiring care is increasing. Greater support for the family may help it to maintain present levels of care, but even looking on the optimistic side, no more than a modest increase in family care can be anticipated. A major problem in Britain is that the government expects more from the informal sector, but appears to be unwilling to provide the necessary finance and support.

Walker (1985: 50) warns against viewing informal support networks 'as a universal panacea for the problems – economic, organisational and operational – of the social services', and continues:

> There are worrying signs in the UK that current policies of privatisation and greater use of informal carers are not based on a responsible assessment of needs and resources but on a dual concern to reduce the financial cost and limit the scope of the social services. It does seem sometimes that in place of 'throwing money' at social problems the government is attempting to 'throw' volunteers at them.

As for the voluntary sector, its coverage is uneven and incomplete and there are problems of accountability and regulation. Brenton (1985: 197) comments: 'To devolve responsibility for the kind of social services we currently enjoy to a mass of informal, ill-organised groups and organisations would constitute so great a dismantling of the personal social services system as to leave its functions solely to hidden providers of informal care'.

With the commercial sector, too, there are serious difficulties in ensuring effective control and regulation. This is of particular significance when a large number of private concerns are subsidized from public funds.

At present, statutory finance and regulation of all three sectors in Britain is haphazard and piecemeal: there are no discernible principles at work. Given the diverse nature of the voluntary and commercial sectors, it is difficult to imagine what acceptable principles for the division of resources among the multitude of agencies could be devised, and the problems of control would remain considerable. The development of a powerful private market sector could damage the voluntary sector.

The conclusion must be that any dramatic shift in the present balance within the mixed economy would be unwise. If the voluntary and informal sectors cannot respond in the ways and to the extent expected of them, then any reduction of statutory activity will merely serve to legitimate cuts in public expenditure and the development of market provision.

There appears to be no viable alternative to statutory dominance in the mixed economy of welfare, but this should not be used as an excuse for maintaining the status quo. The statutory social services, as they are at present constituted, have a number of shortcomings which require urgent attention. They are too bureaucratic and remote, they are too slow to respond to changing needs and they do too little for women and ethnic minorities. We need to look for new ways of organizing, providing and financing welfare. Unfortunately, the debate about the mixed economy of welfare has had the effect of diverting attention from the main task of reforming state services.

To make services more responsive and less remote, decentralization and participation are two related strategies that might be attempted. Decentralization is already well advanced in many West European countries and in the United States. It is seen as a means of reducing the power of the central state and as a prerequisite for successful participation, which is taken to mean involvement in both service delivery and policy making. Two stages of decentralization might be envisaged: from central to local government and from local government to neighbourhoods.

Decentralization is regarded as essential to a participatory system because people feel best able to participate in small local units. Participation in the provision of services is, of course, much easier to achieve than participation in decision making. The latter requires power-holders (locally elected councillors, for example) to surrender some of their autonomy and to negotiate with those previously excluded from the decision-making process.

It would be a mistake to expect too much of participation for two reasons. First, it cannot be assumed that everyone *wants* to participate, and this raises the question of *who* participates. Most participants in formal structures are middle class rather than working class. At the very least, the weakest and most vulnerable members of the community will be excluded and their interests may be ignored.

Secondly, it cannot be assumed that wider participation brings about wider dispersal of power. It is true that participation may give people greater power over their own lives, but involvement at neighbourhood level is not likely to lead to the exercise of political power in national, regional or even local contexts. Power is class-based and built into economic and social structures. As Higgins (1978: 125) says of the poverty programmes: 'Participation alone cannot secure an overall redistribution of income and wealth or the eradication of inequalities of class, status and power. The real danger is that participation, as a means to such ends, becomes an end in itself.'

Decentralization and participation have found support among all shades of political opinion. Such policies are welcomed by conservatives and many welfare pluralists as part of a general policy of reducing the role of the state and transferring respon-sibility to the commercial, voluntary and informal sectors. Those who believe that the state must retain a dominant role in welfare see decentralization and participation, not as a means of *replacing* the state but as a means of making its intervention more accep-table and more responsive. And, I would argue, a debate about how to achieve greater decentralization and participation is likely to prove more fruitful than debates about how to change the welfare mix.

Notes

I wish to thank Robert Goodin, Michael Laver and Alan Ware for their helpful comments on an earlier version of this chapter.

1 This figure must be treated with some caution. It is based on estimates in the Wolfenden Report (1978) that the work done by volunteers was equivalent to 400,000 full-time workers. Of these, 266,000 were in fields related to the personal social services. Calculation: 266,000 × £4 × 40 × 52 = £2.2 billion.

References

Addy, T. and Scott, D. (1988) *Fatal Impacts? The MSC and Voluntary Action*. London: William Temple Foundation.
Bell, D. (1960) *The End of Ideology*. Glencoe, Ill.: The Free Press.
Beresford, P. and Croft, S. (1984) 'Welfare pluralism: The new face of Fabianism', *Critical Social Policy*, no. 9.
Berger, P.L. and Neuhaus, R.J. (1977) *To Empower People: The Role of Mediating Structures in Public Policy*. Washington DC: American Enterprise Institute for Public Policy Research.

Billis, D. and Harris, M. (1986) *An Extended Role for the Voluntary Sector*, PORTVAC Working Paper 3. London: Brunel University.

Brenton, M. (1985) *The Voluntary Sector in British Social Services*. London: Longman.

Campling, J. (1988) 'Social policy digest', *Journal of Social Policy*, 17(2).

Central Statistical Office (1989) *Social Trends*, no. 19. London: HMSO.

Family Policy Studies Centre (1988) *An Ageing Population*. London: Family Policy Studies Centre.

Family Policy Studies Centre (1989) *Family Policy Bulletin*, no. 6. London: Family Policy Studies Centre.

Finch, J. and Groves, D. (1980) 'Community care and the family: A case for equal opportunities?', *Journal of Social Policy*, 9(4): 487–511.

Gilbert, N. (1983) *Capitalism and the Welfare State*. New Haven, Conn.: Yale University Press.

Gilbert, N. (1984) 'Welfare for profit: Moral, empirical and theoretical perspectives', *Journal of Social Policy*, 13(1).

Gladstone, F.J. (1979) *Voluntary Action in a Changing World*. London: Bedford Square Press

Hadley, R. and Hatch, S. (1981) *Social Welfare and the Failure of the State*. London: George Allen & Unwin.

Hatch, S. (1980) *Outside the State*. London: Croom Helm.

Hatch, S. and Mocroft, I. (1983) *Components of Welfare*. London: Bedford Square Press.

Higgins, J. (1978) *The Poverty Business*. Oxford: Blackwell.

Higgins, J. (1988) *The Business of Medicine*. London: Macmillan.

HM Treasury (1987) *The Government's Expenditure Plans 1988–89 to 1990–91*, Cmnd 288. London: HMSO.

Kohl, J. (1981) 'Trends and problems in postwar public expenditure development in Western Europe and North America', in P. Flora and A.J. Heidenheimer (eds), *The Development of Welfare States in Europe and America*. New Brunswick: Transaction Books.

Kramer, R.M. (1981) *Voluntary Agencies in the Welfare State*. Berkeley: University of California Press.

Leat, D. (1987) *Voluntary Organisations and Accountability: Theory and Practice*. Coventry: University of Warwick.

Le Grand, J. (1982) *The Strategy of Equality*. London: George Allen & Unwin.

Le Grand, J. and Robinson, R. (eds), (1984) *Privatisation and the Welfare State*. London: George Allen & Unwin.

MacPherson, S. and Svenson, M. (1988) 'Attrition benefits'. *The Guardian*, 24 February.

Marshall, T.H. (1965) *Social Policy*. London: Hutchinson.

Mishra, R. (1984) *The Welfare State in Crisis*. Brighton: Wheatsheaf.

Parker, R. (1981) 'Tending and social policy', in E.M. Goldberg and S. Hatch (eds), *A New Look at the Personal Social Services*. London: Policy Studies Institute.

Paukert, L. (1984) *The Employment and Unemployment of Women in OECD Countries*. Paris: OECD.

Phillips, D.R., Vincent, J.A. and Blacksell, S. (1988) *Home from Home*. Sheffield: University of Sheffield.

Public Accounts Committee (1988) *Monitoring and Control of Charities in*

England and Wales. London: HMSO.

Sosin, M. (1986) *Private Benefits: Material Assistance in the Private Sector*. London: Academic Press.

Taylor-Gooby, P. (1985) *Public Opinion, Ideology and State Welfare*. London: Routledge & Kegan Paul.

United Nations (1981) *UN Demographic Yearbook*. New York: UN.

University of York (1988) *Cash and Care*, no. 4. York: University of York.

Walker, A. (1985) 'From welfare state to caring society? The promise of informal support networks', in J.A. Yoder, J.M.L. Yonker and R.A.B. Leaper (eds), *Support Networks in a Caring Community*. Dordrecht: Martinus Nijhoff.

Webb, A. and Wistow, G. (1987) *Social Work, Social Care and Planning: The Personal Social Services*. London: Longman.

Wilding, P. (ed.) (1986) *In Defence of the Welfare State*. Manchester: Manchester University Press.

Wilkinson, M. (1986) 'Tax expenditures and public policy in the UK', *Journal of Social Policy*, 15(2).

Willmott, P. (1986) *Social Networks, Informal Care and Public Policy*. London: Policy Studies Institute.

Wolfenden, J. (1978) *the Future of Voluntary Organisations*. London: Croom Helm.

9

Meeting Needs in a Welfare State: Relations between Government and Voluntary Organizations in Norway

Stein Kuhnle and Per Selle

In *Power and Community*, Robert Nisbet (1962) posits an inherent conflict between voluntary organizations and government. He attributes to government much of the responsibility for the weakening of voluntary institutions and the resulting rise of alienation and anomie in the modern world. As Lester M. Salamon (1987) remarks, this theme is expressed in other accounts of the voluntary sector, which portray a 'golden age' of voluntary sector purity that has been corrupted by receipt of government funds. Salamon and other researchers have demonstrated that such accounts do not correspond with the actual development of relations between government and voluntary institutions in the United States. But what about countries where there is a stronger tradition of the legitimacy of state intervention? This chapter is concerned with one such country, Norway, but in considering it, we also raise issues of more general interest for comparative research.

We shall question the common belief that government and voluntary organizations represent two different worlds and thus, implicitly, have been in a state of conflict. We shall explore, in a historical perspective, how different types of voluntary organizations have related to government in Norway and try to explain why different kinds of relationships have developed for various categories of organizations at different times or in different contexts.

Salamon (1987: 100) has provided a corrective to American conventional wisdom that government support of the voluntary sector is a relatively recent development: 'In point of fact [however], government support of voluntary organizations has roots deep in American history'. In 1901, in all but possibly two territories and four western states, private charities were subsidized either by the state or by counties and cities. 'Collaboration, not separation or antagonism, between government and the

Third Sector ... has been the predominant characteristic [throughout most of our history]'; statistics show that non-profit organizations[1] have emerged as major providers of publicly financed services in the US (Salamon, 1987: 102). Government is the largest single source of income for non-profit service organizations, and is twice the size of private giving. Salamon ascribes the lack of attention devoted to the phenomenon of extensive governmental support for voluntary organizations to the influence of the conventional European model stressing the expansion of the centralized bureaucratic state. As a corollary, one might postulate that Europeans have overlooked the historically close interaction between government and voluntary organizations because of the influence of American theories of voluntarism and community which stress the (supposed) existence of a large 'sector' of *independent* voluntary organizations.

In contrast to the United States the Scandinavian countries were set early on a route leading to universal, citizenship-based welfare institutions before the turn of the twentieth century. The urge to make social insurance and security systems include their entire populations was stated more or less explicitly as the ultimate goal in Denmark, Norway and Sweden (Seip, 1984; Kuhnle, 1981). Under a liberal regime in 1913, Sweden introduced the world's first universal old-age pension scheme, but the proposal for such a radical idea had already been published in 1889 – coincidentally in the same year as the Social Democratic Party was founded.

A 'Scandinavian model' of welfare provision (Erikson et al., 1987), with a relatively strong element of citizenship rights and state responsibility for welfare, can be discerned in programmatic statements and partly in practice long before 1949 when T.H. Marshall (1963) delivered his famous and much-quoted speech on the development of civil, political and social citizenship. In contrast to other Scandinavian countries both commercial, market-based organizations and non-profit, charitable organizations were poorly developed in Norway when state social insurance was put on the political agenda (in Norway as in most other European countries) following Bismarck's large-scale insurance schemes for industrial workers in Germany. A new and more active role for the state gained wide acceptance after 1870–80 (Seip, 1984) and, at the time of this ideological change, few private or voluntary organizations offering social insurance or other welfare-related services existed in Norway (Kuhnle, 1981). In this last respect Norway is very different from Britain and the United States.

Although all Scandinavian countries found an active role for the state in welfare matters almost from the beginning, Norway was more inclined than Denmark and Sweden to adopt the then highly controversial principle of compulsory social insurance. It did so because state involvement would reach few groups, and not the most needy ones, if it confined its role to subsidizing voluntary insurance offered by non-governmental organizations (Kuhnle, 1981). Moreover, private philanthropy was sparsely developed and not able to cope with rapidly rising new social needs, and thus did not represent an alternative to public (state) welfare institutions (Kuhnle and Selle, 1990).

The coalescence of the public and voluntary sectors

Although state, provincial and local government institutional solutions dominate the Scandinavian welfare model, there has been and is room for other organizations. Voluntary organizations emerged in the last century, and close relations developed early. In this section we present a brief review of different types of relations.

Ever since the 1820s *public subsidies* have been granted to private organizations.[2] In the 1840s, the emissaries of the teetotallers were given government subsidies. Private schools for the handicapped were also early recipients of public funds. Rifle clubs received state subsidies from the 1860s, as did sports clubs later on. After 1875, public subsidies were increasingly offered to evening schools, workers' academies, and similar enterprises. In other words, from very early on, organizations were integrated with public policy. Of course, in general, voluntary organizations are much more closely integrated in public policy today, but these examples indicate the context in which changes have occurred.

Pressure group activity is also a phenomenon with a long history. Voluntary organizations have always tried to influence public authorities on issues which affect them, not least in legislative matters. The temperance movement and also the linguistic movement (for New Norwegian, *landsmål*, *nynorsk*) to some extent represent key examples of this. The teetotallers regarded a strong temperance movement as a prerequisite for pressing government in legislative matters (NOU, 1988: 51). As organizations grew in numbers and breadth, the scope of pressure group activity naturally increased, but again the change was a matter of quantity rather than of quality.

From the turn of the century organizations already *participated in official committees* of an ad hoc nature and on committees of a more permanent character. Temperance organizations were involved in the national council for temperance education (*Landsrådet for Edruskapsundervisning*) which was established in 1902. The continuation of this close cooperation resulted in the creation of a government council of temperance (*Statens Edruskapsråd*) in 1936, giving the temperance movement a role on a permanent committee for their task at the national level. The movement was even more integrated in public policy in 1969 when the directorate for sobriety was established, although it had lost much of its mobilizing potential in the meantime.

The other area in which early contact between organizations and government developed was cultural, especially in the case of popular academies (*Folkeakademiene*). As early as 1899, the state offered a grant to a committee, composed of representatives of the government and the academies, to appraise and recommend lectures. In the period of economic stagnation in the 1920s public grants were reduced, but they increased again in the 1930s. Cooperation was formally institutionalized through the establishment of the government council for enlightenment of the people (*Statens Folkeopplysningsråd*).

Moreover, in the field of health, there are examples of the early development of institutionalized cooperation. We explain later the role of government and organizations in the fight against tuberculosis. In fact, the government played an important role as initiator of the establishment of one organization: *Nasjonalforeningen for folkehelsen* (1910). The Director of Public Health (*Medisinaldirektøren*) had a permanent seat on the Board, and a number of municipalities became members of the 'voluntary' organization. Another example is the central board for care of the handicapped (*Centralstyre for vanføreomsorgen*) which was created in 1916 with representatives from private organizations. This model of integrated participation was used in 1923 when the central board for centres of remedial measures (*Sentralstyre for hjelpestasjonsvirksomhet*) was formed. In the health sector, a general understanding grew gradually that government should have a superior responsibility, and that organizations were an integrated part of the transformation process towards increased public responsibility.

In the study of welfare provision, it is important to distinguish between the three functions of financing, producing and controlling welfare provision. Even if public authorities today cover almost all expenditure for running welfare institutions, this does not imply that institutions must be publicly owned. In Norway in 1985, 14 per cent of all places in general hospitals, 21 per cent of the places in psychiatric institutions, and as much as 35 per cent of all places for the mentally retarded were owned by voluntary organizations. Furthermore, voluntary organizations own 60 per cent of all places in institutions for alcoholics, and 32 per cent of the places in institutions for child and youth care (NOU, 1988: 17). About 75 per cent of all welfare service centres for the elderly were *run* by voluntary organizations, but publicly *financed*. In the field of non-institutional work, which is subject to less regulation, voluntary organizations perform more extensive tasks than the public sector. It is in this field that voluntary organizations are now expected to expand their activity. They are less likely to build and run more institutions, as this is an area which is strongly regulated and is an inherent part of the health and social planning activity of provincial and local government. Indeed, the public report on voluntary organizations in Norway (NOU, 1988: 17) envisages a reduction in the role of voluntary organizations in institutional care.

Within the rapidly expanding area of non-institutional care, there is a tendency – similar to one observed for institutional care – for voluntary organizations to look after the 'easiest' cases and to perform tasks which place the fewest demands on resources and personnel. A current vision in public reports considering new tasks for voluntary organizations seems to be decentralized facilities based on local community organization. As in a number of other West European countries, a comprehensive programme for reform of the public sector has been outlined (Olsen, 1988).

Compulsory state schemes, based on general taxation and premiums from employers and employees, dominate the field of social insurance/security, and the general health service is basically financed and run by central and provincial governments. But as we have seen, the state has never reigned supreme in the welfare field. Important services are provided by voluntary organizations, but paid for from the public purse. Service provision is integrated in a system basically controlled and financed by public authorities. This brief overview serves to indicate how interwoven the voluntary and public sectors are in Norway.

What are we to make of this? While Salamon (1987) claims that the voluntary sector had no 'golden age' in the USA, this claim would be even more true for a 'state-friendly'[3] country like Norway. Not only have voluntary organizations endeavoured to receive public subsidies, but today it still seems that organizations gladly welcome even insignificant public support simply because such support indicates that their work is appreciated by government and regarded as important. At the level of ideology, we are not able to find examples of organizations in the health and welfare sector (and even generally) which make much of an effort to demarcate themselves ideologically from government. For example, the newly established crisis centres for battered women and children are publicly financed institutions but with complete private control of their activities. Such arrangements also indicate public confidence in voluntary organizations.

The complexity of relations between the state and voluntary organizations in Norway becomes apparent when we consider examples of the three major types of organization operating in the health and welfare sector in the first decades of this century:[4]

1 Organizations for the promotion of welfare for the public in general (*Nasjonalforeningen for folkehelsen*; *Norske Kvinners Sanitetsforening*; *Norges Røde Kors*). These were large charitable organizations with broadly defined objectives. We shall concentrate here on their work to fight tuberculosis.

2 Organizations for the care and treatment of what was perceived as a self-inflicted problem, such as alcoholism (*Blå Kors, Hvite Bånd*). These were more specialized temperance organizations, based on a Christian philosophy of life, which not only tried to fight the spread of the 'evil' of alcohol, but which owned and ran large-scale institutions.

3 Special organizations catering for the welfare needs of people whose problems were perceived as undeserved, such as the blind, the deaf and the physically handicapped (*Norges Blindeforbund, Norske Døves Landsforbund, Norges Vanførelag*).[5]

The organizations we deal with represent either all organizations of their class, or the largest and most important. Thus, the characteristics of relations between government and voluntary organizations that we report must be considered representative of relations of this kind in Norway in the period concerned.

Organizations in categories 1 and 2 shared the characteristic that they worked for the general welfare of the public, and not primarily for their own members.[6] Organizations in category 3, however, worked primarily for the improvement of conditions for their own members, although the original initiatives to organize depended on people without the handicaps in question. This distinction between organizations in the first two categories and those in the third turns out to be important in a period of transition from private (especially families) to public responsibility for welfare. The major findings of the analyses of the three types of organizations are as follows.

First, organizations working for general welfare (categories 1 and 2) were never compelled to cooperate with the government. On the contrary, they themselves were driving forces in the ideological process of change which resulted in overall public responsibility for social welfare. These organizations were much more interested in the improvement of general welfare than in defining limited roles for themselves which might conflict with the role of the government. Their proximity to government is an obvious characteristic of the institutional care provided by organizations in categories 1 and 2. For organizations in category 1, we find no value differences or conflicts whatsoever; organizations were willingly integrated into an overall system of public responsibility. The situation is more or less the same for organizations in category 2; they played an important part in the care for alcoholics, and cooperated closely with the government. Their philosophy of life made the need for organizational autonomy greater, but this fact did not appear to conflict with the interests of the government. Having places for alcoholics in Christian institutions was better than having no institutions, and it was also less expensive. At the time public authorities had great sympathy for the view that a committed philosophy of life (one which was based on religion) could be conducive to temperance.

Secondly, the mode of activity of organizations in category 3 was strongly linked to general ideological currents. They sought to improve the life conditions of their own members. An important part of their activity was social contact, since these were groups of people who experienced varying difficulties in participating in everyday life; furthermore they provided schooling and economic support in a period when, to a large extent, these groups were outside the reach of government and other schemes, and suffered severe deprivation. In the beginning, they were self-help organizations rather than interest organizations. A central objective was that their members should not inconvenience the public. Increased personal autonomy through self-organization was their goal. Thus they wanted to demarcate themselves in relation to the government. But as the general view on public responsibility changed, the organizations developed skills of interest articulation and began exploring the possibility of obtaining public funds. We discern a development from 'internal' to 'external' activity but without organizations giving up their role in welfare provision.

Historically, these organizations have been more concerned with their own autonomy than organizations which have worked for general welfare purposes and for the welfare of others. They came into contact with the state at a later stage. Furthermore, the state was somewhat reluctant to cater for their needs, partly because the organizations had difficulties in portraying the scope of their problems.

A typology of relations between voluntary organizations and the state

The welfare state literature is filled with evidence of the growth of public expenditure, policy areas covered and policy areas affected. No one can question this strong growth, especially after 1945. The public sector has increasingly financed and provided welfare services, partly through voluntary organizations increasingly integrated into a unifying publicly controlled 'welfare package'. But voluntary organizations have not been exhausted for tasks. In fact, in Norway the main increase in the scope of their services occurred during the first two decades after the Second World War, coinciding with the expansion and maturation of the welfare state.

A number of problems arise when we try to interpret earlier developments, because the main concepts used are often broad and imprecise. However, there are two dimensions, indicated in figure 9.1, which are especially important. The first dimension relates to how 'close' organizations are to the state with respect to the communications and contact they have. Organizations may be either *near* (and hence integrated with the state) or *distant* (and hence separate from it). The second dimension relates to the *independence* of organizations from the state – they may be either autonomous or dependent. What we include as 'voluntary organizations' could conceivably be placed in any one of the four boxes in figure 9.1.[7]

Our argument is that most analytical approaches to the study of the development of the welfare state do not capture the dynamics of the inter-sectoral relations because of the a priori assumption of an 'imperialistic' state, or because the concept of 'sector' is used in a static way. This means that many analyses of modern politics make comparisons with an ideal state characterized by complete autonomy of voluntary organizations.

It is this starting point, a mythical 'golden age', which leads easily to a dramatization of the scope of change in relations between sectors. Given a relational perspective, both the state and voluntary or non-governmental organizations would be identified differently in different contexts. This is a fruitful point of departure for comparative analysis.

In many analyses it is argued that because of changes in public policies, voluntary organizations have moved from the relationship

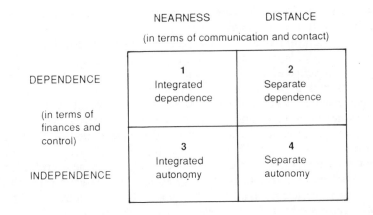

NEARNESS   DISTANCE

(in terms of communication and contact)

	NEARNESS	DISTANCE
DEPENDENCE	**1** Integrated dependence	**2** Separate dependence
INDEPENDENCE	**3** Integrated autonomy	**4** Separate autonomy

DEPENDENCE

(in terms of finances and control)

INDEPENDENCE

Figure 9.1   *Relations between the public and voluntary sectors*

regarded as ideal by advocates of a minimal state (box 4) towards box 1 (primarily labour market organizations), and towards box 2 where the government dominates and organizations have little influence, and have their freedom of action severely limited by public policies. Box 3 constitutes the pluralist ideal: groups of people organize themselves and try to make an impact on public policy on issues which affect them, but without becoming integrated into the decision-making or implementation processes.

Having outlined a typology, the three categories of organizations described in the last section can be fitted into it. We begin with the third category of organizations. The organizations for the physically handicapped were established to reduce personal isolation for those affected. They were dependent on others to arrange ways of coming together. Private citizens or government established schools and supported charitable enterprises (of a religious nature) which developed in the latter half of the last century. Many, but not all of them, were then dissolved as the organizations came of age, and the organizations established were not exclusively for the handicapped. In the beginning, their specified objectives included service provision, and interest promotion, and the provision of information. However, the organization for the deaf had no remit as to its relations with either government or the general public, and it has always been the most 'introverted' organization. Initially the fundamental aim was to change public attitudes about the dependence of the handicapped and to develop self-help. The principle of autonomy vis-à-vis the state was explicit. In general, though, these organizations have switched their emphasis from the provision of welfare services and information (with financial resources based on donations), to a greater use of pressure group activity. This change is also linked to the extension of the area of public responsibility. In the organizations this change is reflected in development towards a strengthened central administration at the expense of local freedom of activity, a change which occurred mainly after the First World War.

As to the relationship between different sectors, it would be correct to regard these voluntary organizations as welfare pioneers. The state entered this field later, taking over many but not all activities. However, the state was also an actor from an early stage, primarily through a school law in 1881 concerning the mentally deficient and the building of institutions for the physically disabled. In the beginning, though, the scope of public subsidies was very limited. However, from the early nineteenth century a number of schools had been created by private citizens before both the state and organizations entered the arena, and such citizens can be regarded as the real pioneers. This is a pattern similar to one reported for other countries (Kramer, 1981).

Organizations soon contacted the government in areas where it had already demonstrated some interest, such as in the case of schooling, subsidies to private institutions, contributions to organizational initiatives, and so on. Apart from schooling, public services for the disabled through economic support for private charity were supplemental to those offered by the organizations in the inter-war period. An official committee in 1924 endorsed the principle of 'government-supported private management'. Although contacts with the government increased, and a tendency to struggle more on behalf of their own interests took place (a tendency which has been strengthened since 1945), it would be reasonable to characterize the period until 1940 as one in which good contacts were established, while at the same time organizations retained a high degree of freedom of action. Lines of communication seem to have been clearly set out (in a society less complex than today's). That is, there existed *nearness* in the sense of easy access, although this fact did not necessarily translate itself into immediate and substantial support for the aims of the organizations. Organizations of this type are not easy to place in our typology. If any organization at all can be placed in box 4, it must be the organization for the deaf, which from its inception was the most 'introverted'. But generally, all three moved gradually towards box 1 which they were to reach many years after 1945.

What about the three large, general charitable organizations of category 1? Some of them developed a wide range of tasks, but we shall focus our attention on their fight against tuberculosis. This was the only task of one of the organizations – *Nasjonalforeningen* – which was set up in 1910 in close cooperation with the Medical Association (*Lægeforeningen*) and the government, and it can be argued that it was really established by the government. Besides the government, the three charitable organizations were the only actors in this fight against the greatest epidemic in Norway since the Black Death. It could be claimed that the nature of the disease required special means, but at the same time the contours of a form of cooperation between government and private ('voluntary') agents that later became increasingly common can be discerned. It is a form of organization which is an expression of the typical *mixed system* which came to dominate from the turn of the century. A steady development towards increased public responsibility occurred. Of great importance was the legislation on tuberculosis in 1900 which was the first of its kind in the world and which ensured the superior responsibility of the government. It also provided for forced hospitalization. That is, it was accepted that disease was no longer a purely private matter. The legislation broke with traditional attitudes about the division between society and the individual citizen, and was politically controversial. There was no alternative to the state assuming responsibility in this area – the other sectors did not have the strength to perform the necessary tasks on the scale required.

Norske Kvinners Sanitetsforening, established in 1896, was the first to take on the problem of tuberculosis. *Nasjonalforeningen for folkehelsen* entered the arena from 1910, as did *Norges Røde Kors* (Red Cross) from about 1920 – the latter transforming itself from an organization for victims of war to a more general welfare organization. The competition between the three organizations at the local level led in 1925 to an agreement about cooperation which decided that new local associations should not be established in areas in which the other organizations already operated. In 1947, they joined together with the last charitable organization to be established, *Norsk Folkehjelp* (1939), to create a 'Council of Cooperation' which secured cooperation between organizations, contact with the government, and effectively prevented other organizations entering the same 'market'. Since 1945, no broad charitable health organization based on individual membership and local associations has been established.

These organizations came to play a major role both in terms of spreading health information and of running institutions. Service provider roles can be characterized by their degree of functional adaptation to the state system. In a great number of fields today, voluntary organizations are not prime or sole suppliers of services, though there are some examples, such as crisis centres for battered women, and mountain rescue services offered by *Røde Kors* and by *Norsk Folkehjelp*. Such a role of sole supplier of services was not usual in the fight against tuberculosis either. With respect to financing there were major transfers of governmental funds from a state lottery and from the state monopoly on the sale of liquor and wine, which emphasized the close relationship between the sectors. The state defined its responsibility also by financing expenditure to institutions providing care, for example, in accordance with laws on tuberculosis (1900), sickness insurance (1909), and through general appropriations over the government budget; by guaranteeing the operation of institutions (for example by paying deficits on operational costs); and by taking over the operation as well as ownership of non-public institutions. The picture which emerges is one of close contact and coordination.

If we return to our figure 9.1, it seems reasonable to argue that *Nasjonalforeningen* may be classified as being in box 1 throughout its existence. The other two organizations active in the fight against tuberculosis also seem most appropriately placed in box 1. Government and organizations are mutually dependent on each other, and relations are close, although no permanent superior board or committee of cooperation exists. Such formal cooperation belongs to the post-Second World War era.

Finally, organizations of the category 2 type are not easy to fit into figure 9.1. These organizations were part of one of the largest mass movements in Norway: the temperance movement. Social and religious objectives were mingled, but the organizations we are examining went beyond preventative efforts. The first institutions were marked by Christian charity. The view on alcoholism changed gradually, and the organizations were important agents of this change. At the turn of the century, the predominant public view was one of moral denunciation; the will to help was non-existent. It was believed that the state had to punish alcoholics who caused public disturbances. The attitude to alcoholics was part of a puritan morality in which a distinction between the deserving and undeserving poor was made. On the other hand the opinion of the two organizations, *Blå Kors* and *Det Hvite Bånd*, was that, although alcoholism was considered a vice, over-indulgence in alcohol gradually developed into an illness.

These organizations came to be the most important actors in the early development of caring institutions for alcoholics. The first attempt through legislation to establish a special relief scheme for compulsive drinkers, morphine-addicts, and other victims of intoxicants dates from 1898: the law permitted a person to be declared as incapacitated (*Lov om umyndiggjøring*). The law offered the possibility of committal in a sanatorium, but generally such institutions were lacking.

The first known sanatorium was created on a private initiative in 1882. Members of the temperance movement and medical practitioners served on the board. The majority in the temperance movement already regarded treatment and care as a public responsibility, because the state generated income from the sale of alcohol, and the temperance movement wanted to concentrate on preventative efforts (Bønes, 1978). Before the turn of the century, some private sanatoria run by doctors were established (paid for by the wealthy), but none of these institutions survived for long (Fuglum, 1972). A real improvement in these services came only when two organizations began to build and run sanatoria, in 1908 and 1913 respectively.

All sanatoria were soon to receive state subsidies. It would seem correct to say that the evolution of care for alcoholics was strongly differentiated on the basis of criteria of morality and illness. Religious and professional interests shaped a system of institutional care, based on financial support from the government, while the government was expected to assume responsibility for the chronic drinkers. During the period of contraction of public expenditure in the inter-war years (until 1935), state subsidies to the organizations were sharply reduced and caused severe problems for them. Private sanatoria took only those who volunteered to go into a sanatorium. Committals were left to the government.

Voluntary organizations still dominate the provision of institutional care for alcoholics. State supply of places (for the most difficult cases) developed only as a supplement to the voluntary effort. The organizations have not only been pioneering, but they have developed their role as the major service provider in close cooperation with the government and are completely dependent on public subsidies. Their activity has been an important and integrated part of a system of care for which a superior public responsibility has been manifest.

The close cooperation between the Christian temperance organizations and the state is interesting not only in itself, but also from an ideological perspective. Not only were these organizations willing to receive public support, but as with the rest of the temperance movement they have always considered it a public task to develop care for alcoholics and have believed that such care could best be established in cooperation with them. At the same time, they have shown much concern for their autonomy. However, public financing has been looked upon more as a right than as a problem for organizational autonomy. Increased public support was not necessarily perceived as a sign of weakness on their part, but rather as an indicator of growing public understanding of the tasks performed by the organizations. They have always favoured formal cooperation, and the adaptation to a superior public system today can in no way be seen as a solution forced on the organizations. Their institutions are still privately owned, with their own boards and administration, but they are fully integrated elements of the public care system. That running expenses and the patients' care in sanatoria are publicly financed does not create any problem for the organization, simply because they are not obsessed by the idea of autonomy. They look upon themselves as important opinion-makers and agents of influence towards public authorities.

Again, this category of organizations is not easily placed in our typology (figure 9.1). These organizations did not have a period of 'separate autonomy', and even if they have been important welfare pioneers, they were closely linked to public policy. A particular philosophy of life demands some autonomy in matters which relate to that philosophy, but it seems that these organizations are at least as integrated in public policy as the charitable organizations engaged in the fight against tuberculosis. Indeed, the degree of integration becomes even more apparent if we take into account the other tasks of the broadly based charitable organizations (*Norske Kvinners Sanitetsforening, Røde Kors*).

The relations between the three types of voluntary organizations in Norway and the Norwegian state are not easily placed in a context of existing theoretical approaches. We have seen that, from the very beginning, the more general charitable organizations, which primarily attend to the problems and needs of *others*, have cooperated closely with public authorities. Organizations have sometimes been pioneers, and the government may have been reluctant to take on tasks, but generally it is not possible to discern a pattern of 'visionary' organizations and a 'reactionary' public bureaucracy. Cooperation rather than conflict has been the rule. A perspective which depicts the state forcing itself into territories previously occupied by voluntary organizations is false. On the contrary, organizations have encouraged the process of ideological and organizational transformation towards increased public responsibility. Public solutions have not come as a result of 'failure' in the other sectors. Voluntary services have generally been regarded positively, as prerequisites for much of what the state has later taken over, and as developments unfolding through contact and in cooperation with public authorities.

Cooperation and ideology

In recent years we have seen tendencies to revise perspectives on public responsibility and on the choice of models or forms of organization. Comprehensive discussions on the modernization of the public sector in the direction of more decentralization, and stronger emphasis on values such as self-help and 'user democracy', are in progress. Among neo-conservatives and (European) liberals, the welfare state is criticized for inefficiency and overregulation. Individual freedom is seen as being constrained, and only seen to be safeguarded through a greater role for the market. Simultaneously, the New Left argues for a kind of 'civil society' – a user democracy where a system of local decision making and increasing degrees of self-government (and possibly self-sufficiency and self-financing) are supposed to go hand in hand. It is this development towards user democracy and decentralization which can offer new possibilities for voluntary organizations and lead to changes in the demarcations between sectors. It seems that we are moving into a decade of experimentation, similar to the early period of this century.

But the *structural* situation is very different today. The period leading up to 1940 represented an 'open' situation in the sense that the concept of the kind of welfare system to be developed was unclear. Gradually the view matured beyond serious dispute that the state should have a superior responsibility (whether executed directly or indirectly) for health, social insurance and social policy in general. This system did not generally evolve in a way which meant that the state took over tasks from the other sectors. It would be more correct to argue that new social needs were uncovered and new rights made 'natural' or obvious. It was realized that only through comprehensive public efforts could the necessary resources for an adequate supply of welfare services be provided. Thus, it makes sense to claim that the system developed in a vacuum with little competition from the other sectors. The voluntary sector was a cooperative driving force in the process of transformation towards increased public responsibility. The expression that the state 'took over', which is frequently used to describe this process of change, is hardly adequate. Public service provision and responsibility have not increased at the expense of the voluntary sector. But the scope and type of public service activity have obviously changed the potential for voluntary action.

Towards the end of the 1980s the situation is different: it is quite possible that the market alternative, both in terms of ideology and resources, is now much stronger, and that a similar case can be made for the voluntary sector. Ideologically there seems to have been a shift towards a view of the public and voluntary sectors as alternatives. Whether sufficient energy and resources to take on new tasks exist, is another matter (Brenton, 1985; Grindheim and Selle, 1989). In any case, there appears to be pressure on the 'Scandinavian welfare model' which is connected to problems of efficiency and legitimacy. The pressure is not only in the direction of changes between levels (that is, from central to local), but also in the direction of changes in the boundary between sectors. The situation now has two characteristics in common with the situation in the period 1900–1940: uncertainty and experimentation. New forms of organization are tried out without a clear picture as to what might develop overall. But the contrast is also striking: in the period leading up to 1940 a development towards increased public responsibility is evident – a development which does not exclude the possibility of voluntary organizations. In the 1950s and 1960s the expansion of the public sector – due to its 'own dynamics', political consensus and a consistently growing economy – was so comprehensive that in spite of the fact that extensive tasks were performed in the voluntary sector, the activity of that sector was almost invisible in official documents and public debate. It is the recent problems of efficiency and legitimacy of the Scandinavian model from the end of the 1970s which make for a realization that other producers and suppliers of welfare have been operating all the time. Furthermore, it prompts debates about the appropriate roles for old and new actors in the voluntary sector. A major ideological change seems to be taking place.

But how should we characterize the relations between sectors in the earlier period? What we observe are voluntary organizations acting as driving forces towards increased public responsibility. Thus, it seems that the organizations in this period both mobilize (that is, emphasize member activity) *and* politicize (that is, try to influence the political culture in favour of greater welfare and democracy) (Engberg, 1986). From very early on, they developed a 'function of cooperation', because there existed a consensus about goals and means of social development. In this period the charitable organizations sought public solutions rather than private ones. But such a choice may be dependent on context, and today it may well be that increasingly voluntary organizations will seek private solutions because the idea of public responsibility is being undermined.

Our postulate, that the organizations – first and foremost those in categories 1 and 2 – stood for a cooperative attitude from the outset, has consequences for the way in which we should understand relations between sectors. Cooperation meant that the understanding as to which tasks had to be dealt with had priority over organizational demands and autonomy. The concepts of 'common interests' and 'the general will' seem appropriate in this case. The organizations seemingly work for the good of 'everybody', for 'the people', 'the nation', and the result seems more important than demarcation between sectors – thus they do not perceive a clash of interests with government.

That organizations which work for the public at large, rather than for their own members, are closely connected to government in the period under study indicates an important contrast between organizations in categories 1 and 2 and organizations in category 3. (In essence, it is a distinction between 'common interest' groups and 'specific interest' groups.) We argue that a kind of 'open' structure existed in the early period, and that it assumed a definite form in the 1950s and 1960s. The strengthening of the state model was not a consequence of ideological compulsion, but rather a consequence of internal organizational processes in a system with a high degree of consensus with respect to ideology and goals. We argue in favour of a consensual view as to how the organization of welfare schemes and services developed. Our view is similar to an argument presented by March and Olsen (1987: 344): '. . . the will of the people is discovered through deliberation by reasoning citizens and rulers seeking to find the general welfare within a context of shared social values'.

But we do not stretch our argument as far as postulating that the 'common interest' or 'general interest' has always ranked higher than special interests in Norway.[8] Our argument is that the organizations which work for others have developed characteristics which clearly resemble those found in a system of popular representation, although in this case 'the general will' is not understood in territorial terms. The voluntary organizations are concerned with general welfare without being in conflict with the fundamental values and goals of government. It is more a question of differences of opinion as to the *scope* (quantity) of welfare rather than to the *substance* (quality) of welfare. The problems for democratic procedures which arise when more special interest organizations gain significant access to public policy making are different from those we have outlined here.

Conclusion

We have argued that historically the relationship between voluntary organizations and government in the welfare area has been one of extensive cooperation and integration rather than of conflict. The main difference between the pre- and post-Second World War periods has been more of a difference in scope than in the structuring of cooperation and integration itself. These conclusions, which stem from a historical and relational approach, lead to a questioning of key assumptions in pluralist and corporatist theories as to what is 'public' or 'private'. We contend that what we see is coordination through shared goals more than through forced hierarchical command, or coordination of a corporative–pluralist type where the state is involved in a political struggle between self-interested, powerful, organized actors (Olsen, 1987). Furthermore, we have argued that this symbiosis has been more comprehensive for the broad general welfare organizations working for others than for the specialized organizations which work mainly for the improvement of the conditions of their own members. Rather than expressing important distinctive values and being in conflict with government, the voluntary organizations have represented a main force in the ideological and organizational transformation towards increased public responsibility. They have sought public solutions rather than private ones. Which values voluntary organizations express, and which organizational solutions they prefer depends, however, on context – on the structuring of the relationship between the different sectors. In a situation with less consensus concerning public responsibility in the welfare area, and with greater ideological and economic strength of the non-public sectors, voluntary organizations could become an important force in a development away from public responsibility.

Notes

1. Like Salamon, we use 'non-profit', 'voluntary' and 'charitable' interchangeably.

2. *Selskapet for Norges Vel* received funds for book collections in the 1820s (Raaum, 1988).

3. The concept refers to the perspective that the state is generally perceived as 'friendly' by the population, fundamentally because the population rarely experienced state authority as repressive or suppressive.

4. This section is based on three dissertations in comparative politics written under our guidance, Hestetun (1985), Grindheim (1986), Onarheim (1988); and on historical overviews by Raaum (1988) and Seip (1984).

5. Since the Second World War, there has been an enormous increase in this third type of organization: only three organizations existed before 1940, while currently there are 48.

6. Organizations in categories 1 and 2 worked with specific problems (and therefore specific groups of people), but were oriented towards the welfare of others.

7. Obviously organizations in boxes 1, 3 and 4 could be further differentiated, but for our purposes here it is not necessary to do so.

8. Such as arguments put forward by Torgersen (1962) and Sejersted (1983) seem to imply.

References

Brenton, Maria (1985) *The Voluntary Sector in British Social Services*. London: Longman.

Bønes, Bergsvein (1978) *Alkoholomsorg i Norge*. Oslo: Statens Institutt for alkoholforskning.

Engberg, Jan (1986) 'Folkerørelserne i välfärdssamhället'. Unpublished dissertation, University of Umeå.

Erikson, Robert et al. (eds) (1987) *The Scandinavian Model: Welfare States and Welfare Research*. New York: M.E. Sharpe.

Fuglum, Per (1972) *Kampen om alkoholen i Norge 1816–1904*. Oslo: Universitetsforlaget.

Grindheim, Jan Erik (1986) 'Velferd eller veldedighet? En analyse av frivillige organisasjoners rolle i utviklingen av alkoholistomsorgen i Norge'. Unpublished dissertation, Department of Comparative Politics, University of Bergen.

Grindheim, Jan Erik and Selle, Per (1989) *The Role of Voluntary Social Welfare Organizations in Norway: A Democratic Alternative to a Bureaucratic Welfare State?* Bergen: Norwegian Research Centre on Management and Organization. (Notat 89/5).

Hestetun, Per Arne (1985) 'Velferdsekspansjon og organisasjonsendring. Ei analyse av frivillige organisasjonar si rolle i arbeidet mot tuberkulosen'. Unpublished dissertation, Department of Comparative Politics, University of Bergen.

Kramer, Ralph (1981) *Voluntary Agencies in the Welfare State*. Berkeley: University of California Press.

Kuhnle, Stein (1981) 'The growth of social insurance programs in Scandinavia: Outside influence and internal forces', in Peter Flora and A.J. Heidenheimer (eds), *The Development of Welfare States in Europe and America*. New Brunswick: Transaction Books.

Kuhnle, Stein and Selle, Per (eds) (1990) *Frivillig organisert velferd – alternativ til offentlig?* Bergen: Alma Mater.

March, James and Olsen, Johan P. (1987) 'Popular sovereignty and the search for appropriate institutions', *Journal of Public Policy*, 6(4): 341–70.

Marshall, T.H. (1963) 'Citizenship and social class', in T.H. Marshall, *Sociology at the Crossroads*. London: Heinemann.

Nisbet, Robert (1962) *Power and Community*. 2nd edn. New York: Oxford University Press.

NOU (1988): 17 *Frivillige organisasjoner*, Statens trykningskontor, Oslo. ('NOU' is *Norges offentlige utredninger* which is 'Norwegian public reports', a series of annual publications.)

Olsen, Johan P. (1987) 'Administrative reform and theories of organization', in

Colin Campbell and B. Guy Peters (eds), *Organizing Governance. Governing Organizations*. Pittsburgh: University of Pittsburgh Press.

Olsen, Johan P. (1988) 'The modernization of public administration in the Nordic countries: Some research questions', *Administrative Studies*, 7: 2–17.

Onarheim, Gunnar (1988) 'Ein analyse av frivillige organisasjonar sitt arbeid for funksjonshemma'. Unpublished dissertation, Department of Comparative Politics, University of Bergen.

Raaum, Johan (1988) 'De frivillige organisasjonenes framvekst og utvikling i Norge', pp. 239–355 in NOU 17.

Salamon, Lester M. (1987) 'Partners in public service: The scope and theory of government – nonprofit relations', in Walter W. Powell (ed.), *The Nonprofit Sector: A Research Handbook*. New Haven, Conn.: Yale University Press.

Seip, Anne-Lise (1984) *Sosialhjelpstaten blir til*. Oslo: Gyldendal.

Sejersted, Francis (1983) 'Politikk som interessegruppe eller styringsproblem', in Trond Bergh (ed.), *Deltagerdemokratiet*. Oslo: Universitetsforlaget.

Torgersen, Ulf (1962) 'The trend towards political consensus: The case of Norway', *Acta Sociologica*, 6: 159–72.

10
Meeeting Needs through Voluntary Action: Does Market Society Corrode Altruism?

Alan Ware

During the 1980s New Right beliefs about the role of markets have been subjected to considerable scrutiny by academic commentators (for example King, 1987). This chapter is concerned with an aspect of New Right thought that has received rather little attention – the compatibility between markets and a social response to needs based primarily on altruistically inspired voluntary action. I want to consider the assumption made by New Right advocates (for example Friedman and Friedman, 1980: 172) that providing for needs through altruism is compatible with a pre-dominantly market basis for social organization.

My argument will be that while there is no conceptual incompatibility, the extension of the market does tend to corrode altruism in a variety of ways. The purpose of this chapter is to classify the various forms of that corrosion, and to show that it is only by ignoring the *institutions* of market societies, and their consequences, that the compatibility of markets and philanthropic activity could seem plausible.

At the outset, however, the parameters of the argument must be made quite explicit. This chapter does not discuss objections to a society relying entirely on the market and individuals' altruistic impulses in meeting needs – objections such as how the acts of 'small decision makers' could possibly be coordinated to provide an optimal response to need.[1] Nor is it argued here that voluntary organizations cannot thrive in market society. Most certainly they can, and one of the main reasons for this is their integration with the state sector – not only, as is shown in chapter 9 of this book, in 'state-friendly' societies like Norway but also in the United States (see Hall, 1987; Salamon, 1987). Nor, again, am I denying that in certain specific circumstances some growth in donations by individuals to relieve the needs of others can be generated as, indeed, seems to have occurred in Britain during the 1980s. (Obviously, as evidence from the US suggests, one way of stimulating financial donations is to reduce the degree of altruism required by providing tax incentives to potential donors (Clotfelter, 1985).) Rather, this chapter is solely about the altruistic elements of voluntary action, and my argument is that, *in general*, the extension of market mechanisms in a society makes it less possible for that society to rely on altruism in meeting needs.

If the New Right assertion of the compatibility of altruism and the market were correct, it would be expected that the more affluent a society became the more its individual members would give to voluntary organizations. Greater personal income would enable individuals to give increasingly larger proportions of their income to meet the needs of others. Yet this expectation of greater philanthropy is not met. Even in the USA, donations form only about one-fifth of the total income of non-religious non-profit organizations. Nor is there any general propensity for the growth in financial gifts to run far ahead of the growth in personal income. Jencks's (1987: table 18.6) data for the US suggest that between the 1930s and the 1950s total contributions to philanthropy increased only from 1.5 to 2 per cent of personal income, and that after that it did not increase at all. This scarcely suggests that wealth begets charity, neither can this failure of philanthropy be explained away, as the New Right often asserts, by the rise of the welfare state. In the US it was not until the 1960s that comprehensive welfare programmes started, by which time a pattern of philanthropic failure was long apparent. The evidence from the US (and elsewhere) shows that philanthropy is not a real alternative to the state paying for welfare services, even in societies experiencing economic growth. The purpose of this chapter is to provide an explanation of this, and it does so by focusing on the ways in which market societies tend to corrode altruism.

The New Right, needs and altruism

There are two main features of a New Right approach to needs. First, the New Right generally rejects a notion of need identified by, among others, Weale (1983: 35), and which links people's needs to the resources required in their own society for them to carry out projects of their own. Instead, the New Right either insists that the idea of a need is incoherent or links needs merely to the sustenance of life itself.[2] Again the New Right claims that while markets can help to provide for most needs, altruism provides the best means for bridging any 'gap' between market provision and needs.

Altruistic activity is preferred by the New Right for several reasons. Most importantly, there is no element of compulsion involved. Unlike universal welfare provision, or compulsory insurance schemes, whether organized by private employers or by the state, no individual *has* to contribute towards meeting the needs of others. Because all individuals retain a choice as to whether to assist others, freedom is maximized. Again, unlike state provision of welfare, provision based on altruism does not undermine the responsibility of the beneficiary for his or her own actions: markets supposedly help to engender this sense of responsibility for needs by allowing choices to be made by individuals which determine whether their needs will be met. Furthermore, and the first part of this claim would not be accepted by all New Right supporters, altruism is a morally superior form of behaviour which is undermined by state provision of welfare. According to this view, state provision diminishes the 'altruistic spirit', because would-be philanthropists can see no point in such activity if they are merely duplicating the supply of goods and services to those in need.

Altruism and its forms

Altruism is a complex concept and it is not possible here to deal fully with the problems this can pose. The term was first coined by Comte and given a quite precise meaning by him, and only later did it come into general usage. One difficulty with the term is that in some contexts in which it has been widely used (notably sociobiology) it has acquired meanings which conflict with our common understanding of what altruistic behaviour involves.

As a first approximation, it may be said that altruistic behaviour is behaviour that benefits another (unrelated) actor and which imposes some cost on its originator. Two points may be made about such a definition: it excludes behaviour to benefit a close relative – someone with whose interests the actor may be presumed to identify, and altruism is defined here in *behavioural* terms and has not been related, as in most ethical theories, to the motives of the actor involved. The reason for focusing on behaviour in a study about provision for social needs is the lack of data on the actual motives of actors whose actions *seem* to be directed towards providing welfare for others at some cost to themselves. However, discussions of altruism in human interactions require that a distinction be drawn which does link altruism to motives and which is not required, for example, by sociobiologists in their analyses of altruism.

The relevant distinction in the case of social interactions can be illuminated by an example. Suppose that two people have car driveways adjacent to each other and that, if there is a heavy fall of snow, it takes less time for one person to clear both driveways than the combined time it takes each of them to clear his/her own. If one of them clears both driveways *in anticipation that the other will reciprocate* the next time there is a snowstorm, this is scarcely recognizable as altruistic behaviour. Calculations of this kind in one-to-one relations are really *exchanges* and not altruism – even though the attempt at exchange can involve loss for the initiator if the other party considers merely his/her own short-term self-interest.[3]

Nevertheless, when it is practised on a much wider scale reciprocity can be seen as a form of altruism. Consider behaviour often found in many small communities. *A* does something for *B* even though *B* may not himself have provided anything for *A*, but, because *A* has had similar benefits from other members of the community (or expects to receive them), he helps *B* as a member of a wider 'reciprocating group'. In this latter case *A* would only fail to help *B* if *B* was a known unrepentant 'defector' who flouted the conventions of reciprocity of the group. Much behaviour that we regard as altruistic is of this second type: it would cease in relation to those individuals who were known to be selfish. I suggest, then, that reciprocity can be treated as altruistic even if (a) the benefactor will cease his gift should the beneficiary respond to him with a selfish act, but only if (b) the benefactor in engaging in it was not commencing or perpetuating a purely *bilateral* relationship of reciprocal assistance.

Having outlined how altruism is conceived in this chapter, I would now suggest that, in analysing altruism as a response to need, it is useful to draw three different distinctions between forms of altruism.

Indiscriminate altruism versus reciprocal altruism

The first distinction has already been alluded to. Indiscriminate altruists want to provide benefits for others irrespective of the latter's behaviour towards them – they 'turn the other cheek' and continue to behave altruistically. Reciprocal altruists, however, 'are willing to help only those who have not acted in a selfish manner towards them in the past' (Colman, 1982: 267). Indiscriminate altruism is sometimes seen as a morally superior form. Indeed, some moral theorists would argue that reciprocal altruism is not altruism at all, precisely because it is conditional upon the behaviour of others, and that it is better described as enlightened self-interest. I have already conceded that some forms of reciprocity cannot be regarded as altruism because they are really a bilateral exchange (involving risk for one party). However, not only do less direct instances of reciprocity have clearly altruistic elements, but it can be argued that very little altruistic behaviour does not depend in *some way* on the response of the beneficiary to the gift. For example, if a pauper were to insist on always selling gifts of food he receives so as to buy addictive drugs, most donors would regard this refusal to have his needs met as a reason for discontinuing the gifts.

Welfare altruism versus participation altruism

This distinction is one developed by Margolis (1982), and it cross-cuts the distinction between indiscriminate and reciprocal altruism. On the one hand, there is welfare altruism, where the potential donor draws satisfaction from other people receiving benefits. The welfare altruist is as satisfied by other people making contributions to those he wants to see benefited as he is by seeing that his own contributions make a difference. He 'gains utility from an increase in the goods available to others: his utility function incorporates a taste for having other people better off' (Margolis, 1982: 21). Conversely, the participation altruist 'gains utility from giving resources away for the benefit of others' (Margolis, 1982: 21); he is made happier only by his own contributions and the contributions of others are irrelevant, for it is the act of giving which is crucial.

Personal altruism versus impersonal altruism

Personal altruism values the connection between the donor and the recipient: the latter owes a special obligation to the former, while the former may be morally or spiritually uplifted in some way by his encounter with the latter. It is this kind of altruism which was valued by the Charity Organization Society (COS) in the nineteenth century. Personal altruism often leads to resentment on the part of recipients that their plight has become a further excuse for the exercise of power over them – the COS, for instance, tried to make the working class conform to middle-class morals. While the proponents of personal altruism value the moral qualities supposedly present in the connection between donor and recipient, it is the very absence of such connections which proponents of impersonal altruism value. Impersonal altruism takes a core element of the parable of the Good Samaritan a stage further – the Samaritan's help becomes morally valuable when he knows that those he benefits do not know who he was, cannot communicate any form of gratitude to him, and may not even know that there was a donor at all. Impersonal altruism is exemplified today, perhaps, in the institutional arrangements for the donating of blood: the beneficiary never knows who is the donor (and vice versa), and because there are no generally recognized 'symbols' to show who is a donor, he or she remains an 'unsung hero'.[4]

This distinction is connected to, though still separate from, the distinction between indiscriminate and reciprocal altruism. The blood-donating impersonal altruist is not in a position to refuse to give blood in the future to those who had received transfusions from his blood in the past but had not subsequently given blood themselves. Nevertheless, there are two approaches that such an impersonal altruist might take when facing a general unwillingness by others in society to donate their blood: if he is also an indiscriminate altruist, he would continue to donate anyway, even in the face of an unwillingness by others to give blood, while at a certain point a reciprocal altruist would cease to make such gifts himself. The wholly personal altruist would not be interested in donating blood today because the arrangements for doing so provide no opportunities for making any contact with the beneficiaries; the latter is unable to respond with gratitude and possibly to accept the 'moral leadership' of the donor.

Similarly this distinction between personal and impersonal altruism is different from that between welfare and participation altruism. If the latter suggests a personal involvement in giving, it does not entail a power relationship of the kind evident in personal altruism; the participation altruist may be fastidiously concerned to remain anonymous to the beneficiaries.

Bearing these distinctions in mind, we can now turn to examine the impact of market systems on altruistic behaviour. Several of the arguments to be introduced have been much discussed by political theorists, but the point of this analysis is to review the arguments in the light of recent debates prompted by the New Right about the role of altruism in social life. In essence there are three main arguments about the adverse effect of market society on altruism:

1 There is a *psychological* argument about how people behave when they try to act on the basis of two conflicting sets of values. While there could be human societies in which these two sets were each related to quite distinct spheres of people's lives, in most advanced market societies this separation is not maintained. The more market transactions there are, therefore, the less likely it is that altruistic principles will be acted upon.

2 There is the argument that market society extends the *territory* in which individuals have their social interactions, and this means that more interactions are taking place outside the arena in which it is easiest to establish and maintain altruistic interactions.
3 There is an argument that increasing the number of transactions in a community changes the *institutional* structure of a society in ways which can undermine its organization of altruism.

These arguments, and their interrelationships, form the subject of the next four sections.

The incompatibility of market values and altruism

This is the argument that the pursuit of self-interest in the market clashes with the ethos of aiding others: the greater the permeation of market relations into social interactions, the more likely it is that self-interested attitudes will displace altruistic beliefs generally. Market activity involves calculating the costs and benefits of aspects of behaviour, so that the more calculations people make the more this mode of operating is likely to intrude into areas of their lives in which previously it played no part. Habits, conventions and principles which support aid for others are weakened when cost/benefit calculations of self-interest are even contemplated by the actor. This argument assumes that it is difficult for people to maintain conflicting principles in different spheres of their lives, so that the more dominant market values become the less likely it is that people will act altruistically outside the market.

We may begin by observing that there is one obvious respect in which this argument might seem to be incorrect. It might be said to apply only to indiscriminate altruism and not to reciprocal altruism. If we suppose that the impact of the market is to make people more cautious of how they interact with others, then it could be argued that the market will probably strengthen the position of reciprocal altruism in relation to indiscriminate altruism. Not only does the former provide a 'less fertile' arena in which selfishness can prosper, but the functioning of a community of reciprocal altruists is actually endangered by the introduction of indiscriminate altruists. In both social and the biological arenas indiscriminate altruism is unbalancing. Its introduction (Colman, 1982: 268) tends:

> . . . to shift the direction of evolution towards selfishness. This is
> because selfish individuals would get more out of interactions with the

indiscriminate altruists than reciprocal altruists would; they would enjoy the benefits without incurring the costs. In other words, the presence of indiscriminate altruists endangers the healthy reciprocal altruist morality by enabling selfishness to prosper . . .

If they help to drive out indiscriminate altruism, the values of the market might be thought to assist in the creation of a more stable reciprocally altruistic community. But there are two objections to accepting this point.

If market values undermine indiscriminate altruism then they are also likely to undermine all but the most formal kinds of reciprocal behaviour. By focusing attention on the promotion of self-interest, the market will tend to encourage free-riding whenever it is difficult for the 'victims' to impose a penalty on free-riders. Consequently, while strict 'tit-for-tat' arrangements between pairs of individuals would survive (and would become even more attractive), many kinds of *reciprocal altruistic* behaviour would be threatened by the growth of defection. Moreover, and this is a point we return to in the next section, by widening the scope of personal interactions beyond local communities, the market tends to weaken the small, tightly knit groups in which reciprocal altruism is most likely to be sustained.

This last point leads us to another area in which the spread of market values will corrode altruism – it will tend to destroy personal altruism because it destroys paternalistic hierarchies based in local communities. The personal altruism usually associated with Victorian philanthropy, and which was exemplified in the approach of the COS, is not compatible with the values of a pure market society in which deference to social hierarchies is absent. Victorian philanthropy was largely predicated upon notions of social obligation which attached to a person's position in society. These supposed obligations were connected to obligations on the part of recipients to heed the moral lessons of their 'betters' – the donors. While the resurrection of 'Victorian values' in the 1980s might conceivably have helped to foster a spirit of self-improvement among some Britons, it could do nothing to revive that other key element of Victorian values – personal altruism. Not surprisingly, then, even in the 1980s when appeals for philanthropic activity increased greatly, donations to charities in Britain, for example, increased relatively little in relation to total personal income. While personal donations appear to have increased at, perhaps, one-and-a-half times the rate of increase in personal income, donations remained at a very low level. Moreover, there was still hardly any variation across income groups in donations as a proportion of donors' income (Ware,

1989: table 4.3.) – the more affluent did not seem to regard it as their particular responsibility to give to others. And if the spread of the market threatens personal altruism especially, impersonal altruism is also affected, of course, in the way already identified, by the strengthening of the ethos of the pursuit of self-interest.

Obviously, it is *possible* that market values and altruism could coexist. (Indeed, some proponents of the New Right (Griffiths, 1984) do argue that a market society requires a strong moral base.) In a highly religious society, for example, it might be possible for individuals to conform with two seemingly contradictory value systems – but in separate spheres; they would abide by non-market values outside strictly economic transactions. This coexistence would be greatly facilitated, of course, by church institutions being centrally involved in the *organization* of altruism, so that the two spheres of action remained as separate as possible. (The Mormon church in Utah might be cited as an instance of communities holding dual principles; tithing to the church is widespread, the church provides some welfare services, and this goes hand-in-hand with high esteem for business success.) Continuing differences between Britain and the US with regard to both financial donations and organized volunteer labour indicate the role of religion in prompting altruistic behaviour. If religious observance was as high in Britain as it is in the US, there can be little doubt that certain forms of giving would be considerably greater; this is suggested, for example, by patterns of volunteering in Britain (Gerard, 1983: 84). But, of the industrialized states, it is only in the multi-ethnic, 'immigrant' ones, most especially the US, and in some predominantly rural states (like Ireland) that high levels of religious observance still persist. And, contrary to the hopes of writers like Griffiths (1984), it is very unlikely even in the US that a strict separation of values appropriate to the market and those appropriate to other areas of social life can be maintained. Consequently, the emphasis on the pursuit of self-interest is likely to undermine support for meeting social needs through altruism.[5]

However, a sceptic might object that these arguments do not mesh with the fact that some forms of impersonal altruism have increased in recent decades (including donations to third world charities) and that donations to charities *overall* did increase in the 1980s. Unfortunately for New Right theorists, there is no evidence whatsoever that this can be attributed to the influence of the market, and especially to the beneficence of those who have done well out of market transactions. To the contrary, a more likely explanation of this philanthropy would relate it to the growing acceptance of 'social citizenship' rights in the twentieth century and of the obligations which citizens have.[6] But, of course, this idea of 'social citizenship' is anathema to the New Right because it justifies a wide range of state intervention.

The expansion of social relations beyond smaller communities

The growth of markets not only changes values in communities in the way just described, it does so indirectly as well through extending social relations beyond the realm of immediate social contacts.[7] By 'opening up' local communities, markets provide many advantages for their inhabitants; but the expansion of social relations beyond these communities also produces disbenefits, among them a reduced willingness to support the provision of welfare for those in need in the communities. There are three main ways in which this will occur.

First, by widening the scope of social interactions, markets weaken the basis for personal altruism. In the first place, commercialization is likely to draw some local elites away from their purely local concerns and into major economic relations in areas beyond that of their residence. Unless they retain a strong emotional attachment to their original locale – through, for example, keeping their main residence there – these elites are likely to become less concerned with the welfare of the members of these communities. Noblesse oblige is largely a manifestation of *territorially-based* social relations, and once these relations are weakened personal altruism is more likely to collapse than to be transformed. However, there are two important qualifications to be made to this argument.

One qualification is that elites may try to re-create personal altruism of the traditional rural community in new, and predominantly urban, communities. This was the approach of the COS in mid-to-late-nineteenth-century urban Britain – as it was for the COS in American cities when the idea was introduced there a decade later. To substitute for the complex social links which tied peasants to lords, the COS chose 'friendly visits' by their members to those in need. 'Friendly visiting' was to yield a form of social control of the masses by providing them with moral guidance (Lubove, 1965: 16). But, ultimately, the kind of social control sought by the COS was unattainable in the absence of other ties between visitor and client – the 'visitor' was a pale imitation of the rural 'patron', if for no other reason than geographical separation. Since visitors were, in any case, ill equipped to adduce the needs of their clients, the visitor system gradually became transformed in the early twentieth century into one of professional social workers. The attempt to recreate a system of personal altruism quite simply failed.

Another qualification is that the elites may so much value the territorial exercise of social power that becoming a member of the territorial elite may become an objective for those successful in commerce. Indeed, nineteenth-century businessmen's attraction to the lifestyle and values of a landed aristocracy has been a major theme of some interpretations of the peculiarly British experience of industrialization (Wiener, 1981). However, the impact of this sustenance of traditional aristocratic values on the meeting of needs in Britain was relatively small, precisely because the reduction of the agriculturally dependent workforce and the depopulation of rural areas in Britain had occurred at such an early stage of industrialization; to a large degree the former really preceded what is conventionally thought of as the period of the 'British Industrial Revolution'.[8]

The other way in which the wider scope of social interaction created by markets weakens the basis for personal altruism is that it erodes the support for deferential behaviour. All actors in a market are equally actors – only the differences in their economic resources are relevant. This ethos clashes with notions of obligation founded in dependence on sociopolitical elites. The more they become involved in markets the more individuals will dismiss any notion of duty that they owe to these elites. But the decline of deferential behaviour is likely to discourage the practice of personal altruism. 'Lady Bountifuls' who do not receive the gratitude they anticipate are more likely to withdraw their largesse.

Secondly, the expanded scope of social interactions does little to encourage impersonal altruism – providing benefits for fellow human beings on an anonymous basis. Interactions in markets feature actors who usually have no relation to each other except in their commercial transactions. Unlike those in the peasant village, for instance, actors in a market are unlikely to reflect on the needs they share – partly because their circumstances are so different (Goodin, 1988: 114). The newly unemployed business executive may have to sell his Porsche and move to a smaller house, but his perceptions of the uncertainties of life will almost certainly be very different from those of an unemployed 16-year-old with no educational qualifications. In market societies there are relatively few areas of life in which all are exposed to the same uncertainties.[9] Yet it is the sharing of uncertainty which could prompt both a view of a common humanity, and also a correct perception of which needs cannot be met by markets, so that a sufficient response by impersonal altruists could be generated. This is why Titmuss's (1971) study of blood donation is an analysis of a rather unusual aspect of altruistic behaviour. As with many kinds of disease, in the case of blood it is all too obvious to the individual that he may be as equally likely to be in need as anyone else. His potential vulnerability is much the same as everyone's – people with whom he interacts in the market and those he does not. In the absence of a market in blood, the rich can no more assure themselves of the supply of blood than the poor. They are all dependent on the altruism of blood donors. Moreover, blood also differs from many other needs in that, except in wartime or in major national disasters, needs can be met through the actions of a relatively small proportion of the population.

When needs are shared universally, as with blood, the similarity of the position in which each person finds himself can stimulate the ethic of the Good Samaritan. Blood transfusions are one area of need in Britain which so far has been met entirely by altruism. It can be argued too that the widespread sharing of a need is one of the reasons, though certainly not the only one, for the success of medical research charities in the last few decades. There were only a handful of such charities before the Second World War, but today they account for about one-eighth of all donations to British charities.[10]

Thirdly, the expansion of social interactions beyond local communities weakens the conditions which foster reciprocal altruism. In particular, there is a high level of personal mobility associated with advanced market economies. This is a point emphasized by Hirsch (1977: 78):

> The huge increase in personal mobility in modern economies . . . [makes] . . . sociability more of a public and less of a private good. The more people move, the lower are the chances of social contacts being reciprocated directly on a bilateral basis. A casual favour or gesture is less likely to be returned. There also is then less scope for a long run view to be taken in bilateral friendship exchange; before my gesture to you today has been reciprocated by you tomorrow, you may have moved away . . . This influence is strongest with geographical mobility, but increased social mobility – moving out of one's class – has the same general effect.

Geographical mobility destroys the bilateral basis for multilateral social relations based on reciprocity in several ways. There is the point made specifically by Hirsch – people's jobs now take them from one community to another, so that there is less incentive for developing complex reciprocal links to others in that community.

But even when people do spend all their lives in the same community, motorized transport means that many individual economic transactions can be conducted miles away. This can create a collective action problem for would-be altruists. Thus, the reciprocal altruist who would wish to help out his poor non-car-owning neighbours by spending money at the village shop, in order to keep it in business, faces such a problem. He can buy his own goods elsewhere at a lower price, and while he may be prepared to subsidize the village shop to help others, his own purchases by themselves cannot ensure its survival. Thus, the reciprocal altruist may well conclude that particular acts, which he may know are the ones that would most help his neighbours, are not worth engaging in. The possibility of 'exit' by some actors to other sources of economic goods restricts the framework within which patterns of reciprocal altruism can be developed.

Finally, motorized transport means that many personal relationships can be conducted over great distances. This adversely affects reciprocal altruism, in that when these relationships are conducted within a confined territory, it becomes more possible for complex, multilateral, patterns of reciprocity to develop because there are more interactions. *A* knows that *B* helped *C*, and some aspect of *A*'s gratitude to *C*'s earlier assistance to himself may then be manifested in *A* subsequently aiding *B*. But when *A*, *B* and *C* live in separate communities, even though they all know each other, they are less likely to be aware of many of the minor aspects of reciprocal aid involving the other two. Moreover, others are also less likely to know of, and respond to, altruistic acts involving pairs of actors. While bilateral reciprocity can survive this physical extension of personal relationships, multilateral reciprocity is far more difficult to sustain.

The extension of economic activity in previously marginal areas

In an underdeveloped economy services such as health care, education, adequate housing, and many others can be afforded by only a small minority of the population.[11] But in societies at all levels of economic development there are goods or services, the provision of which is widely regarded as valuable, yet which the market system distributes to only a few of the potential customers. These are 'marginal' areas of the economy; they are particularly important in relation to needs, because it is in areas where the market does not supply all the goods necessary for everyone to enjoy at least the minimum standard of subsistence for that community, that debates about how to fill the 'gap' left by the market become prominent. When mutual benefit organizations (such as cooperatives) do not emerge to fill this 'gap', the state or individuals and organizations may provide funds to enable the good or service to be supplied by an organization, and (when a charge is made) at a price below that which would generate a normal rate of profit in the market.

There are four rather different reasons why the market may fail to distribute what is believed to be an optimal supply of services such as health care, education, adequate housing and so on, and why subsidies have to be employed:

1 The level of income of most customers is so low in relation to the price of the product as to make it irrational (and even impossible) for purchases to be made.

2 Even if the product can be afforded by most potential customers, the patterns of their demand for goods is such that they choose to purchase less of it than either other individuals or the state believes to be desirable. Private philanthropy or state grants could be the basis of subsidy to facilitate greater consumption by lowering the price. Stated in this way, the argument might seem to be essentially paternalistic in character: 'People don't know what is good for them'. But it need not be; the purpose of encouraging greater consumption of the product might not be for the good of the consumers, but, say, to create a greater domestic market as the basis for an export drive.

3 The consumers may be insufficient in number, for example because of their geographical dispersal, to provide a normal rate of return for the supplier. A village shop requires a minimum number of customers to make it viable; the decline of agricultural employment, combined with the migration to rural areas of commuters who can do their shopping in towns, has resulted in many villages no longer being able to sustain a shop. 'Traditional' village residents find that they can no longer purchase the goods they require.

4 Because of hostility to a service being supplied by for-profit firms, proprietorial firms can supply only a relatively small proportion of those who want the service. Fears about 'contract failure' may keep some customers out of the market, and these fears may well be understood by entrepreneurs in the for-profit sector.[12] For example, Nelson and Krashinsky (1973: 55), citing Ruderman (1958), say of day care facilities for children in the

US, 'even many businessmen believe that this is an unsatisfactory way of providing the service'.

One solution to the problem of the inability of the market to supply a good on a scale that is regarded as desirable is through direct provision by the state, or through state subsidy of commercial enterprises. But sometimes private organizations, such as business corporations and charitable trusts, have also sought to remove these 'gaps' in supply on an altruistic basis. But what happens when marginal areas of the economy become less marginal for many people, and supply on a commercial basis becomes more widespread? There are two ways in which altruistic responses to the meeting of needs may be undermined.

The first is that there is goal displacement in the organizations originally established to provide for those in need, so that they concentrate their activities much more on providing services to full-fee-paying clients than to those in need who pay at a subsidized rate or who receive the service at no charge at all. This switch towards commercial activities does not necessarily mean that there is still not some difference between how fully commercial and other organizations behave in the supply of services. The latter may still provide more cross-subsidization for the needy, from the income provided by full-fee-payers, than the former. For example, it has been widely argued (despite the claims of Herzlinger and Krasker (1987) to the contrary) that investor-owned hospitals in the US provide less care for the poor than non-profit hospitals.[13] But there are other instances where the organizations concerned have completely abandoned their original client-groups in favour of servicing full-fee-payers. Among the best examples of this are public (i.e. private) schools and grammar schools in Britain. Originally established to provide free education to the poor, these charitable schools underwent a transformation in the eighteenth and nineteenth centuries; they came to cater primarily for a fee-paying middle-class clientele (Moffat, 1989: 197). In the case of the grammar schools, the legal basis of the organizations involved was changed so as to permit a transformation to a full-fee-paying clientele. But goal transformation can still occur simply through the emphasis an organization chooses to give to the different aspects of its work – this was the case with the public schools which also switched away from educating the poor.

The second way in which altruistic responses may be undermined as commercial supply of a particular good or service becomes more viable is through potential donors ceasing to see this as an appropriate focus for altruism. It is more likely to be perceived as a product which *could* be bought by most people, and those who cannot purchase it are thereby likely to be overlooked. As is the case in the US, the more that hospitals are referred to as the 'hospital industry', the less likely donors are to see the provision of medical treatment for the indigent as a need, at least in comparison with other social needs that have to be met. There may still be a lot of people who could not afford to pay for hospital treatment, but this would be less likely to be understood by others.

This second argument, that commercialization of the supply of a service reduces its probable appeal as a source of donations, must be distinguished from a quite separate argument associated with Titmuss's study of blood donation. Some people have argued that, if blood could be sold, those who might consider donating it would believe that in some sense their donation was 'tainted'. (When we are all in need, paying some people for a product may well appear to donors as degrading their act of giving; when only some people are in need there is no incongruity between giving for those in need and paying people to supply similar goods for one's own use.) But my point is a different one – it is that the existence of a large market may serve to conceal the fact that not all individuals can participate in that market.

The effects of the institutionalization of altruism

Extending the role of the market in a society tends to further the institutionalization of altruistic responses to need and, in turn, this tends to constrain the role of altruism in meeting needs. To explain this point, it is important to realize that the institutionalization of altruism is brought about by a number of factors, but there are two ways in which the expansion of the market contributes to this.

In undermining traditional social relations, market economies create problems of social control especially for new socioeconomic elites. For example, the market may eliminate the livelihood of various kinds of economic actors, promote undesirable behaviour and so on. One aspect of elite response to this takes the form of laws, as with the poor laws, to regulate such behaviour. But another aspect of this response is likely to involve the creation of forms of altruism which best permit social control to be effected in a more indirect way. The COS in the nineteenth century attempted to have charitable donations channelled through itself, so that 'scientific charity' could be practised and the 'undeserving' would be excluded from such gifts. But the failure of the COS to achieve its objective produced in the US another response by socioeconomic elites – a response which, for a variety of reasons, did not have a counterpart in Britain. This was the consolidation of fund-raising efforts by charities, first practised successfully in Cleveland, Ohio. The movement became nationwide during the First World War, with many towns and cities developing 'Community Chests'; there were fund-raising drives once a year with local charities participating in the drives and in the distribution of funds. Because they selected which organizations to support with donations, the business-led Community Chests (later to become the United Way) tried to drive out radical charities by making it difficult for them to raise funds.

Moreover, organizations formed to channel altruistic responses from the public tend to copy the organizational styles of commercial businesses. In particular, as businesses themselves become suppliers of funds to these organizations, they tend to demand that they conform to many of the organizational practices of the commercial sector. In the 1980s there is clear evidence of a major shift in the organizational infrastructure among charities in Britain in response to the need to attract corporate sponsorship to boost funds (Wilson, 1989; Butler and Wilson, 1988).

Institutionalization has a number of benefits for bodies formed to channel gifts to those in need: it can help to stabilize the flow of income, it can make bodies more attractive to corporate donors and so on. But there are also reasons for believing that institutionalization helps to weaken altruistic responses to need in crucial respects.

The conversion of charities (and similar organizations) into more hierarchical structures may diminish the contribution of participation altruists. As we noted earlier, these sorts of altruists want to give their own resources away to benefit others. But they are not merely 'self-deniers' – they want to see some connection between their donations (whether of money or labour) and results. One of the main ways in which they establish this connection is through control over the organization to which they give money or time. Not surprisingly, then, these sorts of organizations have tended to be more decentralized and more participation-oriented than commercial firms. However, as charities move more towards managerial styles which are copied from the commercial sector, the more participation altruists are likely to become disenchanted with these organizations. Many, of course, will simply move to other bodies (probably newer ones) which they find more congenial, but it is quite probable that the experience of dealing with 'inappropriately hierarchical' structures may help to diminish generally the ethic of participation altruism within society.

Institutionalization can also make it more difficult for responses to new needs to be successful; it can contribute to the erection of barriers to altruistic initiatives to meet such needs. An excellent illustration of this point is the different response to the Live Aid concerts (held in London and Philadelphia) which Bob Geldof (1986: 356) encountered in 1985:

> We discovered that, unlike in Britain where everyone was working for nothing, in the States almost everyone expected to be paid. Only the bands and the promoters and Mitchell's crowd, Worldwide Sports and Entertainments, were working without payment; all the technical people, the PA and light companies, and everybody who was a member of a union had to be paid. . . . We cursed, but we realized that we just had to live with it. Philadelphia cost $3.5 million. Wembley cost $250,000.

The problem faced by Geldof was not, of course, antagonism to voluntary activity in the US; most studies agree that the propensity to donate money and to volunteer is considerably greater in the US than in Britain. Rather Geldof's plan did not fit into the philanthropic organizational structure which individuals and institutions in the US were used to facing, and they responded by treating it as a commercial proposition. In Britain the much weaker penetration of society by organized charities meant that there was much greater scope for persuading people to provide their services free of charge. Businesses and employees in Britain were in some doubt as to who should be doing something about the Ethiopian tragedy, and were prepared to assume some responsibility themselves through the Geldof project. Persuasion is more difficult to implement when decision makers have more clear-cut views about whose responsibility a particular problem is, and how their own activity relates to that.

The institutionalization of altruism, then, makes it less likely that altruism can play its most distinctive role in contemporary society: acting as a catalyst to stimulate responses by those organizations best placed to provide for those in need. In many circumstances altruistic activity is the best mechanism for drawing attention to the emergence of new needs. Its institutionalization, however, may make it less likely that the accepted public agenda as to 'who is in need' can be re-ordered to take account of new needs. The likely price of requiring organizations originally founded on altruism to provide more goods and services for those in need is to reduce their effectiveness in signalling changes in people's needs.

Concluding remarks

In this chapter I have introduced a number of arguments to suggest that the New Right view of the compatibility of the market and altruism is unfounded. Of course, altruism can survive in market societies, and indeed there are innumerable examples where it still thrives; it has not been completely undermined by the market, and it can even be argued that, by increasing leisure time for individuals, free market economies have contributed to a growth in volunteer labour. But overall my argument is that, while markets are probably an inevitable feature of social organization, and may bring many benefits with them, extending the market too far into social life will nonetheless undermine the role of altruism in meeting needs. Since, in any case, altruism is a poor basis for actually meeting many needs in contemporary societies, it may be argued that the New Right view of meeting needs is merely a chimera. But, if this is so, why at the level of popular political debate has it not been dismissed as unfounded?

One reason is that profound differences between contemporary industrial societies and Victorian society are not fully appreciated by the public. New Right theorists often look back to the nineteenth century as a model of society–state relations. But the economic individualism of which they approve was interlinked with pre-industrial social structures and attitudes which are much weaker today. Personal altruism, for example, thrived in the Victorian period, but cannot be re-created today, because it reflected older attitudes towards a social hierarchy; the triumph of the 'egalitarianism' of the market was far from complete then. Similarly, the size of nineteenth-century towns and the smaller scale of commercial firms meant that patterns of social relations were much more confined than now, and in those circumstances altruistic behaviour was more likely to be sustained.

However, another reason for the New Right not having been completely discredited is that the role of altruism is often confused in the popular imagination with the role of voluntary or charitable organizations in meeting needs. In the 1980s the British government has made much greater use of these organizations in the delivery of goods and services – at the same time as it has cut back on its own direct supply of welfare services. Central government funding of these services has helped to sustain them. In this way the British government has emulated the American approach during the expansion of its welfare services in the 1960s: 'third parties' are being used as instruments of government policy.

But the American experience in the 1980s is itself revealing of the problem for a welfare policy that relies on voluntary organizations. In the early 1980s, when the Reagan administration cut back on welfare services, and called on voluntary effort to fill the gap, the increase in donations (whether financial or in the form of labour) came nowhere close to matching the cuts in federal government expenditure. Although many of these organizations were able to increase their non-governmental sources of income, they did so primarily by raising their fee income. In other words, they tended to switch towards providing services for those who could pay for them – people who, by definition, are not those most in need.

In neither the British nor the American case, then, does the fact that voluntary organizations are 'doing more' in the provision of welfare services indicate any potential for a much increased role for altruism overall in the meeting of needs. To the contrary, it provides further evidence of the limited role that altruism can play. The common dismissal of the supply of welfare through voluntary organizations as merely a variant of the market (for example, Rose, 1985: 46) may be a simplification, but it is not misleading. This is not to say that all forms of altruism are in decline in contemporary societies – the rapid growth of third world charities is a case in point. But it is doubtful whether such sentiments can produce more than a tiny fraction of the resources required for social needs. Moreover, it is difficult to see how the growth of such altruism can be connected in any way to the expansion of the market system. To the contrary, it seems much more plausible to link such developments to the general acceptance of 'social citizenship', and to the rights that this generates, than to the spread of the market. The general effect of the expansion of the market system has been to corrode altruism, in the ways identified in this chapter, and it will surely continue to do so.

Notes

Earlier versions of this chapter were presented at the Political Theory Workshop. University of Warwick and at the ECPR Workshop on 'Needs, Contributions, and Welfare' in Paris. I am very grateful for the helpful comments of the members of these workshops and also for the written comments of Bob Goodin and Desmond King.

1. On 'small decision making', see Hirsch (1977: 40).

2. The claim that the idea of need is not coherent certainly does not mean that the New Right has nothing to say on the subject of needs. Their substantive points can be couched in terms of the idea of welfare – which is acceptable to New Right thinkers.

3. 'Relinquishing something "in exchange" for something, and in order to obtain that other thing, is no more a gift than is a forced contribution' (Kolm, 1983: 57).

4. Of course, the example of donating blood is not the most extreme example of impersonal altruism: here everyone knows that the good was provided by (unknown) donors. The extreme case is one where only the donor knows that a donation was made at all, and where all others assume the good was supplied by some other means. The classic study of blood donation is by Titmuss (1971).

5. One area in which the impact of the pursuit of self-interest (in competitive situations) on other social values has been debated is competitive sports involving children. See, for example, Meakin (1981).

6. On the justification 'social citizenship' provides for the provision of welfare, see King and Waldron (1988).

7. Conversely, of course, an emphasis on economic self-sufficiency for local communities tends to make these communities more inward-looking. This point is made, for example, by Shue (1988: 134–5) in her discussion of the effects of the Chinese policy of grain self-sufficiency in the 1960s and 1970s.

8. 'Even by the mid-eighteenth century the proportion of labour force inputs employed in agriculture may have been less than 50 per cent' (Crafts, 1985: 2). By 1800 the urbanization level in Britain was already nearly 34 per cent compared with a European norm of 23 per cent (Crafts, 1985: 62).

9. The welfare state as a risk-sharing device had its origins in the Second World War precisely because that was a period in which there was a considerable sharing of experiences involving similar risks. On the welfare state as risk-sharing, see Dryzek and Goodin (1986).

10. On British medical research charities generally, see Deans (1989).

11. The first part of this section was originally published in Ware (1989: ch. 3).

12. On the idea of 'contract failure', see Hansmann (1980).

13. The selective use of data by these authors was much commented on when their article was published, and the debate received considerable publicity in the American press; for example see *New York Times*, 2 April 1987. Data indicating that the behaviour of non-profit and for-profit hospitals differs is presented, among other places, in Marmor et al. (1987). For evidence that, in the area of mental health care, for-profit firms provide fewer staff resources for patient care and fewer services with community-wide benefits, see Schlesinger and Dorwart (1984).

References

Butler, R.J. and Wilson, D.C. (1988) *Managing Voluntary Organizations*. London: Routledge.

Clotfelter, Charles T. (1985) *Federal Tax Policy and Charitable Giving*. Chicago: University of Chicago Press.

Colman, Andrew M. (1982) *Game Theory and Experimental Games*. Oxford: Pergamon.

Crafts, N.F.R. (1985) *British Economic Growth during the Industrial Revolution*. Oxford: Oxford University Press.

Deans, Tom (1989) 'Organizing medical research: The role of charities and the state', pp. 139–68 in Alan Ware (ed.), *Charities and Government*. Manchester: Manchester University Press.

Dryzek, John and Goodin, Robert E. (1986) 'Risk sharing and social justice: The motivational foundations of the welfare state', *British Journal of Political Science*, 16(1): 1–34.

Friedman, Milton and Friedman, Rose (1980) *Free to Choose*. Harmondsworth: Penguin.

Geldof, Bob (1986) *Is That It?* Harmondsworth: Penguin.

Gerard, David (1983) *Charities in Britain*. London: Bedford Square Press/NCVO.

Goodin, Robert, E. (1988) *Reasons for Welfare*. Princeton, NJ: Princeton University Press.

Griffiths, Brian (1984) *The Creation of Wealth*. London: Hodder & Stoughton.

Hall, Peter Dobkin (1987) 'A historical overview of the private nonprofit sector', pp. 3–26 in Walter W. Powell (ed.), *The Nonprofit Sector*. New Haven, Conn.: Yale University Press.

Hansmann, Henry (1980) 'The role of non-profit enterprise', *Yale Law Journal*, 89(5): 835–901.

Herzlinger, Regina E. and Krasker, William S. (1987), 'Who profits from nonprofits?', *Harvard Business Review*, 65(1): 93–106.

Hirsch, Fred (1977) *Social Limits to Growth*. London and Henley: Routledge.

Jencks, Christopher (1987) 'Who gives to what?', pp. 321–39 in Walter W. Powell (ed.), *The Nonprofit Sector*. New Haven: Yale University Press.

King, Desmond S. (1987) *The New Right*. London: Macmillan.

King, Desmond S. and Waldron, Jeremy (1988) 'Citizenship, social citizenship and the defence of welfare provision', *British Journal of Political Science*, 18(4): 415–53.

Kolm, Serge-Christophe (1983) 'Altruism and efficiency', *Ethics*, 94(1); 18–65.

Lubove, Roy (1965) *The Professional Altruist*. Cambridge, Mass: Harvard University Press.

Margolis, Howard (1982) *Selfishness, Altruism and Rationality*. Cambridge: Cambridge University Press.

Marmor, Theodore R., Schlesinger, Mark and Smithey, Richard W. (1987) 'Nonprofit organizations and health care', pp. 221–39 in Walter W. Powell (ed.), *The Nonprofit Sector*. New Haven, Conn.: Yale University Press.

Meakin, Derek (1981) 'Physical education: An agency of moral education', *Journal of the Philosophy of Education*, 15(2): 241–53.

Moffat, Graham (1989) 'Independent schools, charity and government', pp. 190–221 in Alan Ware (ed.), *Charities and Government*. Manchester: Manchester University Press.

Nelson, Richard and Krashinsky, Michael (1973) 'Two major issues of public policy: Public subsidy and organization of supply', pp. 47–69 in Dennis R. Young and Richard R. Nelson (eds), *Public Policy for Day Care of Young Children*. Lexington, Mass: D.C. Heath.

Rose, Richard (1985) *The State's Contribution to the Welfare Mix*. Glasgow: Centre for the Study of Public Policy, University of Strathclyde.

Ruderman, F. (1958) *Child Care and Working Mothers*, Child Welfare League of America.

Salamon, Lester M. (1987) 'Partners in public service: The scope and theory of government–nonprofit relations', pp. 99–117 in Walter W. Powell (ed.), *The Nonprofit Sector*. New Haven, Conn.: Yale University Press.

Schlesinger, Mark and Dorwart, Robert (1984) 'Ownership and mental health care', *New England Journal of Medicine*, 311: 959–65.

Shue, Vivienne (1988) *The Reach of the State*. Stanford: Stanford University Press.

Titmuss, Richard (1971) *The Gift Relationship*. New York: Pantheon.

Ware, Alan (1989) *Between Profit and State: Intermediate Organizations in Britain and the United States*. Cambridge: Polity Press.

Weale, Albert (1983) *Political Theory and Social Policy*. London: Macmillan.

Wiener, Martin J. (1981) *English Culture and the Decline of the Industrial Spirit, 1850–1980*. Cambridge: Cambridge University Press.

Wilson, David C. (1989) 'New trends in the funding of charities', pp. 55–81 in Alan Ware (ed.), *Charities and Government*. Manchester: Manchester University Press.

Index

Index compiled by Meg Davies (Society of Indexers)

Notes on the Contributors

Brian Barry is Professor of Political Science at the London School of Economics. His most recent books are *Theories of Justice* (1989), volume I (1989) of a three-volume *Treatise on Social Justice* and a book of collected essays, *Democracy, Power and Justice* (1989).

Michael Freeden is a Fellow in Politics at Mansfield College, Oxford. His publications include *The New Liberalism: An Ideology of Social Reform* (1978). *Liberalism Divided: A Study in British Political Thought 1914–1939* (1986) and *J.A. Hobson: A Reader* (1988). He is currently writing a comparative study of modern ideologies as a British Academy Research Reader.

Robert E. Goodin, until recently Reader in Government at the University of Essex, is now Professorial Fellow in Philosophy at the Australian National University's Institute of Advanced Studies. He has served as one of the editors of both the *British Journal of Political Science* and *Ethics.* His most recent books are *Reasons for Welfare* (1988) and *No Smoking: The Ethical Issues* (1989).

Norman Johnson is a Senior Lecturer in Social Policy at the University of Keele. His publications include *Voluntary Social Services* (1981), *Marital Violence* (1985) and *The Welfare State in Transition* (1987). He is currently working on a book entitled *Reconstructing the Welfare State.*

Peter Jones is a Senior Lecturer in politics at the University of Newcastle-upon-Tyne. He has written on a number of issues concerning political philosophy and public policy, and is currently writing a book on rights.

Stein Kuhnle is a Professor in Comparative Politics at the University of Bergen. He is the author of numerous books and articles on the development of Scandinavian welfare states, social and political mobilization in Scandinavia and political science in Norway.

Joakim Palme is a Research Associate at the Swedish Institute for Social Research in Stockholm University. His research focuses on social policy and inequality in a comparative perspective.

Richard Parry is a Lecturer in Social Policy at the University of Edinburgh. His publications include the United Kingdom sections of *Growth to Limits: The European Welfare States since World War II* (1986–8) and 'The viability of the welfare state', in Derek Urwin and W.E. Paterson (eds), *Politics in Western Europe Today* (1990).

Per Selle is an Associate Professor of Comparative Politics at the University of Bergen. At present he is attached to the Norwegian Centre in Organization and Management in Bergen where he is working on a study of the relationship between government and voluntary organizations.

Alan Ware, until recently a Senior Lecturer in Politics at the University of Warwick, is now a Fellow of Worcester College, Oxford. His most recent books are *Citizens, Parties and the State* (1987), *Between Profit and State* (1989) and (as editor) *Charities and Government* (1989).